THE

POETICAL WORKS

OF

SAMUEL BUTLER.

VOLUME I.

BOSTON:
LITTLE, BROWN AND COMPANY.
SHEPARD, CLARK AND BROWN.
CINCINNATI: MOORE, WILSTACH, KEYS AND CO.
M.DCCC.LVII.

CAMBRIDGE:
PRINTED BY ALLEN AND FARNHAM

STEREOTYPED BY STONE AND SMART.

CONTENTS.

VOL. I.

HUDIBRAS.

TO THE REV. WILLIAM LISLE BOWLES,

CANON OF SALISBURY, ETC.

UNHONOUR'D lay poor Butler's nameless grave,
One line, the hand of pitying friendship gave.
'Twas his with pure confiding heart to trust
The flattering minions of a monarch's lust;
And hope that faith a private debt would own,
False to the honour of a nation's throne.
Such were the lines insulted virtue pour'd,
And such the wealth of wit's exhaustless hoard:
Of keenest wisdom dallying with her scorn,
And playful jest of indignation born;
And honest hatred of that godless crew,
To king, to country—to themselves untrue:
The hands that laid the blameless mitre low,
That gave great Wentworth to the headsman's blow,
And theirs the deed immortalized in shame,
Which raised a monarch to a martyr's name.
Oh! friend! with me thy thoughtful sorrows join,
Thy heart will answer each desponding line;
Say, when thy hand o'er KEN'S neglected grave
At once the flowers of love and learning gave;

Or when was heard, beneath each listening tree,
The lute sweet Archimage had lent to thee:
Say, while thy day was like a summer dream,
And musing leisure mét thee by the stream,
Where thro' rich weeds the lulling waters crept,
And the huge forest's massive umbrage slept,
And, summon'd by thy harp's aerial spell,
The shadowy tribes came trooping from their cell;
(For still 'twas thine, with all a poet's art,
To paint the living landscape of the heart;
And still to nature's soft enchantments true,
Feel every charm, and catch each varying hue;)
Couldst thou foresee how soon the poet's strain
Would wake its satire into truth again;
How soon the still-revolving wheel of time
Recall the past — each folly, and each crime;
Again the petty tyrant boast his flame,
And raise, on fancied ills, a patriot's name;
How soon the trembling altar fade away,
The hallow'd temple prove the spoiler's prey;
The throne its proud ancestral honours yield;
And faction shake the senate and the field;
How folly seize, while bleeding freedom wept,
That sacred ark which jealous wisdom kept;
Which, virtuous Falkland! saw thy banners wave,
Which Somers lived, and Chatham died to save;
While history points her awful page in vain,
And sees all Butler scorn'd, revive again.

J. M.

BENHALL, Feb. 1835.

LIFE OF SAMUEL BUTLER.

BY THE REV. JOHN MITFORD.

Samuel Butler, the author of Hudibras, was born in the parish of Strensham, in Worcestershire, in 1612,* and christened February the 14th. A. Wood says, that his father was competently wealthy; † but the anonymous author of a life prefixed to his Poems describes him as in the condition of a yeoman, possessing a very small estate, and renting another; who with difficulty found means to educate his son at the grammar-school at Worcester, under Mr. Henry Bright, a man of high reputation as a scholar, and a Prebendary of the Cathedral. Butler is said to have

* This date is contradicted by Charles Longueville, the son of Butler's friend, and who declared that the poet was born in 1600. Nash dates his baptism February 8, 1612, and says it is entered in the writing of Nash's father, who was churchwarden : he had four sons and three daughters; the three daughters and one son older than the poet.

† Dr. Nash discovered that his father was owner of a house and a little land, worth about 10*l.* a year, still called *Butler's tenement*, of which he has given an engraving in the title page of his first volume. A. Wood affirms that he had a competent estate of nearly 300*l.* a year, but held on *lease* of William Russell, lord of the manor of Strensham.

gone from thence to Cambridge,* with the character of a good scholar; but the period and place of his residence seem alike unknown, and indeed it appears doubtful whether he ever received the advantages of an academical education.

For some time he was clerk to Mr. Jefferys, of Earls Croomb, in Worcestershire, an eminent justice of the peace. He employed the ample leisure which his situation afforded in study; while he also cultivated the arts of painting and music. "The Hogarth of poetry," says Walpole, "was a painter too:" his love of the pencil introduced him to the acquaintance of the celebrated Samuel Cooper.† Some pictures were shown by the family as his, but we presume of no great excellence, as they were subsequently employed to stop broken windows. Dr. Nash says that he heard of a portrait of Oliver Cromwell by him. After this, he was recommended to the notice of the Countess of Kent, living at Wrest, in Bedfordshire, where he had not only the advantage of a library,‡ but enjoyed the conversation of the most learned man

* A. Wood had his information from Butler's brother; some of his neighbours sent him to Oxford. Mr. Longueville asserted that Butler never resided at Oxford.

† Of our English poets, Flatman and George Dyer were painters. Pope also used the brush under the tuition of Jervas. I recollect no further union of the arts.

‡ "Butler was not acquainted with the Italian poets. Of Ruggiero he might have truly asserted what he has falsely told of Rinaldo." — See Neve on the English Poets, p. 79.

of his age, the great Selden. Why he subsequently left so advantageous and honourable a situation does not appear, but we find him domesticated under the roof of Sir Samuel Luke, at Cople, or Wood end, a gentleman of a very ancient family in Bedfordshire, one of Cromwell's officers, and a rigid Presbyterian. It is in this place and at this time that he is said to have commenced his celebrated poem. His patron's house afforded him a gallery of living portraits, and he was fortunately permitted to see Puritanism in one of its strong holds. The keenness of his observation secured the fidelity of his descriptions, and enabled him to fill up his outline with those rich and forcible details, which a familiar acquaintance with the originals afforded.

At the restoration of the exiled monarch, when loyalty expected the reward of its fidelity and the recompense of its losses, Butler appears to have suffered the same disappointment that met other claimants; and silently and unobtrusively retreating from the conflict of avarice and importunity,* he accepted the Secretaryship to Richard,

* It is supposed that Sir Samuel Luke is ridiculed under the character of Hudibras: the reason of the conjecture is founded on Hudib. P. i. c. 1. ver. 904:—

'Tis sung, there is a valiant Mamaluke,
In foreign land yclep'd —;

and the ballad entitled "A Tale of the Cobbler and Vicar of Bray," in the posthumous works, p. 285, but this ballad is

Earl of Carbury, Lord President of the Principality of Wales, who made him Steward of Ludlow Castle, where the court of the marches was removed. About this time, he married Mrs. Herbert,* a gentlewoman of good family, but who had lost most of her fortune, by placing it on bad securities, in those very dangerous and uncertain times. A. Wood says, that he was Secretary to George, Duke of Buckingham, when he was Chancellor of Cambridge; that the Duke treated him with kindness and generosity; and

not proved to be genuine. Nash says, "he was informed by a bencher of Gray's Inn, who had it from an acquaintance of Butler's, that the person intended was Sir Henry Rosewell, of Torr Abbey, in Devonshire," but adds, "these would be probable reasons to deprive Bedfordshire of the hero, did not Butler, in his Memoirs of 1649, give the same description of Sir Samuel Luke, and in his Dunstable Downs expressly style Sir Samuel Luke, Sir Hudibras;" the name was borrowed from Spenser, F. Q. 11. i. 17.

He that made love unto the eldest dame
Was hight Sir Hudibras, an hardy man.

It is supposed that Lilly the astrologer was represented under the person of Sidrophel; though Sir Paul Neal, who denied Butler to be the author of Hudibras, has been mentioned as the person intended. Vide Grey's Hudibras, ii. 388. 105. 1st edit.; and Nash's Hudibras, vol. ii. p. 308. That *Whachum* was meant for Sir George Wharton, does not appear to rest on any proof; v. Biographia, Art. Sherborne, note (B).

* A. Wood says, that she was a widow, and that Butler supported himself by her jointure, deriving nothing from the practice of the law.

that, in common with almost all men of wit and learning, he enjoyed the friendship of the celebrated Earl of Dorset. The author of his Life, prefixed to his Poems, says, that the integrity of his life, the acuteness of his wit, and the easiness of his conversation, rendered him acceptable to all; but that he avoided a multiplicity of acquaintance. The accounts both of the patronage of the Duke of Buckingham and the Secretaryship are disbelieved by Dr Johnson, on the following grounds: — "Mr. Wycherley," says Major Packe, "had always laid hold of an opportunity which offered of representing to the Duke of Buckingham how well Mr. Butler had deserved of the royal family, by writing his inimitable Hudibras, and that it was a reproach to the Court that a person of his loyalty and wit should suffer in obscurity, and under the wants he did. The Duke always seemed to hearken to him with attention enough, and after some time undertook to recommend his pretensions to his Majesty. Mr. Wycherley, in hopes to keep him steady to his word, obtained of his Grace to name a day, when he might introduce that modest and unfortunate poet to his new patron. At last an appointment was made, and the place of meeting was agreed to be the Roebuck. Mr. Butler and his friend attended accordingly; the Duke joined them, but as the devil would have it, the door of the room where they sat was open, and his Grace, who had seated himself near it, observing a pimp of his acquaintance (the creature too was a knight) trip by with a brace of ladies, immediately quitted his engagement to follow another kind of business, at which he was more ready than to do good offices to those of desert, though no one was better qualified than he, both in regard to his fortune and understanding, to protect them; and from that time to the day of his death, poor Butler never found the least effect of his promise."

This story may be believed or not; to me, I confess, it appears more like a well-dressed fiction of Wycherley's than the truth; why the accidental interruption of the interview should never after have been repaired, does not appear; but there is a better testimony in some verses of Butler, which were published by Mr. Thyer: "which are written (says Johnson) with a degree of acrimony, such as neglect and disappointment might naturally excite, and such as it would be hard to imagine Butler capable of expressing against a man who had any claim to his gratitude."

In 1663, the first part of Hudibras, in three cantos, was published,* when more than fifty years

* Some verses in the first edition of Hudibras were afterwards omitted for reasons of state, as

Did not the learned Glynne and Maynard,
To make good subjects traitors, strain hard.
Was not the king, by proclamation,
Declared a traitor through the nation.

had matured the author's genius, and given large scope to his experience of mankind. It was speedily known at Court, through the influence of the Earl of Dorset.* The king praised, the courtiers, of course, admired, and the royalists greeted a production which certainly covered their now fallen enemies with all the derision and contempt which wit and genius could command. In 1664, the second part appeared; and the author, as well as the public, watched with anxiety for the reward which he was to receive from the gratitude of the king; like the other expectants of Charles's bounty, which was drained off into very different channels, they watched in vain. Clarendon, says Wood, gave him reason to hope for places and employments of value and credit, but he never received them; and the story of the king's presenting him with a purse of three hundred guineas appears also to rest on no competent authority. To compensate for the neglect of the court, and of a king, who, in truth, cared for no one but himself, and who possessed neither public honour nor private principle, it is difficult to say, whether Butler may have been satisfied with the approbation of the people; or how far the love of his art, confidence in his own genius, and a natural fondness for a successful production, may have induced him to continue his poem; certainly

* See Prior's Dedication to his Poems.

in four years more he published the third part, which still leaves the work unfinished. What he ultimately intended, it is impossible to conjecture from a narrative which has no consistent plan, or progress. He may have been wearied of it, or he may not have had time to continue it; for he died two years after its appearance, on the 25th of September, in the year 1680;* and was buried very privately by his friend Mr. Longueville, in the church-yard of St. Paul, Covent Garden, at his private expense; for he had in vain solicited an honourable and public funeral in Westminster Abbey. About seven or eight persons followed his remains. His grave, which, according to his desire, was six feet deep, was at the west end of the church-yard on the north side; and the burial service was read over him by the learned Dr. Patrick, then minister of the parish, and afterwards Bishop of Ely. Dr. Johnson says, that Mr. Lowndes of the Treasury informed Dr. Zachary Pearce,† that Butler was allowed a yearly pension of a hundred pounds; but this, as Johnson says, is contradicted

* A. Wood says he died of a consumption; Oldham says he was carried off by a fever; but as he was near fourscore, we may be spared any further investigation. Mr. Longueville says he lived for some years in Rose Street, Covent Garden, and probably died there: that notwithstanding his disappointments he was never reduced to want or beggary, and that he did not die in any person's debt.

† See Granger's Biog. Hist. of England, vol. iv. p. 40.

by all tradition, by the complaints of Oldham,* and the reproaches of Dryden. About sixty years after, Mr. Barber, whose name is familiar to all persons conversant with the literature of that time, who was printer and mayor of London, erected a monument in Westminster Abbey to the poet's memory; the inscription will prove how warmly he approved his principles.

M. S.
SAMUELIS BUTLERI,
Qui Strenshamiæ in agro Vigorn. nat. 1612,
obiit Lond. 1680.

Vir doctus imprimis, acer, integer;
Operibus ingenii, non item præmiis fœlix:
Satyrici apud nos carminis artifex egregius;
Quo simulatæ religionis larvam detraxit,
Et perduellium scelera liberrime exagitavit;
Scriptorum in suo genere, primus et postremus.
Ne, cui vivo deerant ferè omnia,
Deessit etiam mortuo tumulus,
Hoc tandem posito marmore, curavit
Johannes Barber, civis Londinensis, 1721.†

* See Oldham's 'Satire against Poetry,' and Dryden's 'Hind and Panther,' and Otway's 'Prologue to the Tragedy of Constantine the Great.' Butler twice transcribed the following distich in his Common-place Book:

To think how *Spenser* died, how *Cowley* mourn'd,
How *Butler's* faith and service were return'd.

† In the additions to Pope's works, published by George Steevens, i. p. 13, are some lines said to be written by Pope on this monument erected by Barber.

Respect to Dryden Sheffield justly paid,
And noble Villars honour'd Cowley's shade.

After his death, three small volumes were pub lished bearing the title of his posthumous pieces in verse and prose;* they are, however, all spurious, except the ode on Duval and two of the prose tracts: but the volumes subsequently given to the world by Mr. Thyer, keeper of the public library at Manchester, are genuine † and valuable. "As

But whence this Barber? that a name so mean
Should, join'd with Butler's, on a tomb be seen;
The pyramid would better far proclaim
To future ages humbler Settle's name;
Poet and patron then had been well pair'd,
The city printer and the city bard.

The lines also by Samuel Wesley are well known (vide Poems, 4to. 1736, p. 62.)

While Butler, needy wretch, was yet alive,
No generous patron would a dinner give;
See him, when starved to death and turn'd to dust,
Presented with a monumental bust.
The poet's fate is here in emblem shown,
He ask'd for bread, and he received a stone.

* See Delineation of Butler's Monument in Dart's Westminster Abbey, pl. 3, tom. 1, pp. 78, 79. With regard to the monument erected in 1786, when the church was repaired, at the expense of some of the parishioners, on the south side of the church (inside) with the inscription, see Nash's Life of Butler, xiii. See engraving of it in Nash's Life of Butler, p. xxxix. An engraving of the monument in Westminster Abbey is in the same work, p. 678.

† What genuine remains of Butler Thyer did *not* publish, were all in the hands either of Dr. R. Farmer or Dr. Nash, and had been seen by Atterbury. See Life by Nash, xvi. James Massey, Esq. of Rosthern, Cheshire, had Butler's Common place Book. Some law cases from Coke upon Littleton, drawn

to these *remains* of Butler," says Warburton in his Letters (cxxxi), "they are certainly his; but they would not strike the public, if that public was honest; but the public is a malicious monster, which cares not what it affords to dead merit, so it can but depress the living. There was something singular in this same Butler; besides an infinite deal of wit, he had great sense and penetration, both in the sciences and in the world. Yet with all this, he could never plan a work or tell a story well. The first appears from his Hudibras; the other from his Elephant in the Moon. He evidently appears to be dissatisfied with it, by turning it into long verse, but that was his forte; the fault lay in the manner of telling, not but he might have another reason for trying his hand at heroic verse — emulation. Dryden had burst out in a surprising manner; and, in such a case, the poetic world, as we have seen by a late instance, is always full of imitations. But Butler's heroics are poor stuff; indeed only doggerel made languid by heavy expletives. This attempt in the change of his measure was the sillier, not only as he acquired the mastery in the short measure, but as that measure, somehow or other, suits best with his sort of wit. His characters are full of cold puerilities, though intermixed with abundance of

up in Norman-French by Butler, were bought by Dr. Nash of Butler's relation in Buckinghamshire. He had also a French dictionary compiled by him, and part of a tragedy of Nero.

wit and with a great deal of good sense. He is sometimes wonderfully fine both in sentiment and expression, as when he defines 'the Proud Man to be a Fool in fermentation;' and when speaking of the Antiquary, he says, 'he has a great veneration for words that are stricken in years and are grown so aged that they have outlived their employments:' but the great fault in these characters is that they are a bad and false species of composition.* As for his editor he is always in the wrong when there was a possibility of his mistaking. I could not but smile at his detecting Pope's plagiarisms about the Westphalia hogs, when I reflected, that in a very little time, when the chronology is not well attended to, your fine note about the ambergris will be understood by every one as a ridicule upon it; and, indeed, an excellent one it is: notwithstanding, I wish this fellow would give us a new edition of Hudibras, for the reason he mentions."

A. Wood ascribed to Butler two pamphlets, supposed, he says, falsely to be William Prynn's. The one entitled "Mola Asinaria," or the unreasonable and insupportable Burden pressed upon the Shoulders of this groaning Nation. London, 1659, in one sheet 4to. The other, Two Letters; one from John Audland, a quaker, to William

* See some excellent observations on this style of writing in Retrosp. Rev. vol. iii. art. iv. 'Fuller's Church History.'

Prynn; the other, Prynn's Answer; in three sheets in folio, 1672. The author of his life also adds, that he had seen a small poem, of one sheet in quarto, on Duval the highwayman, said to be written by Butler. These formed part of the posthumous pieces above mentioned; to which may be added the fragment given to Mr Aubrey by the poet himself, and printed by the writer of his life. It is said that Butler did not shine in conversation till he had taken a cheerful glass, though he was no intemperate drinker. The following story is told in the British Biography:— "Before he (Butler) was personally known to the Earl of Dorset, that nobleman had a great desire to spend an evening with him as a private gentleman; and with that view prevailed on Mr. Thetwood Shepherd to introduce him into his company, at a tavern which they used, in the character only of a common friend. This being done, Mr. Butler, we are told, whilst the first bottle was drinking, appeared very flat and heavy, at the second bottle extremely brisk and lively, full of wit and learning, and a most pleasant agreeable companion, but before the third bottle was finished sunk again into such stupidity and dulness, that hardly any body could have believed him to be the author of Hudibras, a book abounding with so much wit, learning, and pleasantry. Next morning Mr. Shepherd asked his lordship's opinion of Mr. Butler, who answered, "He is like a ninepin, little at both ends, but great in the middle."* Johnson sums up the personal history of the poet by saying, "In this mist of obscurity passed the life of Butler, a man whose name can only perish with his language. The date of his birth is doubtful, the mode and place of his education are unknown, the events of his life are variously related, and all that can be told with certainty is that he was poor."

A list of the portraits of Butler, in painting and engraving, may be found in Granger's History of England; † a portrait of him by Lely is in the Picture Gallery at Oxford; and another, by the same hand, formerly in the possession of Mr. Longueville, became the property of Mr. Hayter of Salisbury. Another likeness of him by Zoort, was formerly in the collection of the celebrated Mr. Charles Jennins. Several prints of him by Vertue are also prefixed to different editions of his works.

The merit of Hudibras (it has been well observed),‡ certainly lies in its style and execution,

* A. Wood says, "Butler was a boon and witty companion, especially among the company he knew well."

† See vol. iv. p. 38, &c. A mezzotint print of Lord Grey has been altered to Butler.

‡ See Campbell's Specimens of Br. Poets, vol. iv. p. 205. The principal actions of the poem, says Nash, are four. 1. Hudibras's victory over Crowdero. 2. Trulla's victory over Hudibras. 3. Hudibras's victory over Sidrophel. 4. The Widow's antimasquerade. The rest is made up of the adven-

and by no means in the structure of the story. The action of the poem as it stands, and interrupted as it is, occupies but three days, and it is clear from the opening line, "When civil dudgeon first grew high," that it was meant to bear date with the civil wars. Yet after two days and nights are completed, the Poet skips at once, in the third part, to Oliver Cromwell's death, and then returns to retrieve his hero, and conduct him through the last canto. Before the third part of Hudibras appeared, a great space of time had elapsed, since the publication of the first. Charles the Second had been fifteen years asleep on the throne, and Butler seems to have felt that the ridicule of the sectaries was a stale subject. The final interest of the piece, therefore, dwindles into the Widow's repulse of Sir Hudibras, a topic which has been suspected to allude not so much to the Presbyterians, as to the reigning monarch's dotage upon his mistresses. "Burlesque," says Shenstone, "may perhaps be divided into such as turns chiefly on the thought and such as depends more on the expression, or we may add a third kind, consisting in thoughts ridiculously dressed, in language much above or below their dignity. The Splendid Shilling of Phillips, and the Hudibras of Butler are the most obvious instances. Butler,

tures of the Bear, of the Skimmington, Hudibras's conversations with the Lawyer and Sidrophel, and his long disputations with Ralpho and the Widow.

however, depended much on the ludicrous effect of his double rhymes; in other respects, to declare your sentiments, he is rather a witty writer, than a humorous one."* The defect of Butler's poem undoubtedly consists in what has been already mentioned,—the poverty of the incidents, and the incompleteness and irregularity of the design. The slender strain of narrative which is just visible in the commencement,† soon dwindles away aud is lost. It is true that the poem abounds with curious and uncommon learning, with original thoughts, happy images, quaint and comic turns of expression, and new and fanciful rhymes. But the humour, instead of being diffused quietly and unostentatiously over the whole poem, in rich harmonious colouring, is collected into short epigrammatic sentences, pointed apothegms, and unexpected allusions. It has the same merits and defects as a poem of a very different kind—Young's Night Thoughts,—copious invention, new and pleasing images, and brilliant thoughts; with a want of sufficient connexion in the subject,

* Shenstone's Works, vol. ii. p. 182, third ed.

† "Butler set out on too narrow a plan, and even that design is not kept up. He sinks into little true particulars about the Widow, &c. The enthusiastic Knight, and the ignorant Squire, over religious in two different ways, and always quarrelling together, is the chief point of view in it."—(Pope) v. Spence's Anecdotes, p. 208. It appears from some passages in Warburton's Correspondence, that *Gray* did not much admire this poem of Butler's.

and progress in the story. There is no poem at all resembling Hudibras in character in our language; but parts of it are not dissimilar to the style and manner of some prose writings of the time, which were published under the name of 'Characters,' and which, like Butler's poem, dazzle rather than delight by successive flashes of wit, and a rapid play of fancy. It may be observed that the defects and merits of this work are *practically* made known by the manner in which it is read. Its want of story and incident seldom permits a continued perusal; while the abundance of its wise * and witty sayings insures a constant recurrence to its pages. As little can be added to the character of the work which Johnson has given, and as it would be presumptuous to hope to express his thoughts in any language but his own, we shall conclude with extracting from his Life of Butler the following critical opinion of his work.

"The poem of Hudibras is one of those compositions of which a nation may justly boast; as the images which it exhibits are domestic, the sentiments unborrowed and unexpected, and the strain of diction original and peculiar. We must not, however, suffer the pride, which we assume

* "Though scarcely any author was ever able to express his thoughts in so few *words* as Butler, he often employs too many thoughts on one subject, and thus becomes prolix after an unusual manner." — See Hume's Hist. of England, vol. viii. p. 337.

as the countrymen of Butler, to make any encroachment upon justice, nor appropriate those honours which others have a right to share. The poem of Hudibras is not wholly English; the original idea is to be found in the history of Don Quixote; a book to which a mind of the greatest powers may be indebted without disgrace. Cervantes shows a man, who, having by the incessant perusal of incredible tales subjected his understanding* to his imagination, and familiarized his mind by pertinacious meditation to trains of incredible events and scenes of impossible existence, goes out in the pride of knighthood to redress wrongs and defend virgins, to rescue captive princesses, and tumble usurpers from their thrones, attended by a squire, whose cunning, too low for the suspicion of a generous mind, enables him often to cheat his master.

"The hero of Butler is a Presbyterian justice, who, in the confidence of legal authority and the rage of zealous ignorance, ranges the country to repress superstition and correct abuses, accompanied by an *Independent* clerk, disputatious and obstinate, with whom he often debates, but never conquers him.

"Cervantes had so much kindness for Don Quixote, that, however he embarrasses him with absurd distresses, he gives him so much sense and

* Would not "reason" be the more proper word?

virtue, as may preserve our esteem. Wherever he is or whatever he does, he is made by matchless dexterity, commonly ridiculous, but never contemptible.

"But for poor Hudibras, his poet had no tenderness, he chooses not that any pity should be shewn, or respect paid him. He gives him up at once to laughter and contempt, without any quality that can dignify or protect him. In forming the character of Hudibras, and describing his person and habiliments, the author seems to labour with a tumultuous confusion of dissimilar ideas. He had read the history of the mock knights-errant, he knew the notions and manners of a Presbyterian magistrate, and tried to unite the absurdities of both, however distant, in one personage.* Thus he gives him that pedantic ostentation of knowledge, which has no relation to chivalry, and

* "One great object," says Nash, "of our Poet's satire, is to unmask the hypocrite and to exhibit in a light at once odious and ridiculous, the Presbyterians and Independents, and all other sects, which in our Poet's days amounted to near two hundred, and were enemies to the king; but his further view was to banter all the false and erase all the suspicious pretences to learning that prevailed in his time, such as astrology, sympathetic medicine, alchymy, transfusion of blood, trifling experimental philosophy, fortune-telling, incredible relations of travellers, false wit and injudicious affectation of ornament to be found in the poets, romance writers; thus he frequently alludes to Purchas's Pilgrims, Sir K. Digby's books, Bulwar's Artificial Changeling, Brown's Vulgar Errors, Burton's Melancholy, the early Transactions of the Royal Society, &c."

loads him with martial encumbrances, that can add nothing to his civil dignity. He sends him out a *colonelling*, and yet never brings him within sight of war. If Hudibras be considered as the representative of the Presbyterians, it is not easy to say why his weapons should be represented as ridiculous or useless; for whatever judgment might be passed on their knowledge, or their arguments, experience had sufficiently shown that their swords were not to be despised. The hero, thus compounded of swagger and pedant, of knight and justice, is led forth to action, with his Squire Ralpho, an Independent enthusiast. Of the contexture of events planned by the author, which is called the action of the poem, since it is left imperfect, no judgment can be made. It is probable that the hero was to be led through many luckless adventures, which would give occasion, like his attack on the Bear and Fiddle, to expose the ridiculous rigour of the sectaries; like his encounter with Sidrophel and Whachum, to make superstition and credulity contemptible; or like his recourse to the low retailer of the law, discover the fraudulent practices of different professions.

"What series of events he would have formed, or in what manner he would have rewarded or punished his hero, it is now vain to conjecture. His work must have had, it seems, the defect which Dryden imputes to Spenser, the action could not have been one: those could only have been a succession of incidents, each of which might have happened without the rest, and which could not all co-operate to any single conclusion. The discontinuity of the action might, however, have been easily forgiven, if there had been action enough; but I believe every reader regrets the paucity of events, and complains that in the poem of Hudibras, as in the History of Thucydides, there is more said than done. The scenes are too seldom changed, and the attention is tired with long conversation. It is indeed much more easy to form dialogues than to contrive adventures. Every position makes way for an argument, and every objection dictates an answer. When two disputants are engaged on a complicated and extensive question, the difficulty is not to continue, but to end the controversy. But whether it be, that we comprehend but few of the possibilities of life, or that life itself affords little variety, every man who has tried, knows how much labour it will cost to form such a combination of circumstances as shall have at once the grace of novelty and credibility, and delight fancy without violence to reason. Perhaps the dialogue of this poem is not perfect. Some power of engaging attention might have been added to it, by quicker reciprocation, by seasonable interruptions, by sudden questions, and by a nearer approach to dramatic sprightliness; without which fictitious speeches will always tire, however sparkling with sentences, and however variegated with allusions. The great source of pleasure is variety. Uniformity must tire at last, though it be an uniformity of excellence. We love to expect, and when expectation is disappointed, or gratified, we want to be again expecting. For this impatience of the present, whoever would please must make provision. The skilful writer, *irritat, mulcet,* makes a due distribution of the still and animated parts. It is for want of this artful intertexture, and those necessary changes, that the whole of a book may be tedious, though all the parts are praised.

"If inexhaustible wit could give perpetual pleasure, no eye could ever leave half-read the work of Butler; for what poet has ever brought so many remote images so happily together? It is scarcely possible to peruse a page without finding some association of images that was never found before. By the first paragraph the reader is amused, by the next he is delighted, and by a few more strained to astonishment, but astonishment is a toilsome pleasure. He is soon weary of wandering, and longs to be diverted.

> Omnia vult belle Matho dicere, dic aliquando
> Et bene, dic neutrum, dic aliquando male.

Imagination is useless without knowledge; nature gives in vain the power of combination, unless study and observation supply materials to be combined. Butler's treasures of knowledge appear proportioned to his expense. Whatever topic employs his mind, he shows himself qualified to expand and illustrate it with all the accessories that books can furnish. He is found not only to have travelled the beaten road, but the bye paths of literature; not only to have taken general surveys, but to have examined particulars with minute inspection. If the French boast the learning of Rabelais, we need not be afraid of confronting them with Butler. But the most valuable parts of his performance are those which retired study and native wit cannot supply. He that merely makes a book from books may be useful, but can scarcely be great. Butler had not suffered life to glide by him unseen or unobserved. He had watched with great diligence the operations of human nature, and traced the effects of opinion, humour, interest, and passion. From such remarks proceeded that great number of sententious distichs, which have passed into conversation, and are added as proverbial axioms to the general stock of practical knowledge. When any work has been viewed and admired, the first question of intelligent curiosity is, how was it performed? Hudibras was not a hasty effusion; it was not produced by a sudden tumult of imagination, or a short paroxysm of violent labour. To accumulate such a mass of sentiments at the call of accidental desire, or of sudden necessity, is beyond the reach and power of the most active and comprehensive mind. I am informed by Mr. Thyer, of Manchester, that excellent editor of this author's reliques, that he could show something like Hudibras in prose. He has in his possession the common-place book in which Butler reposited, not such events and precepts as are gathered by reading, but such remarks, similitudes, allusions, assemblages, or inferences, as occasion prompted, or meditation produced, those thoughts that were generated in his own mind, and might be usefully applied to some future purpose. Such is the labour of those who write for immortality: * but

* Butler crowds into his confined circle all the treasures of art and the accumulations of learning. He gives full measure to his readers, heaped up and running over. Thought crowds upon thought, and witticism on witticism, in rapid and dazzling succession. Every topic and every incident is made the most of: his bye-play always tells. Many of his happiest sallies appear to escape him as if by accident. Many of his hardest hits appear to be merely chance-blows. A description of a bear-ward brings in a sneer at Sir K. Digby, and his powder of sympathy; and an account of a tinker's doxy introduces a pleasantry on Sir W. Davenant's Gondibert. There is always an under-current of satiric allusion beneath the main stream of his satire. The juggling of astrology, the besetting folly of alchymy, the transfusion of blood, the sympathetic medicines, the learned trifling of experimental philosophers, the knavery of fortune-tellers, and the folly of their dupes, the marvellous relations of travellers, the subtleties of the school divines, the freaks of fashion, the fantastic extravagancies of lovers, the affectations of piety, and the absurdities of romance, are interwoven with his subject, and soften down and relieve his dark delineation of fanatical violence and perfidy. * * Butler was by no means deficient

human works are not easily found without a perishable part. Of the ancient poets, every reader feels the mythology tedious and oppressive; of Hudibras, the manners, being founded on opinions, are temporary and local, and therefore become every day less intelligible and less striking. What Cicero says of philosophy is true likewise of wit and humour, that time effaces the fictions of opinion, and confirms the determinations of nature. Such manners as depend upon standing relations and general passions are co-extended with the race of man; but those modifications of life and peculiarities of practice, which are the progeny of error and perverseness, or at best, of some accidental influence, or transient persuasion, must perish with their parents. Much, therefore, of that humour which transported the last century with merriment is lost to us, who do not know the sour solemnity, the sullen superstition, the gloomy moroseness, and the stubborn scruples of the ancient Puritans; or, if we know them, derive our information only from books, or from tradition; have never had them before our eyes, and cannot but by recollection and study understand the lines in which they are satirized. Our grandfathers

in humour, but it is cast into a dim eclipse by the predominance of his wit. His characters do not show themselves off unconsciously as fools or coxcombs: they are set up as marks at which the author levels all the shafts of his ridicule and sarcasm. *v.* Retrosp. Rev. vol. iii. p. 333.

knew the picture from the life; we judge of the life by contemplating the picture.

"It is scarcely possible, in the regularity and composure of the present time, to image the tumult of absurdity and clamour of contradiction, which perplexed doctrine, disordered practice, and disturbed both public and private quiet, in that age when subordination was broken, and awe was hissed away; when any unsettled innovator, who could hatch a half-formed notion, produced it to the public; when every man might become a preacher, and almost every preacher could collect a congregation. The wisdom of the nation is very reasonably supposed to reside in the parliament; what can be concluded of the lower classes of the people, when, in one of the parliaments summoned by Cromwell, it was seriously proposed, that all the records in the Tower should be burned, that all memory of things passed should be effaced, and that the whole system of life should commence anew! We have never been witnesses of animosities excited by the use of mince pies and plum porridge, nor seen with what abhorrence those who could eat them at all other times of the year, should shrink from them in December. An old Puritan, who was alive in my childhood, being, at one of the feasts of the Church, invited by a neighbour to partake his cheer, told him that if he would treat him at an alehouse with beer brewed for all times and seasons, he should accept his kindness, but would have none of his superstitious meats and drinks. One of the puritanical tenets was the illegality of all games of chance, and he that reads Gataker upon Lots, may see how much learning and reason one of the first scholars of his age thought necessary to prove that it was no crime to throw a die, or play at cards, or hide a shilling for the reckoning. Astrology, however, against which so much of the satire is directed, was not more the folly of the Puritans than of others; it had in that time a very extensive dominion; its predictions raised hopes and fears in minds which ought to have rejected it with contempt. In hazardous undertakings care was taken to begin under the influence of a propitious planet; and when the king was prisoner in Carisbrook Castle, an astrologer was consulted what hour would be found most favourable to an escape. What effect this Poem had upon the public, whether it shamed imposture, or reclaimed credulity, is not easily determined; cheats can seldom stand long against laughter; it is certain that the credit of planetary intelligence wore fast away, though some men of knowledge, and Dryden among them, continued to believe that conjunctions and oppositions had a great part in the distribution of good or evil, and in the government of sublunary things.

"Poetical action ought to be probable upon

certain suppositions; and such probability as burlesque requires is here violated only by one incident. Nothing can show more plainly the necessity of doing something, and the difficulty of finding something to do, than that Butler was reduced to transfer to his hero the flagellation of Sancho, not the most agreeable fiction of Cervantes, very suitable indeed to the manners of that age and nation, which ascribed wonderful efficacy to voluntary penances; but so remote from the practice and opinions of the Hudibrastic time, that judgment and imagination are alike offended. The diction of this poem is grossly familiar, and the numbers purposely neglected, except in a few places where the thoughts by their native excellence secure themselves from violation, being such as mean language cannot express. The mode of versification has been blamed by Dryden, who regrets that the heroic measure was not rather chosen. To the critical sentence of Dryden the highest reverence would be due, were not his decisions often precipitate, and his opinions immature. When he wished to change the measure, he probably would have been willing to change more. If he intended that when the numbers were heroic, the diction should still remain vulgar, he planned a very heterogeneous and unnatural composition. If he preferred a general stateliness both of sound and words, he can only be understood to wish Butler had undertaken a different work. The measure is quick, sprightly, and colloquial, suitable to the vulgarity of the words, and the levity of the sentiments, but such numbers and such diction can gain regard only when they are used by a writer whose vigour of fancy and copiousness of knowledge entitle him to contempt of ornaments, and who in confidence of the novelty and justness of his conceptions, can afford to throw metaphors and epithets away. To another that conveys common thoughts in careless versification, it will only be said, 'Pauper videri Cinna vult, et est pauper.' The meaning and diction will be worthy of each other, and criticism may justly doom them to perish together. Nor even though another Butler should arise, would another Hudibras obtain the same regard. Burlesque consists in a disproportion between the style and the sentiments, or between the adventitious sentiments and the fundamental subject. It, therefore, like all bodies compounded of heterogeneous parts, contains in it a principle of corruption. All disproportion is unnatural, and from what is unnatural we can derive only the pleasure which novelty produces. We admire it awhile as a strange thing; but when it is no longer strange we perceive its deformity. It is a kind of artifice which by frequent repetition detects itself: and the reader, learning in time what he is to expect, lays down his book, as the spectator turns away from a second exhibition of those tricks, of which the only use is to show they can be played."

NOTES.

Page ix. On Sir Samuel Luke being represented by Hudibras, see Dr. Grey's Preface, p. iv., where by a reverend and learned person, *Warburton* is meant ; see D'Israeli's Curiosities of Literature (new series), vol. i. p. 235, on this point. The Grub Street Journal says, one Col. Rolle, a Devonshire man. The old tutelar saint of Devonshire was Hugh de Bras, see Edinburgh Review, No. LXVII. 159. The author of a curious article in the Censor, No. XVI. (v. Gent. Mag.) called "Memoirs of Sir Samuel Luke," observes, An unauthenticated story prevails that Butler once lived in the service of Sir Samuel Luke, and has increased with a succession of writers, like a rolling ball of snow. Wood and Aubrey, who had both access to credible information, say nothing about it ; and it first occurs in an anonymous life prefixed to his poems. Towneley, in his Memoir, insinuates that he behaved with ingratitude ; 'Il me semble qu'il doit épargner le chevalier Luke, son bienfaiteur, que la gratitude et la reconnaissance auraient du mettre a couvert contre les traits de la satire de votre auteur.' But for the climax of this representation we are indebted to the Edinb. Review (Art. Hogg's Jacobite Relics), in which the critic roundly asserts that "Butler lived in the family, supported by the bounty of Sir Samuel Luke, one of Cromwell's captains, at the very time he planned his Hudibras, of which he was pleased to make his kind friend and hospitable patron the Hero." Now (he continues) we defy the history of whiggism to match this anecdote, or to produce so choice a specimen of the human nettle!

P. xiii. Gratitude of the king.] According to the verses in Butler's 'Hudibras at Court' (v. Remains).

Now you must know, Sir Hudibras
With such perfections gifted was,
And so peculiar in his manner,
That all that saw him, did him honor.
Among the rest this prince was one
Admired his conversation.
This prince, whose ready wit and parts
Conquer'd both men and women's hearts:
Was so o'ercome with Knight and Ralph,
That he could never clear it off.
He never eat, nor drank, nor slept,
But Hudibras still near him kept;
Nor would he go to church, or so,
But Hudibras must with him go.
Nor yet to visit concubine,
Or at a city feast to dine;
But Hudibras must still be there,
Or all the fat were in the fire.
Now after all, was it not hard
That he should meet with no reward,
That fitted out this Knight and Squire,
This monarch did so much admire;
That he should never reimburse
The man for th' equipage and horse,
Is sure a strange ungrateful thing
In any body but a king;
But this good king, it seems, was told
By some that were with him too bold,
If e'er you hope to gain your ends,
Caress your foes, and trust your friends.

Such were the doctrines that were taught
Till this unthinking king was brought
To leave his friends to starve and die,
A poor reward for loyalty.

Oldham, in his Satire against Poetry, writes thus:

On Butler who can think without just rage,
The glory and the scandal of the age.
Fair stood his hopes, when first he came to town,
Met every where with welcomes of renown.
Courted and loved by all, with wonder read,
And promises of princely favour fed.
But what reward for all had he at last,
After a life in dull expectance past.
The wretch, at summing up his misspent days,
Found nothing left but poverty and praise.
Of all his gains by verse he could not save
Enough to purchase flannel and a grave.
Reduced to want, he in due time fell sick,
Was fain to die, and be interred on tick,
And well might bless the fever that was sent
To rid him thence, and his worse fate prevent.

And Dryden, in the Hind and Panther:

Unpitied Hudibras, your champion friend,
Has shown how far your charities extend.
This lasting verse shall on his tomb be read,
He shamed you living, and upbraids you dead.

P. xv. Epitaph on Butler, by John Dennis, never before published, in D'Israeli's Curiosities of Literature (new series), vol. i. p. 240.

Near this place lies interred
The body of Mr. S. Butler,
Author of Hudibras.
He was a whole species of poets in one,
Admirable in a manner,
In which no one else has been tolerable;
A manner which began and ended with him,
In which he knew no guide,
And found no followers.

P. xxiii. On the versification of Hudibras, see Dryden's Ded. to Juvenal, 1735, p. 100; to which Johnson alludes. See also Addison's Spectator, vol. i. No. ix. See also Prior's Alma (c. ii. init.).

But shall we take the muse abroad,
To drop her idly on the road?
And leave our subject in the middle,
As Butler did his bear and fiddle?
Yet he, consummate master, knew
When to recede and when pursue.
His noble negligences teach
What others' toils despair to reach.
He, perfect dancer, climbs the rope,
And balances your fear and hope;
If, after some distinguish'd leap,
He drops his pole, and seems to slip,
Straight gathering all his active strength,
He rises higher half his length.
With wonder you approve his slight,
And owe your pleasure to your fright.
But like poor Andrew I advance,
False mimic of my master's dance.
Around the cord awhile I sprawl,
And thence, though low, in earnest fall.

APPENDIX.

I. BUTLER's Hudibras; the first part printed by T. G. for Richard Marriott, under St. Dunstan's Church, Fleet Street, 1663, 8vo. p. 268.* In the Mercurius Aulicus, Jan. 1–8, 1662, is an advertisement: — There is stolen abroad a most false and imperfect copy of Hudibras, without name, either of printer or bookseller; the true and perfect edition printed by the author's original, is sold by Richard Marriott, near St. Dunstan's Church, in Fleet Street. That other nameless impression is a cheat, and will but abuse the buyer as well as the author, whose poem deserves to have fallen into better hands.

II. Hudibras, the second part, 1663. This spurious second part was published after Butler had printed his first part, and before he printed the second, and is very scarce. It ran through three editions in the same year; the first two do not differ except in the type. But there was another edition still, "Hudibras, the second part, with the continuation of the third canto, to which is added a fourth canto."

* I have also met with 'Mercurius Menippeus, the Loyal Satirist, or Hudibras in Prose; written by an unknown hand, in the time of the late rebellion, but never till now published, 1682,' a curious tract.

Hudibras; the second part, by the author of the first; printed by T. R. for John Martyn and James Allestrey, at the Bell, in St. Paul's Church-yard, 1664, 8vo. and 12mo. It has on the title page a wood-cut, with the publishers' device, a bell, and the letters at the bottom, M: A. In the Mercurius Publicus for Nov. 20, 1663, is this very singular advertisement: — "Newly published, the second part of Hudibras, by the author of the former, which (if possible) has outdone the first." — In the B. Museum (Misc. Pap. Bibl. Birch. No. 4293) is the following injunction: — Charles R., our will and pleasure is, and we do hereby strictly charge and command, that no printer, bookseller, stationer, or other person whatsoever, within our kingdom of England, or Ireland, do print, reprint, utter, or sell, or cause to be printed, reprinted, uttered, or sold, a book or poem, called Hudibras, or any part thereof, without the consent and approbation of Samuel Boteler, Esq. or his assigns, as they, and every of them will answer the contrary at their perils. Given at our Court at Whitehall, the 10th day of September, in the year of our Lord God 1677, and in the 29th year of our reign, by his Majesty's command. T. Berkenhead.

Hudibras; the third and last part, written by the author of the first and second parts; printed for Simon Miller, at the sign of the Star, at the west end of St. Paul's, 1678, 8vo. p. 285. This part had no notes during the author's life, and who inserted them afterwards is not known.

The first and second parts were republished in 1674. Hudibras, the first and second parts, written in the time of the late wars, corrected and amended with several additions and annotations, London, 1674, part i. p. 202; part ii. pp. 223–412.

III. See some lines from the first canto of Hudibras, admirably translated into Latin verse by Christopher Smart, published in the Student; or, Oxford and Cambridge Miscellany, published by Thornton in 1750.— See Beloe's Anecdotes, vol. vi. p. 419. Some also by Dr. Harmer, Greek Professor at Oxford, may be seen in the notes to the Biographia Britannica.

IV. Dr. Grey's edition of Hudibras was published first in 1744. See on it Gent. Mag., 1819, vol. xii. N. S. p. 416, Dr. Grey's valuable but *incorrect* edition. In Grey's edition the Meditations of Justice Adam Overdo in the stocks are inserted from B. Jonson's Bartholomew Fair. The soliloquy is ingeniously split into a dialogue, and one-half given to *Adam*, the other half to *Overdo*. The consulship of Julius and Cæsar was nothing to this. Dr. Grey left large additional notes, designed for a new edition, which were in the hands of Mr Nichols. As regards the posthumous works of Butler (*v.* Life, p. xv.) it appears from the authority of Mr. Thyer that very few (only three) of them are authentic. Jacob, in his Lives of the Dramatic Poets, p. 21, says, "not one line of those poems lately published under his (Butler's) name is genuine." See also Gent. Mag. May, 1819, vol. xii. N. S. p. 417, and Thyer's Remains, vol. i. p. 145, 302, 327. One passage occurs in the speech of the Earl of Pembroke which is curious from its strong verbal coincidence with a passage in Burke's will—"My will is that I have no monument, for then I must have epitaphs and verses, but all my life long I have had too much of them," v. Burke's Will, in Bisset's Life, p. 578. "I desire that no *monument* beyond a middle-sized tablet, with a small and simple inscription on the church-wall, or on the flag stone, be erected; but *I have had in my life time* but *too much of noise and compliment.*"

V. John Townley, the translator of Hudibras, was an officer of the Irish brigade, and a knight of the military order of St. Louis; he was uncle to Charles Townley, Esq. who possessed the marbles and statues. See Nichol's Hogarth, p. 145, and Notice sur la vie et les écrits de M. Larcher, p. 135, in Class. Journal, No. xix. When the critical reviewers reviewed Tytler's Essay on Translation, they would not believe in the existence of this book, it was so scarce. See Beloe's Anecdotes, i. p. 216, 220. The publication was superintended by M. L'Abbé Turberville Needham, and illustrated with notes by Larcher. There is an engraving of Mr. Townley by Skelton, with the following inscription: —

Ad impertiendum amicis inter Gallos
Linguæ Anglicanæ nonnihil peritis
Facetum poema Hudibras dictum
Accurate, festiveque gallice convertit
Hic Johannes Towneley
Caroli Towneley de Towneley
In agro Lancastriensi armigeri filius
Nat. A. D. 1679. Denat. A. D. 1782.
Grato, pioque animo fieri curavit
Johannes Towneley, nepos 1797.

Reprinted, Paris, 1819, 12mo. 3 vols. said to be a faithful reprint with the *addition* of notes by Larcher, and a Key to Hudibras by Zottin le jeune, and some account of the translator.

From the Literary Cyclopædia, p. 83.

VI. In estimating the poem of Hudibras, we should consider that genius takes every variety of form, adapts itself to every change of circumstance, and out of every object selects, according to its purpose, what is most essential to the view of truth, the exhibition of beauty, or the chastisement of folly. There are conventional notions on the subject which would restrict the honours of genius to the few master minds which have led to the discovery of some great laws of nature, or displayed the highest forms of creative imagination. But it is sometimes as great proof of genius to draw pictures from daily and familiar life, and to work upon its elements, as it is to soar above them; and it is still a question for the philosophical critic to decide, whether to raise a gorgeous pyramid of dreams out of the abstractions of thought, be a higher task than to master the fallacies of existence, and paint reality in all its strange and grotesque combinations. The author of Hudibras might alone afford scope to a controversy of this nature, for while he presents few, if any, of those characteristics which belong to the loftier class of minds, he so wonderfully adopts whatever is to be found in the actual world, or learnt from books, as to make his memorable lesson against bigotry one of the most remarkable productions of human ingenuity. But whatever may be the class to which Butler belongs in the Temple of Fame, there can only be one opinion respecting the value of his works, as a rich collection of lively sarcasms, often intermingled with wit, on those errors and foibles of human nature, which at once verge upon extravagance and mischief. A practical observer of the world, and an active sharer in its concerns, Butler never forgets the pleasant and every day character of mankind. His mind was thoroughly impressed with the subject on which he wrote, and that subject embraced the whole circle of motives, which set society in action at the period when he lived. His wit is consequently often spent upon follies which are no longer conspicuous, and his experience made lessons which it would now be unprofitable to study. There is yet so much imperishable wisdom in his writings — so many warnings against evil tempers and absurdities, of which the seeds have never to this hour been eradicated from human nature, that Butler may still be estimated as one of the noblest writers of sentential maxims to be found in the English language.

VII. *From Retrospective Review*, vol. iii. 307.

LIST OF THE IMITATIONS OF HUDIBRAS.

1 Hudibras, second part . . . . London 1663
2 Butler's Ghost; or, Hudibras, the fourth part . . 1682
3 Hogan Moganides; or, the Dutch Hudibras . . . 1674
4 The Irish Hudibras; or, Fingallian Prince, &c. . . 1689
5 The Whig's Supplication, by S. Colvil 1695
6 Pendragon; or, the Carpet Knight, his Kalendar . 1698
7 The Dissenting Hypocrite; or, Occasional Conformist 1704
8 Vulgus Britannicus; or, the British Hudibras, in fifteen cantos, &c. by the Author of the London Spy, second edition 1710
9 Hudibras Redivivus, &c. by E. Ward, no date.
10 The Republican Procession; or, the Tumultuous Cavalcade, second edition 1714
11 The Hudibrastic Brewer, a satire on the former (No. 10) 1714
12 Four Hudibrastic Cantos, being poems on four of the greatest heroes 1715

13 Posthumous Works in Prose and Verse of Mr. S. Butler, 3 vols. 12mo. 1720, and in 1 vol. . . . 1754
14 England's Reformation, &c., a Poem, by Thomas Ward 1747
15 The Irish Hudibras, Hesperi-neso-graphia, by William Moffet, 1755, a reprint of No. 4.
16 The Poetical Works of William Meston. 1767
17 The Alma of Matthew Prior.

For a very judicious and elegant criticism on the merits and defects of these various poems, the reader is advised to consult the article in the work from which our list is taken. The present editor, who has carefully read most of the above poems, bears his testimony to the truth and justice of the observations upon them.

"Pope, in classing the English poets for his projected discourse on the rise and progress of English Poetry, has considered Sir John Mennis and Thomas Baynal as the original of Hudibras. See Dr. Warton's Essays. Some of these pieces certainly partake of the wit, raillery, and playful versification of Butler; and this collection, it is just to remember, made its appearance eight years before the publication of Hudibras. Dr. Farmer has traced much of Butler in Cleveland." Musarum Deliciæ, first printed, 1655.

VIII. *An Epitaph on James Duke of Hamilton.*

He that three kingdoms made one flame,
Blasted their beauty, burnt the frame,
Himself now here in ashes lies,
A part of this great Sacrifice:
Here all of HAMILTON remains,
Save what the other world contains.

But (*Reader*) it is hard to tell
Whether that world be Heav'n, or Hell.
A *Scotch* man enters Hell at 's birth,
And 'scapes it when he goes to earth,
Assur'd no worse a Hell can come
Than that which he enjoyed at home.
Now did the Royall Workman botch
This Duke, halfe-*English* and halfe-*Scotch!*
A Scot an English Earldom fits,
As *Purple* doth your Marmuzets;
Suits like *Nol Cromwell* with the Crown,
Or *Bradshaw* in his Scarlet-gown.
Yet might he thus disguis'd (no lesse)
Have slipt to Heav'n in 's *English* dresse,
But that he'in hope of life became
This mystick *Proteus* too as well
Might cheat the Devill 'scape his Hell,
Since to those pranks he pleas'd to play
Religion ever pav'd the way;
Which he did to a *Faction* tie,
Not to reforme but crucifie.
'Twas he that first alarm'd the *Kirke*
To this prepost'rous bloody worke,
Upon the *King's* to place *Christ's throne*,
A step and foot-stoole to his owne;
Taught Zeal a hundred tumbling tricks,
And Scriptures twin'd with Politicks;
The Pulpit made a Jugler's Box,
Set Law and Gospell in the Stocks,
As did old *Buchanan* and *Knox*,
In those daies when (at once*) the *Pox*

* *The Pox, Presbytery, and Jesuitisme, are of the same standing.*

And Presbyters a way did find
Into the world to plague mankind.
'Twas he patch'd up the new Divine,
Part *Calvin* and part Catiline,
Could too transforme (without a spell)
Satan into a *Gabriel;*
Just like those pictures which we paint
On this side Fiend, on that side *Saint.*
Both this, and that, and every thing
He was ; for and against the King :
Rather than he his ends would misse,
Betray'd his master with a kisse,
And buri'd in one common Fate
The glory of our *Church* and *State:*
The *Crown* too levell'd on the ground ;
And having rook't all parties round,
'Faith it was time then to be gone,
Since he had all his business done.
Next on the fatall *Block* expir'd,
He to this *Marble-Cell* retir'd ;
Where all of HAMILTON remains
But what Eternity contains.

Digitus Dei, or God's Justice upon Treachery and Treason, exemplified in the Life and Death of the late James Duke of Hamilton, whereto is added an Epitaph upon him. 4to. London, 1649.

This poem is ascribed to Marchamont Needham. It is curious as being much in the style of Butler, and being published fourteen years before Hudibras appeared.

APPENDIX.

As it has been said, on the authority of Pope, that Butler was indebted for the peculiarities of his style to "Musarum Deliciæ, or Wit's Recreation;" and as that work is not in the possession of any but a few persons who are curious in poetry, it has been thought advisable to afford an extract or two from it. It was first printed in 1655.

"A letter to Sir John Mennis, when the Parliament denied the King money to pay the army, unless a priest, whom the King had reprieved, might be executed. Sir John at the same time wanting the money for provisions for his troop, desired me by his letter to goe to the priest, and to persuade him to dye for the good of the army, saying,

> What is't for him to hang an houre,
> To give an army strengthe and power?"

THE REPLY.

> By my last letter, John, thou see'st
> What I have done to soften priest,
> Yet could not with all I could say
> Persuade him hang, to get thee pay.
> Thou swad, quoth he, I plainly see
> The army wants no food by thee.
> Fast oft'ner, friend, or if you'll eate,
> Use oaten straw, or straw of wheate;
> They'll serve to moderate thy jelly,
> And (which it needs) take up thy belly.
> As one that in a taverne breakes
> A glasse, steales by the barre and sneaks,

At this rebuke, with no less haste, I
Trudg'd from the priest and prison hasty.
The truth is, he gave little credit
To th' armies wants, because I said it;
And if you'll press it further, John,
'Tis fit you send a learned man.
For thou with ease can friends expose,
For thy behoof, to fortune's blows.
Suppose we being found together,
Had pass'd for birds of the same feather
I had perchance been shrewdly shent,
And maul'd too by the Parliament.
Have you beheld the unlucky ape
For roasted chestnuts mump and gape,
And offering at them with his pawes,
But loath he is to scorch his clawes.
When viewing on the hearth asleep
A puppy, gives him cause to weep,
To spare his own, he takes his helpe,
And rakes out nuts with foot of whelpe;
Which done, as if 'twere all but play,
Your name-sake looks another way.
The cur awakes, and finds his thumbs
In paine, but knows not whence it comes;
He takes it first to be some cramp,
And now he spreads, now licks his vamp.
Both are in vain, no ease appeares;
What should he doe? he shakes his eares;
And hobling on three legs, he goes
Whining away with aking toes.
Not in much better case perhaps,
I might have been to serve thy chaps,
And have bestrewed my finger's end
For groping so in cause of friend;
Whilst thou wouldst munch like horse in manger,
And reach at nuts with others' danger,
Yet have I ventured far to serve
My friend that says — he's like to starve.

"An answer to a letter from Sir John Mennis, wherein he jeeres him for falling so quickly to the use of the Directory."

Friend, thou dost lash me with a story,
A long one, too, of Directory;
When thou alone deserves the birch,
That brought'st the bondage on the Church.
Didst thou not treat for Bristow City
And yield it up? — the more's the pity.
And saw'st thou not, how right or wrong
The Common Prayer-Book went along?
Didst thou not scource, as if enchanted,
For articles Sir Thomas granted;
And barter, as an author saith,
Th' articles o' th' Christian faith?
And now the Directory jostles
Christ out o' th' church and his Apostles,
And teares down the communion rayles,
That men may take it on their tayles.
Imagine, friend, *Bochus* the King,
Engraven on *Sylla's* signet ring,
Delivering open to his hands
Jugurth, and with him all the lands,
Whom *Sylla* tooke and sent to Rome,
There to abide the Senate's doome.

In the same fortune, I suppose
John standing in 's doublet and hose;
Delivering up amidst the throng
The common prayer and Wisdom's song
To hands of *Fairfax*, to be sent
A sacrifice to the Parliament.
Thou little thought'st what geare begun
Wrapt in that treaty, *busie John.*
There lurked the fire that turned to cinder
The Church — her ornaments to tinder.
There bound up in that treaty lyes
The fate of all our Christmas pyes.

Our holy-dayes then went to wrack,
Our wakes were layd upon their back,
Our gossips' spoones away were lurch'd,
Our feastes, and fees for woemen church'd;
All this and more ascribe we might
To thee at Bristow, wretched knight.
Yet thou upbraidst and raylst in rime
On me, for that, which was thy crime.
So froward children in the sun
Amid their sports, some shrewd turne done,
The faulty youth begins to prate
And layes it on his harmlesse mate.
Dated
From *Nymptom*, where the Cyder smiles,
And *James* has horse as lame as *Gyles.*
The fourth of *May:* and dost thou heare,
'Tis, as I take it, the eighth yeare
Since *Portugall* by *Duke Braganza*
Was cut from *Spaine* without a handsaw.

J. S.

Account of Mr. Samuel Butler, from Aubrey's Letters, in the Bodleian Library, edited by Dr. Bliss.

IX. Mr. Samuel Butler was borne at Pershore, in Worcestershire, as we suppose; * his brother lives there: went to schoole at Worcester. His father a man but of slender fortune, and to breed him at schoole was as much education as he was able to reach to. When but a boy, he would make observations and reflections on every thing one sayd or did, and censure it to be either well or ill. He never was at the university for the reason alledged. He came when a young

* He was born in Worcestershire, hard by Barton-bridge, ½ a mile from Worcester, in the parish of St John, Mr. Hill thinkes, who went to schoole with him.

man to be a servant to the Countesse of Kent,* whom he served severall yeares. Here, besides his study, he employed his time much in painting † and drawing, and also in musique. He was thinking once to have made painting his profession.‡ His love to and skill in painting made a great friendship between him and Mr. Samuel Cowper (the prince of limners of this age). He then studyed the common lawes of England, but did not practise. He married a good jointuresse, the relict of .... Morgan, by which meanes he lives comfortably. After the restauration of his ma[tie], when the courte at Ludlowe was againe sett up, he was then the king's steward at the castle there. He printed a witty poeme called *Hudibras*, the first part A° 166. which tooke extremely, so that the king and Lord Chanc. Hyde would have him sent for, and accordingly he was sent for. (The L[d] Ch. Hyde hath his picture in his library over the chimney.) They both promised him great matters, but to this day he has got no employment, only the king gave him .... lib.

He is of a middle stature, strong sett, high coloured, a head of sorrell haire, a severe and sound judgement:

* Mr. Saunders (y[e] Countesse of Kent's kinsman) sayd that Mr. J. Selden much esteemed him for his partes, and would sometimes employ him to write letters for him beyond sea, and to translate for him. He was secretairie to the D. of Bucks, when he was Chancellor of Cambridge. He might have had preferments at first; but he would not accept any but very good, so at last he had none at all, and dyed in want.

† He painted well, and made it (sometime) his profession. He wayted some yeares on the Countess of Kent. She gave her gent. 20 lib. per an. a-piece.

‡ From Dr. Duke.

a good fellowe. He hath often sayd that way (e. g. Mr. Edw. Waller's) of quibling with sence will hereafter growe as much out of fashion and be as ridicule* as quibling with words. 2d. N. B. He hath been much troubled with the gowt, and particularly, 1679, he stirred not out of his chamber from October till Easter.

He † dyed of a consumption Septemb. 25 (Anno Dni 1680, 70 circiter), and buried 27, according to his owne appointment in the churchyard of Covent Garden; sc. in the north part next the church at the east end. His feet touch the wall. His grave, 2 yards distant from the pillaster of the dore, (by his desire) 6 foot deepe.

About 25 of his old acquaintance at his funeral: I myself being one.

HUDIBRAS UNPRINTED.

No Jesuite ever took in hand
To plant a church in barren land;
Or ever thought it worth his while
A Swede or Russe to reconcile.
For where there is not store of wealth,
Souls are not worth the chandge of health.
Spaine and America had designes
To sell their Ghospell for their wines,
For had the Mexicans been poore,
No Spaniard twice had landed on their shore.
'Twas Gold the Catholic Religion planted,
Which, had they wanted Gold, they still had wanted.

He had made very sharp reflexions upon the court in his last part.

* [Siv. Edit.]
† [Evidently written some time after the former part. E.]

Writt my Lord (John *) Rosse's Answer to the Marquesse of Dorchester.

Memorandum. Satyricall witts disoblige whom they converse with, &c. consequently make to themselves many enemies and few friends, and this was his manner and case. He was of a leonine-coloured haire, sanguine, cholerique, middle sized, strong.

* [In the hand-writing of Anthony à Wood. Edit.]

HUDIBRAS.

HUDIBRAS.

PART I. CANTO I.

THE ARGUMENT.

Sir Hudibras his passing worth,
The manner how he sally'd forth,
His arms and equipage are shown,
His horse's virtues and his own:
Th' adventure of the Bear and Fiddle
Is sung, but breaks off in the middle.*

WHEN civil dudgeon first grew high,
And men fell out they knew not why;
When hard words, jealousies, and fears,
Set folks together by the ears,
And made them fight, like mad or drunk,

* A ridicule on Ronsarde and Davenant.

Ver. 1. Var. 'Civil fury.'—To take in 'dudgeon' is inwardly to resent some injury or affront, and what is previous to actual fury.

V. 2. It may be justly said, 'They knew not why;' since, as Lord Clarendon observes, "The like peace and plenty, and universal tranquillity, was never enjoyed by any nation for ten years together, before those unhappy troubles began."

V. 3. By 'hard words' he probably means the cant words used by the Presbyterians and sectaries of those times; such as Gospel-walking, Gospel-preaching, Soul-saving, Elect, Saints, the Godly, the Predestinate, and the like; which they applied to their own preachers and themselves.

For Dame Religion as for punk;
Whose honesty they all durst swear for,
Though not a man of them knew wherefore;
When Gospel-trumpeter, surrounded
With long-ear'd rout, to battle sounded;
And pulpit, drum ecclesiastic,
Was beat with fist instead of a stick;
Then did Sir Knight abandon dwelling,
And out he rode a-colonelling.
A wight he was, whose very sight would
Entitle him Mirror of Knighthood,
That never bow'd his stubborn knee
To any thing but chivalry,
Nor put up blow, but that which laid
Right Worshipful on shoulder blade;
Chief of domestic knights and errant,

V. 11, 12. Alluding to their vehement action in the pulpit, and their beating it with their fists, as if they were beating a drum.

V. 13. Our author, to make his Knight appear more ridiculous, has dressed him in all kinds of fantastic colours, and put many characters together to finish him a perfect coxcomb.

V. 14. The Knight (if Sir Samuel Luke was Mr. Butler's hero) was not only a Colonel in the Parliament army, but also Scoutmaster-general in the counties of Bedford, Surrey, &c. This gives us some light into his character and conduct; for he is now entering upon his proper office, full of pretendedly pious and sanctified resolutions for the good of his country. His peregrinations are so consistent with his office and humour, that they are no longer to be called fabulous or improbable.

V. 17, 18. *i. e.* He kneeled to the king, when he knighted him, but seldom upon any other occasion.

Either for chartel or for warrant;
Great on the bench, great in the saddle,
That could as well bind o'er as swaddle;
Mighty he was at both of these
And styl'd of War, as well as Peace:
(So some rats, of amphibious nature,
Are either for the land or water).
But here our Authors make a doubt
Whether he were more wise or stout:
Some hold the one, and some the other,
But, howsoe'er they make a pother,
The diff'rence was so small, his brain
Outweigh'd his rage but half a grain;
Which made some take him for a tool
That knaves do work with, call'd a Fool.
For 't has been held by many, that
As Montaigne, playing with his cat,
Complains she thought him but an ass,
Much more she would Sir Hudibras:
(For that's the name our valiant Knight
To all his challenges did write).
But they're mistaken very much;
'Tis plain enough he was not such.
We grant, although he had much wit,
H' was very shy of using it,
As being loth to wear it out,

V. 22. 'Chartel' is a challenge to a duel.

V. 23. In this character of Hudibras all the abuses of human learning are finely satirised: philosophy, logic, rhetoric, mathematics, metaphysics, and school-divinity.

And therefore bore it not about;
Unless on holydays or so,
As men their best apparel do.
Beside, 'tis known he could speak Greek
As naturally as pigs squeak;
That Latin was no more difficile,
Than to a blackbird 'tis to whistle:
Being rich in both, he never scanted
His bounty unto such as wanted;
But much of either would afford
To many that had not one word.
For Hebrew roots, although they're found
To flourish most in barren ground,
He had such plenty as suffic'd
To make some think him circumcis'd;
And truly so he was, perhaps,
Not as a proselyte, but for claps.
He was in logic a great critic,
Profoundly skill'd in analytic;
He could distinguish, and divide
A hair 'twixt south and south-west side;
On either which he would dispute,
Confute, change hands, and still confute:
He'd undertake to prove, by force
Of argument, a man's no horse;

V. 55, 56. This is the property of a pedantic coxcomb, who prates most learnedly amongst illiterate persons, and makes a mighty pother about books and languages, where he is sure to be admired, though not understood.

V. 63, 64. Var. 'And truly so perhaps he was,
'Tis many a pious Christian's case.'

He'd prove a buzzard is no fowl,
And that a lord may be an owl;
A calf an alderman, a goose a justice,
And rooks Committee-men and Trustees.
He'd run in debt by disputation,
And pay with ratiocination:
All this by syllogism, true
In mood and figure he would do.
For rhetoric, he could not ope
His mouth, but out there flew a trope;
And when he happen'd to break off
I' th' middle of his speech, or cough,
H' had hard words ready to show why,
And tell what rules he did it by;
Else, when with greatest art he spoke,
You'd think he talk'd like other folk;
For all a rhetorician's rules

V. 75. Such was Alderman Pennington, who sent a person to Newgate for singing (what he called) 'a malignant psalm.' Lord Clarendon observes, "That after the declaration of No more addresses to the King, they who were not above the condition of ordinary constables six or seven years before, were now the justices of the peace." Dr. Bruno Ryves informs us, "That the town of Chelmsford in Essex was governed, at the beginning of the Rebellion, by a tinker, two cobblers, two tailors, and two pedlers."

V. 76. In the several counties, especially the Associated ones (Middlesex, Kent, Surrey, Sussex, Norfolk, Suffolk, and Cambridgeshire) which sided with the Parliament, committees were erected of such men as were for the Good Cause, as they called it, who had authority, from the members of the two Houses at Westminster, to fine and imprison whom they pleased.

Teach nothing but to name his tools.
But, when he pleas'd to show 't, his speech,
In loftiness of sound, was rich;
A Babylonish dialect,
Which learned pedants much affect;
It was a party-colour'd dress
Of patch'd and pyebald languages;
'Twas English cut on Greek and Latin,
Like fustian heretofore on satin;
It had an odd promiscuous tone,
As if h' had talk'd three parts in one;
Which made some think, when he did gabble,
Th' had heard three labourers of Babel,
Or Cerberus himself pronounce
A leash of languages at once.
This he as volubly would vent,
As if his stock would ne'er be spent:
And truly, to support that charge,
He had supplies as vast and large;
For he could coin or counterfeit
New words with little or no wit;
Words so debas'd and hard, no stone
Was hard enough to touch them on;
And when with hasty noise he spoke 'em,
The ignorant for current took 'em;

V. 109. The Presbyterians coined a great number, such as Out-goings, Carryings-on, Nothingness, Workings-out, Gospel-walking-times, &c. which we shall meet with hereafter in the speeches of the Knight and Squire, and others, in this Poem; for which they are bantered by Sir John Birkenhead.

That had the orator, who once
Did fill his mouth with pebble stones
When he harangu'd, but known his phrase,
He would have us'd no other ways.
In mathematics he was greater
Than Tycho Brahe or Erra Pater;
For he, by geometric scale,
Could take the size of pots of ale;
Resolve by sines and tangents straight
If bread or butter wanted weight;
And wisely tell what hour o' th' day
The clock does strike, by Algebra.
Beside, he was a shrewd philosopher,
And had read ev'ry text and gloss over;
Whate'er the crabbed'st author hath,
He understood b' implicit faith:
Whatever sceptic could enquire for,
For ev'ry why he had a wherefore;
Knew more than forty of them do,
As far as words and terms could go;
All which he understood by rote,
And, as occasion serv'd, would quote;
No matter whether right or wrong;
They might be either said or sung.
His notions fitted things so well,

V. 115. Demosthenes is here meant, who had a defect in his speech.

V. 120. An eminent Danish mathematician; and William Lilly, the famous astrologer of those times.

V. 131. Var. 'Inquere.'

That which was which he could not tell,
But oftentimes mistook the one
For th' other, as great clerks have done;
He could reduce all things to acts,
And knew their natures by abstracts;
Where Entity and Quiddity,
The ghosts of defunct bodies, fly;
Where truth in person does appear,
Like words congeal'd in northern air.
He knew what's what, and that's as high
As metaphysic wit can fly:
In school-divinity as able
As he that hight Irrefragable;
A second Thomas, or, at once
To name them all, another Dunce:

V. 145. Var. 'He'd tell where Entity and Quiddity.'

V. 152. Alexander Hales was born in Gloucestershire, and flourished about the year 1236, at the time when what was called School-divinity was much in vogue; in which science he was so deeply read, that he was called 'Doctor Irrefragabilis;' that is, the 'Invincible Doctor,' whose arguments could not be resisted.

V. 153. Thomas Aquinas, a Dominican friar, was born in 1224, studied at Cologne and at Paris. He new-modelled the school-divinity, and was therefore called the 'Angelic Doctor,' and 'Eagle' of divines. The most illustrious persons of his time were ambitious of his friendship, and put a high value on his merits, so that they offered him bishoprics, which he refused with as much ardour as others seek after them. He died in the fiftieth year of his age, and was canonized by Pope John XXII. We have his works in eighteen volumes, several times printed.

V. 154. Johannes Dunscotus was a very learned man,

Profound in all the Nominal
And Real ways beyond them all:
For he a rope of sand could twist
As tough as learned Sorbonist,
And weave fine cobwebs, fit for skull
That's empty when the moon is full;
Such as take lodgings in a head
That's to be let unfurnished.

who lived about the end of the thirteenth and beginning of the fourteenth century. The English and Scots strive which of them shall have the honour of his birth. The English say he was born in Northumberland; the Scots allege he was born at Dunse in the Merse, the neighbouring county to Northumberland, and hence was called 'Dunscotus:' Moreri, Buchanan, and other Scotch historians, are of this opinion, and for proof cite his epitaph:

Scotia me genuit, Anglia suscepit,
Gallia edocuit, Germania tenet.

He died at Cologne, Nov. 8, 1308. In the 'Supplement' to Dr. Cave's 'Historia Literaria,' he is said to be extraordinary learned in physics, metaphysics, mathematics, and astronomy; that his fame was so great when at Oxford, that 30,000 scholars came thither to hear his lectures: that when at Paris, his arguments and authority carried it for the immaculate conception of the Blessed Virgin, so that they appointed a festival on that account, and would admit no scholars to degrees but such as were of this mind. He was a great opposer of Thomas Aquinas's doctrine; and for being a very acute logician, was called 'Doctor Subtilis,' which was the reason also that an old punster always called him the 'Lathy Doctor.'

V. 155, 156. Gulielmus Occham was father of the Nominals, and Johannes Dunscotus of the Reals.

V. 157, 158. Var. 'And with as delicate a hand
Could twist as tough a rope of sand.'

He could raise scruples dark and nice,
And after solve 'em in a trice;
As if Divinity had catch'd
The itch, on purpose to be scratch'd;
Or, like a mountebank, did wound
And stab herself with doubts profound,
Only to show with how small pain
The sores of Faith are cur'd again;
Altho' by woful proof we find
They always leave a scar behind.
He knew the seat of Paradise,
Could tell in what degree it lies,
And, as he was dispos'd, could prove it
Below the moon, or else above it;
What Adam dreamt of, when his bride
Came from her closet in his side;
Whether the Devil tempted her
By a high Dutch interpreter;
If either of them had a navel;
Who first made music malleable;
Whether the Serpent, at the Fall,
Had cloven feet, or none at all:
All this, without a gloss or comment,
He could unriddle in a moment,
In proper terms, such as men smatter
When they throw out and miss the matter.
  For his religion, it was fit

V. 181. Several of the Ancients have supposed that Adam and Eve had no navels; and, among the Moderns, the late learned Bishop Cumberland was of this opinion.

To match his learning and his wit:
'Twas Presbyterian true blue;
For he was of that stubborn crew
Of errant saints, whom all men grant
To be the true Church Militant;
Such as do build their faith upon
The holy text of pike and gun;
Decide all controversies by
Infallible artillery;
And prove their doctrine orthodox,
By Apostolic blows and knocks;
Call fire and sword, and desolation,
A godly, thorough Reformation,
Which always must be carry'd on,
And still be doing, never done;
As if Religion were intended
For nothing else but to be mended:

V. 193, 194. Where Presbytery has been established, it has been usually effected by force of arms, like the religion of Mahomet: thus it was established at Geneva in Switzerland, Holland, Scotland, &c. In France, for some time, by that means, it obtained a toleration; much blood was shed to get it established in England: and once, during that Grand Rebellion, it seemed very near gaining an establishment here.

V. 195, 196. Upon these Cornet Joyce built his faith, when he carried away the King, by force, from Holdenby: for, when his Majesty asked him for a sight of his Instructions, Joyce said, he should see them presently; and so drawing up his troop in the inward court, "These, Sir (said the Cornet), are my Instructions."

V. 199, 200. Many instances of that kind are given by Dr. Walker, in his 'Sufferings of the Episcopal Clergy.'

A sect whose chief devotion lies
In odd perverse antipathies;
In falling out with that or this,
And finding somewhat still amiss;
More peevish, cross, and splenetic,
Than dog distract, or monkey sick:
That with more care keep holyday
The wrong, than others the right way;
Compound for sins they are inclin'd to,
By damning those they have no mind to:
Still so perverse and opposite,
As if they worshipp'd God for spite:
The self-same thing they will abhor
One way, and long another for:
Freewill they one way disavow,
Another, nothing else allow:
All piety consists therein
In them, in other men all sin:
Rather than fail, they will defy
That which they love most tenderly;
Quarrel with minc'd-pies, and disparage
Their best and dearest friend, plum-porridge;
Fat pig and goose itself oppose,
And blaspheme custard through the nose.

V. 207. The religion of the Presbyterians of those times consisted principally in an opposition to the Church of England, and quarrelling with the most innocent customs then in use, as the eating Christmas-pies and plum-porridge at Christmas; which they reputed sinful.

V. 213, 214. They were so remarkably obstinate in this respect, that they kept a fast upon Christmas-day.

Th' apostles of this fierce religion,
Like Mahomet's, were ass and widgeon,
To whom our Knight, by fast instinct
Of wit and temper, was so linkt,
As if hypocrisy and nonsense
Had got th' advowson of his conscience.
Thus was he gifted and accoutred,
We mean on th' inside, not the outward:
That next of all we shall discuss;
Then listen, Sirs, it follows thus.
His tawny beard was th' equal grace
Both of his wisdom and his face;
In cut and die so like a tile,
A sudden view it would beguile;
The upper part whereof was whey,
The nether orange, mix'd with grey.

V. 235, 236. Dr. Bruno Ryves gives a remarkable instance of a fanatical conscience in a captain, who was invited by a soldier to eat part of a goose with him; but refused, because, he said, it was stolen: but being to march away, he who would eat no stolen goose made no scruple to ride away upon a stolen mare; for, plundering Mrs. Bartlet of her mare, this hypocritical captain gave sufficient testimony to the world that the old Pharisee and new Puritan have consciences of the self-same temper, "To strain at a gnat, and swallow a camel."

V. 241. Mr. Butler, in his description of Hudibras's beard, seems to have had an eye to Jaques's description of the Country Justice, in 'As you like it.' It may be asked, Why the Poet is so particular upon the Knight's beard, and gives it the preference to all his other accoutrements? The answer seems to be plain: the Knight had made a vow not to cut it till the Parliament had subdued the King; hence it became necessary to have it fully described.

This hairy meteor did denounce
The fall of sceptres and of crowns;
With grisly type did represent
Declining age of government,
And tell, with hieroglyphic spade,
Its own grave and the State's were made:
Like Samson's heart-breakers, it grew
In time to make a nation rue;
Though it contributed its own fall,
To wait upon the public downfall:
It was monastic, and did grow
In holy orders by strict vow.
Of rule as sullen and severe,
As that of rigid Cordeliere:
'Twas bound to suffer persecution,
And martyrdom, with resolution;
T' oppose itself against the hate
And vengeance of th' incensed state,
In whose defiance it was worn,
Still ready to be pull'd and torn,
With red-hot irons to be tortured,
Revil'd, and spit upon, and martyr'd;
Maugre all which 'twas to stand fast
As long as Monarchy should last;
But when the state should hap to reel,
'Twas to submit to fatal steel,
And fall, as it was consecrate,
A sacrifice to fall of state,

V. 257. Var. 'It was canonic.'

Whose thread of life the Fatal Sisters
Did twist together with its whiskers,
And twine so close that Time should never,
In life or death, their fortunes sever,
But with his rusty sickle mow
Both down together at a blow.
So learned Taliacotius, from
The brawny part of porter's bum,
Cut supplemental noses, which
Would last as long as parent breech,
But when the date of Nock was out
Off dropt the sympathetic snout.
His back, or rather burthen, show'd
As if it stoop'd with its own load:
For as Æneas bore his sire
Upon his shoulders through the fire,
Our Knight did bear no less a pack
Of his own buttocks on his back;
Which now had almost got the upper-
Hand of his head for want of crupper.
To poise this equally, he bore
A paunch of the same bulk before,

V. 281. Gasper Taliacotius was born at Bononia, A. D. 1553, and was Professor of physic and surgery there. He died 1599. His statue stands in the Anatomy theatre, holding a nose in its hand. — He wrote a treatise in Latin called 'Chirurgia Nota,' in which he teaches the art of ingrafting noses, ears, lips, &c. with the proper instruments and bandages. This book has passed through two editions. See 'Græfe de Rhinoplastice, sive arte curtum Nasum ad Vivum restituendi Commentatio,' 4to. Berolin, 1818.

Which still he had a special care
To keep well-cramm'd with thrifty fare,
As white-pot, butter-milk, and curds,
Such as a country-house affords;
With other victual, which anon
We further shall dilate upon,
When of his hose we come to treat,
The cupboard where he kept his meat.
His doublet was of sturdy buff,
And though not sword, yet cudgel-proof,
Whereby 'twas fitter for his use
Who fear'd no blows but such as bruise.
His breeches were of rugged woollen,
And had been at the siege of Bullen;
To Old King Harry so well known,
Some writers held they were his own:
Through they were lin'd with many a piece
Of ammunition bread and cheese,
And fat black-puddings, proper food
For warriors that delight in blood.
For, as we said, he always chose
To carry vittle in his hose,
That often tempted rats and mice
The ammunition to surprise;
And when he put a hand but in
The one or t'other magazine,
They stoutly in defence on't stood,
And from the wounded foe drew blood;
And, till th' were storm'd and beaten out,
Ne'er left the fortify'd redoubt.

And though knights-errant, as some think,
Of old did neither eat nor drink,
Because when thorough deserts vast
And regions desolate they past,
Where belly-timber above ground
Or under was not to be found,
Unless they graz'd there's not one word
Of their provision on record;
Which made some confidently write,
They had no stomachs but to fight:
'Tis false; for Arthur wore in hall
Round table like a farthingal,
On which, with shirt pulled out behind,
And eke before, his good knights din'd:
Though 'twas no table some suppose,
But a huge pair of round trunk-hose,
In which he carry'd as much meat
As he and all the knights could eat,
When, laying by their swords and truncheons,
They took their breakfasts or their nuncheons.
But let that pass at present, lest
We should forget where we digrest,
As learned authors use, to whom
We leave it, and to th' purpose come.
  His puissant sword unto his side,
Near his undaunted heart, was tied,
With basket-hilt that would hold broth,
And serve for fight and dinner both;
In it he melted lead for bullets
To shoot at foes, and sometimes pullets,

To whom he bore so fell a grutch,
He ne'er gave quarter t' any such.
The trenchant blade Toledo trusty
For want of fighting was grown rusty,
And ate into itself for lack
Of somebody to hew and hack:
The peaceful scabbard, where it dwelt,
The rancour of its edge had felt;
For of the lower end two handful
It had devoured, 'twas so manful,
And so much scorn'd to lurk in case,
As if it durst not show its face.
In many desperate attempts
Of warrants, exigents, contempts,
It had appear'd with courage bolder
Than Serjeant Bum invading shoulder:
Oft had it ta'en possession,
And pris'ners too, or made them run.
This sword a dagger had, his page,
That was but little for his age,
And therefore waited on him so
As dwarfs upon knights-errant do.
It was a serviceable dudgeon,
Either for fighting or for drudging:
When it had stabb'd, or broke a head,
It would scrape trenchers, or chip bread;
Toast cheese or bacon; though it were
To bate a mouse-trap, 'twould not care:
'Twould make clean shoes, and in the earth
Set leeks and onions, and so forth:

It had been 'prentice to a brewer,
Where this and more it did endure,
But left the trade as many more
Have lately done on the same score.
  In th' holsters at his saddle-bow
Two aged pistols he did stow,
Among the surplus of such meat
As in his hose he could not get:
These would inveigle rats with th' scent,
To forage when the cocks were bent,
And sometimes catch 'em with a snap,
As cleverly as th' ablest trap.
They were upon hard duty still,
And every night stood sentinel,
To guard the magazine i' th' hose
From two-legg'd and from four-legg'd foes.
  Thus clad and fortify'd Sir Knight
From peaceful home set forth to fight.
But first with nimble active force
He got on th' outside of his horse:
For having but one stirrup ty'd
T' his saddle on the further side,
It was so short h' had much ado
To reach it with his desp'rate toe;
But after many strains and heaves,
He got up to the saddle-eaves,
From whence he vaulted into th' seat
With so much vigour, strength, and heat,
That he had almost tumbled over
With his own weight, but did recover

By laying hold on tail and mane,
Which oft he us'd instead of rein.
But now we talk of mounting steed,
Before we further do proceed,
It doth behove us to say something
Of that which bore our valiant Bumkin.
The beast was sturdy, large, and tall,
With mouth of meal and eyes of wall,
I would say eye, for h' had but one,
As most agree, though some say none.
He was well stay'd, and in his gate
Preserv'd a grave, majestic state;
At spur or switch no more he skipt
Or mended pace than Spaniard whipt,
And yet so fiery, he would bound
As if he griev'd to touch the ground;
That Cæsar's horse, who, as fame goes,
Had corns upon his feet and toes,
Was not by half so tender hooft,
Nor trod upon the ground so soft:
And as that beast would kneel and stoop
(Some write) to take his rider up;
So Hudibras his ('tis well known)
Would often do to set him down.
We shall not need to say what lack
Of leather was upon his back,
For that was hidden under pad,
And breech of Knight gall'd full as bad.
His strutting ribs on both sides show'd
Like furrows he himself had plough'd;

For underneath the skirt of pannel,
'Twixt ev'ry two there was a channel.
His draggling tail hung in the dirt,
Which on his rider he would flirt,
Still as his tender side he prickt,
With arm'd heel, or with unarm'd, kickt:
For Hudibras wore but one spur,
As wisely knowing could he stir
To active trot one side of 's horse,
The other would not hang an arse.
A Squire he had whose name was Ralph,
That in th' adventure went his half,
Though writers, for more stately tone,
Do call him Ralpho, 'tis all one;
And when we can, with metre safe,
We'll call him so; if not, plain Ralph;
(For rhyme the rudder is of verses,
With which, like ships, they steer their courses):
An equal stock of wit and valour
He had laid in, by birth a tailor.
The mighty Tyrian queen, that gain'd
With subtle shreds a tract of land,
Did leave it with a castle fair
To his great ancestor, her heir;

V. 457. Sir Roger L'Estrange ('Key to Hudibras') says, this famous Squire was one Isaac Robinson, a zealous butcher in Moorfields, who was always contriving some new querpo cut in church government: but, in a 'Key' at the end of a burlesque poem of Mr. Butler's, 1706, in folio, p. 12, it is observed, "That Hudibras's Squire was one Pemble, a tailor, and one of the Committee of Sequestrators."

From him descended cross-legg'd knights,
Fam'd for their faith and warlike fights
Against the bloody Cannibal,
Whom they destroy'd both great and small.
This sturdy Squire he had, as well
As the bold Trojan knight, seen hell,
Not with a counterfeited pass
Of golden bough, but true gold-lace:
His knowledge was not far behind
The Knight's, but of another kind,
And he another way came by 't,
Some call it Gifts, and some New-light;
A lib'ral art, that costs no pains
Of study, industry, or brains.
His wit was sent him for a token,
But in the carriage crack'd and broken;
Like commendation nine-pence crookt
With — To and from my love — it lookt.
He ne'er consider'd it, as loth
To look a gift-horse in the mouth,
And very wisely would lay forth
No more upon it than 'twas worth;
But as he got it freely, so

V. 485. Var. 'His wits were sent him.'

V. 487, 488. Until the year 1696, when all money, not milled, was called in, a ninepenny piece of silver was as common as sixpences or shillings, and these ninepences were usually bent as sixpences commonly are now, which bending was called, To my love and from my love; and such ninepences the ordinary fellows gave or sent to their sweethearts as tokens of love.

He spent it frank and freely too:
For saints themselves will sometimes be,
Of gifts that cost them nothing, free.
By means of this, with hem and cough,
Prolongers to enlighten'd stuff,
He could deep mysteries unriddle,
As easily as thread a needle:
For as of vagabonds we say,
That they are ne'er beside their way,
Whate'er men speak by this new light,
Still they are sure to be i' th' right.
'Tis a dark lantern of the Spirit,
Which none see by but those that bear it;
A light that falls down from on high,
For spiritual trades to cozen by;
An *ignis fatuus*, that bewitches,
And leads men into pools and ditches,
To make them dip themselves, and sound
For Christendom in dirty pond;
To dive like wild-fowl for salvation,
And fish to catch regeneration.
This light inspires and plays upon
The nose of saint, like bagpipe drone,
And speaks through hollow empty soul,
As through a trunk or whisp'ring hole,
Such language as no mortal ear
But spirit'al eaves-droppers can hear:

V. 511. Alluding to Ralpho's religion, who was probably an Anabaptist or Dipper.

So Phœbus, or some friendly Muse,
Into small poets song infuse,
Which they at second-hand rehearse,
Through reed or bagpipe, verse for verse.
Thus Ralph became infallible
As three or four-legg'd oracle,
The ancient cup, or modern chair,
Spoke truth point blank, though unaware.
For mystic learning, wondrous able
In magic, talisman, and cabal,
Whose primitive tradition reaches
As far as Adam's first green breeches;
Deep-sighted in intelligences,
Ideas, atoms, influences;
And much of *Terra Incognita*,
Th' intelligible world, could say;
A deep occult philosopher,
As learn'd as the Wild Irish are,
Or Sir Agrippa, for profound
And solid lying much renown'd:
He Anthroposophus, and Floud,
And Jacob Behmen, understood;
Knew many an amulet and charm,
That would do neither good nor harm;
In Rosycrucian lore as learned
As he that *Verè adeptus* earned:
He understood the speech of birds
As well as they themselves do words;

V. 546. Alluding to the Philosophers' stone.

Could tell what subtlest parrots mean,
That speak and think contrary clean;
What member 'tis of whom they talk
When they cry Rope, and Walk, Knave, walk.
He'd extract numbers out of matter,
And keep them in a glass, like water,
Of sov'reign pow'r to make men wise;
For, dropt in blear thick-sighted eyes,
They'd make them see in darkest night,
Like owls, though purblind in the light.
By help of these (as he profest)
He had First Matter seen undrest:
He took her naked, all alone,
Before one rag of form was on.
The Chaos, too, he had descry'd,
And seen quite through, or else he ly'd:
Not that of Pasteboard, which men shew
For groats at fair of Barthol'mew;
But its great grandsire, first o' th' name,
Whence that and Reformation came,
Both cousin-germans, and right able
T' inveigle and draw in the rabble:
But reformation was, some say,
O' th' younger house to Puppet-play.
He could foretell whats'ever was
By consequence to come to pass;

V. 573. The rebellious clergy would in their prayers pretend to foretell things, to encourage people in their rebellion. I meet with the following instance in the prayers of Mr. George Swathe, minister of Denham, in Suffolk: "O my good Lord

As death of great men, alterations,
Diseases, battles, inundations:
All this without th' eclipse o' th' sun,
Or dreadful comet, he hath done
By inward light, a way as good,
And easy to be understood;
But with more lucky hit than those
That use to make the stars depose,
Like Knights o' th' Post, and falsely charge
Upon themselves what others forge;
As if they were consenting to
All mischiefs in the world men do,
Or, like the devil, did tempt and sway 'em
To rogueries, and then betray 'em.
They'll search a planet's house, to know

God, I praise thee for discovering the last week, in the day-time, a vision, that there were two great armies about York, one of the malignant party about the King, the other party Parliament and professors: and the better side should have help from Heaven against the worst; about, or at which instant of time, we heard the soldiers at York had raised up a sconce against Hull, intending to plant fifteen pieces against Hull; against which fort Sir John Hotham, Keeper of Hull, by a garrison, discharged four great ordnance, and broke down their sconce, and killed divers Cavaliers in it. — Lord, I praise thee for discovering this victory, at the instant of time that it was done, to my wife, which did then presently confirm her drooping heart, which the last week had been dejected three or four days, and no arguments could comfort her against the dangerous times approaching; but when she had prayed to be established in faith in thee, then presently thou didst, by this vision, strongly possess her soul that thine and our enemies should be overcome."

Who broke and robb'd a house below;
Examine Venus and the Moon,
Who stole a thimble or a spoon;
And though they nothing will confess,
Yet by their very looks can guess,
And tell what guilty aspect bodes,
Who stole, and who receiv'd the goods:
They'll question Mars, and, by his look,
Detect who 'twas that nimm'd a cloak;
Make Mercury confess, and 'peach
Those thieves which he himself did teach.
They'll find i' th' physiognomies
O' th' planets, all men's destinies,
Like him that took the doctor's bill,
And swallow'd it instead o' th' pill;
Cast the nativity o' th' question,
And from positions to be guest on,
As sure as if they knew the moment
Of Native's birth, tell what will come on't.
They'll feel the pulses of the stars,
To find out agues, coughs, catarrhs,
And tell what crisis does divine
The rot in sheep, or mange in swine;
In men, what gives or cures the itch,
What makes them cuckolds, poor or rich;
What gains or loses, hangs or saves;
What makes men great, what fools or knaves,
But not what wise, for only of those
The stars (they say) cannot dispose.
No more than can the astrologians;

There they say right, and like true Trojans:
This Ralpho knew, and therefore took
The other course, of which we spoke.
  Thus was th' accomplish'd Squire endu'd
With gifts and knowledge per'lous shrewd:
Never did trusty squire with knight,
Or knight with squire, e'er jump more right.
Their arms and equipage did fit,
As well as virtues, parts, and wit:
Their valours, too, were of a rate;
And out they sally'd at the gate.
Few miles on horseback had they jogged
But Fortune unto them turn'd dogged;
For they a sad adventure met,
Of which anon we mean to treat.
But ere we venture to unfold
Achievements so resolv'd and bold,
We should, as learned poets use,
Invoke th' assistance of some Muse,
However critics count it sillier
Than jugglers talking to familiar;
We think 'tis no great matter which,
They're all alike, yet we shall pitch
On one that fits our purpose most,
Whom therefore thus do we accost.
  Thou that with ale, or viler liquors,
Didst inspire Withers, Pryn, and Vickars,
And force them, though it was in spite
Of Nature, and their stars, to write;
Who (as we find in sullen writs,

And cross-grain'd works of modern wits)
With vanity, opinion, want,
The wonder of the ignorant,
The praises of the author, penn'd
B' himself or wit-insuring friend,
The itch of picture in the front,
With bays and wicked rhyme upon't,
(All that is left o' th' Forked hill
To make men scribble without skill)
Canst make a poet, spite of Fate,
And teach all people to translate,
Though out of languages in which
They understand no part of speech;
Assist me but this once, I 'mplore,
And I shall trouble thee no more.
  In western clime there is a town,
To those that dwell therein well known,
Therefore there needs no more be said here,
We unto them refer our reader;
For brevity is very good,
When w' are, or are not understood.
To this town people did repair
On days of market or of fair,

V. 665. Brentford, which is eight miles west from London, is here probably meant, as may be gathered from Part II. Cant. iii. v. 995, &c. where he tells the Knight what befell him there:

> And though you overcame the Bear,
> The dogs beat you at Brentford fair,
> Where sturdy butchers broke your noddle.

And to crack'd fiddle and hoarse tabor,
In merriment did drudge and labour:
But now a sport more formidable
Had rak'd together village rabble;
'Twas an old way of recreating,
Which learned butchers call Bear-baiting;
A bold advent'rous exercise,
With ancient heroes in high prize;
For authors do affirm it came
From Isthmian or Nemæan game;
Others derive it from the Bear
That's fix'd in northern hemisphere,
And round about the pole does make
A circle, like a bear at stake,
That at the chain's end wheels about,
And overturns the rabble-rout:
For, after solemn proclamation
In the bear's name (as is the fashion

V. 687. This game is ushered into the Poem with more solemnity than those celebrated ones in Homer and Virgil. As the Poem is only adorned with this game, and the Riding Skimmington, so it was incumbent on the Poet to be very particular and full in the description: and may we not venture to affirm, they are exactly suitable to the nature of these adventures; and, consequently, to a Briton, preferable to those in Homer or Virgil.

V. 689, 690. Alluding to the bull-running at Tutbury in Staffordshire; where solemn proclamation was made by the Steward, before the bull was turned loose; "That all manner of persons give way to the bull, none being to come near him by forty foot, any way to hinder the minstrels, but to attend his or their own safety, every one at his peril." Dr. Plot's 'Staffordshire.'

According to the law of arms,
To keep men from inglorious harms)
That none presume to come so near
As forty foot of stake of bear,
If any yet be so fool-hardy
T' expose themselves to vain jeopardy,
If they come wounded off, and lame,
No honour's got by such a maim,
Although the bear gain much, being bound
In honour to make good his ground
When he's engag'd, and takes no notice,
If any press upon him, who 'tis,
But lets them know, at their own cost,
That he intends to keep his post.
This to prevent and other harms
Which always wait on feats of arms
(For in the hurry of a fray
'Tis hard to keep out of harm's way),
Thither the Knight his course did steer,
To keep the peace 'twixt Dog and Bear,
As he believ'd he was bound to do
In conscience and commission too;
And therefore thus bespoke the Squire:
  We that are wisely mounted higher

V. 714. This speech is set down as it was delivered by the Knight, in his own words; but since it is below the gravity of heroical poetry to admit of humour, but all men are obliged to speak wisely alike, and too much of so extravagant a folly would become tedious and impertinent, the rest of his harangues have only his sense expressed in other words, unless

Than constables in curule wit,
When on tribunal bench we sit,
Like speculators should foresee,
From Pharos of authority,
Portended mischiefs further than
Low Proletarian tithing-men;
And therefore being inform'd by bruit
That Dog and Bear are to dispute,
For so of late men fighting name,
Because they often prove the same
(For where the first does hap to be,
The last does *coincidere*);
Quantum in nobis, have thought good
To save th' expense of Christian blood,
And try if we by mediation
Of treaty and accommodation,
Can end the quarrel, and compose
The bloody duel without blows.
Are not our liberties, our lives,
The laws, religion, and our wives,

in some few places where his own words could not be so well avoided.

V. 715. Had that remarkable motion in the House of Commons taken place, the constables might have vied with Sir Hudibras for an equality at least; "That it was necessary for the House of Commons to have a High Constable of their own, that will make no scruple of laying his Majesty by the heels:" but they proceeded not so far as to name any body, because Harry Martyn (out of tenderness of conscience in this particular) immediately quashed the motion, by saying, the power was too great for any man.

Enough at once to lie at stake
For Cov'nant and the Cause's sake?
But in that quarrel Dogs and Bears,
As well as we, must venture theirs?
This feud, by Jesuits invented,
By evil counsel is fomented;
There is a Machiavilian plot
(Though ev'ry nare olfact it not)
And deep design in't to divide
The well-affected that confide,
By setting brother against brother,

V. 736. This was the Solemn League and Covenant, which was first framed and taken by the Scottish Parliament, and by them sent to the Parliament of England, in order to unite the two nations more closely in religion. It was received and taken by both Houses, and by the City of London; and ordered to be read in all the churches throughout the kingdom; and every person was bound to give his consent, by holding up his hand, at the reading of it.

V. 736. 'And the Cause's sake.' Sir William Dugdale informs us that Mr. Bond, preaching at the Savoy, told his auditors from the pulpit, "That they ought to contribute and pray, and do all they were able to bring in their brethren of Scotland for settling of God's cause: I say (quoth he) this is God's cause; and if our God hath any cause, this is it; and if this be not God's cause, then God is no God for me; but the Devil is got up into Heaven." Mr. Calamy, in his speech at Guildhall, 1643, says, "I may truly say, as the Martyr did, that if I had as many lives as hairs on my head, I would be willing to sacrifice all these lives in this cause;"

Which pluck'd down the King, the Church, and the Laws,
To set up an idol, then nick-nam'd The Cause,
Like Bell and the Dragon to gorge their own maws;

as it is expressed in "The Rump Carbonaded."

To claw and curry one another.
Have we not enemies *plus satis*,
That *cane et angue pejus* hate us?
And shall we turn our fangs and claws
Upon our own selves, without cause?
That some occult design doth lie
In bloody cynarctomachy,
Is plain enough to him that knows
How Saints lead Brothers by the nose.
I wish myself a pseudo-prophet,
But sure some mischief will come of it,
Unless by providential wit,
Or force, we averruncate it.
For what design, what interest,
Can beast have to encounter beast?
They fight for no espoused Cause,
Frail Privilege, Fundamental Laws,
Nor for a thorough Reformation,
Nor Covenant, nor Protestation,
Nor Liberty of consciences,
Nor Lords' and Commons' Ordinances;

V. 765. Var. 'Nor for free Liberty of Conscience.' The word 'free' was left out in 1674; and Mr. Warburton thinks for the worse; 'free liberty' being a most beautiful and satirical periphrasis for licentiousness, which is the idea the Author here intended to give us.

V. 766. The King being driven from the Parliament, no legal acts of Parliament could be made; therefore when the Lords and Commons had agreed upon any bill, they published it, and required obedience to it, under the title of An Ordinance of Lords and Commons, and sometimes, An Ordinance of Parliament.

Nor for the Church, nor for Church-lands,
To get them into their own hands;
Nor evil Counsellors to bring
To justice, that seduce the King;
Nor for the worship of us men,
Though we have done as much for them.
Th' Egyptians worshipp'd dogs, and for
Their faith made internecine war;
Others ador'd a rat, and some
For that church suffer'd martyrdom;
The Indians fought for the truth
Of th' elephant and monkey's tooth,
And many, to defend that faith,
Fought it out *mordicus* to death;
But no beast ever was so slight,
For man, as for his God, to fight:
They have more wit, alas! and know
Themselves and us better than so.
But we, who only do infuse
The rage in them like *boute-feus*,
'Tis our example that instils
In them th' infection of our ills.
For, as some late philosophers
Have well observ'd, beasts that converse
With man take after him, as hogs
Get pigs all th' year, and bitches dogs;
Just so, by our example, cattle
Learn to give one another battle.
We read in Nero's time, the Heathen,
When they destroy'd the Christian brethren,

They sew'd them in the skins of bears,
And then set dogs about their ears;
From whence, no doubt, th' invention came
Of this lewd antichristian game.
  To this quoth Ralpho, verily
The point seems very plain to me;
It is an antichristian game,
Unlawful both in thing and name.
First, for the name; the word Bear-baiting
Is carnal, and of man's creating,
For certainly there's no such word
In all the Scripture on record;
Therefore unlawful, and a sin:
And so is (secondly) the thing;
A vile assembly 'tis, that can
No more be proved by Scripture than
Provincial, Classic, National,
Mere human creature cobwebs all.
Thirdly, it is idolatrous;
For when men run a-whoring thus
With their inventions, whatsoe'er
The thing be, whether Dog or Bear,
It is Idolatrous and Pagan,
No less than worshipping of Dagon.
  Quoth Hudibras, I smell a rat;
Ralpho, thou dost prevaricate:
For though the thesis which thou lay'st
Be true *ad amussim*, as thou say'st;
(For that Bear-baiting should appear
Jure divino lawfuller

Than Synods are, thou dost deny
Totidem verbis, so do I)
Yet there's a fallacy in this;
For if by sly *homœosis*,
Tussis pro crepitu, an art
Under a cough to slur a f—t,
Thou wouldst sophistically imply
Both are unlawful, I deny.
  And I, quoth Ralpho, do not doubt
But Bear-baiting may be made out,
In gospel-times, as lawful as is
Provincial, or Parochial Classis;
And that both are so near of kin,
And like in all, as well as sin,
That put 'em in a bag, and shake 'em,
Yourself o' th' sudden would mistake 'em,
And not know which is which, unless
You measure by their wickedness;
For 'tis not hard t' imagine whether
O' th' two is worst, tho' I name neither.
  Quoth Hudibras, thou offer'st much,
But art not able to keep touch;
Mira de lente, as 'tis i' th' adage,
Id est, to make a leek a cabbage:
Thou wilt at best but suck a bull,
Or shear swine, all cry and no wool;

V. 851. Var. 'Thou canst at best but overstrain
A paradox and thy own brain;'
and
'Thou'lt be at best but such a bull,' &c.

For what can Synods have at all,
With Bear that's analogical?
Or what relation has debating
Of Church-affairs with Bear-baiting?
A just comparison still is
Of things *ejusdem generis*;
And then what *genus* rightly doth
Include and comprehend them both?
If animal, both of us may
As justly pass for Bears as they;
For we are animals no less,
Although of diff'rent specieses.
But, Ralpho, this is no fit place,
Nor time, to argue out the case:
For now the field is not far off
Where we must give the world a proof
Of deeds, not words, and such as suit
Another manner of dispute:
A controversy that affords
Actions for arguments, not words;
Which we must manage at a rate
Of prowess and conduct adequate
To what our place and fame doth promise,
And all the Godly expect from us.
Nor shall they be deceiv'd, unless
We're slurr'd and outed by success;
Success, the mark no mortal wit,

V. 860. Var. 'Comprehend them inclusive both.'
V. 862. Var. 'As likely.'

Or surest hand, can always hit:
For whatsoe'er we perpetrate,
We do but row, w' are steer'd by Fate,
Which in success oft disinherits,
For spurious causes, noblest merits.
Great actions are not always true sons
Of great and mighty resolutions;
Nor do the bold'st attempts bring forth
Events still equal to their worth;
But sometimes fail, and in their stead
Fortune and cowardice succeed.
Yet we have no great cause to doubt,
Our actions still have borne us out;
Which though they're known to be so ample,
We need not copy from example;
We're not the only person durst
Attempt this province, nor the first.
In northern clime a val'rous knight
Did whilom kill his Bear in fight,
And wound a Fiddler: we have both
Of these the objects of our wroth,
And equal fame and glory from
Th' attempt, or victory to come.
'Tis sung there is a valiant Mamaluke,
In foreign land yclep'd—

V. 904. The writers of the 'General Historical Dictionary,' vol. vi. p. 291, imagine, "That the chasm here is to be filled with the words 'Sir Samuel Luke,' because the line before it is of ten syllables, and the measure of the verse generally used in this Poem is of eight."

To whom we have been oft compar'd
For person, parts, address, and beard;
Both equally reputed stout,
And in the same cause both have fought:
He oft in such attempts as these
Came off with glory and success;
Nor will we fail in th' execution,
For want of equal resolution.
Honour is like a widow, won
With brisk attempt and putting on;
With ent'ring manfully, and urging,
Not slow approaches, like a virgin.
This said, as yerst the Phrygian knight,
So ours, with rusty steel did smite
His Trojan horse, and just as much
He mended pace upon the touch;
But from his empty stomach groan'd
Just as that hollow beast did sound,
And angry answer'd from behind,
With brandish'd tail and blast of wind.
So have I seen, with armed heel,
A wight bestride a Commonweal,
While still the more he kick'd and spurr'd,
The less the sullen jade has stirr'd.

PART I. CANTO II.

THE ARGUMENT.

The catalogue and character
Of th' enemies' best men of war,
Whom in a bold harangue the Knight
Defies and challenges to fight:
H' encounters Talgol, routs the Bear,
And takes the Fiddler prisoner,
Conveys him to enchanted castle,
There shuts him fast in wooden Bastile.

There was an ancient sage philosopher
That had read Alexander Ross over,
And swore the world, as he could prove,
Was made of fighting and of love.
Just so Romances are, for what else
Is in them all but love and battles?
O' th' first of these w' have no great matter
To treat of, but a world o' th' latter,
In which to do the injured right
We mean, in what concerns just fight.
Certes our authors are to blame
For to make some well-sounding name
A pattern fit for modern knights
To copy out in frays and fights
(Like those that a whole street do raze
To build a palace in the place).

They never care how many others
They kill, without regard of mothers,
Or wives, or children, so they can
Make up some fierce dead-doing man,
Compos'd of many ingredient valours,
Just like the manhood of nine tailors:
So a wild Tartar, when he spies
A man that's handsome, valiant, wise,
If he can kill him, thinks t' inherit
His wit, his beauty, and his spirit;
As if just so much he enjoy'd,
As in another is destroy'd:
For when a giant's slain in fight,
And mow'd o'erthwart, or cleft downright,
It is a heavy case, no doubt,
A man should have his brains beat out,
Because he's tall and has large bones,
As men kill beavers for their stones.
But as for our part, we shall tell
The naked truth of what befell,
And as an equal friend to both
The Knight and Bear, but more to Troth,
With neither faction shall take part,
But give to each his due desert,
And never coin a formal lie on't
To make the knight o'ercome the giant.
This b'ing profest, we've hopes enough,
And now go on where we left off.
  They rode, but authors having not
Determin'd whether pace or trot

(That is to say, whether tollutation,
As they do term 't, or succussation),
We leave it, and go on, as now
Suppose they did, no matter how;
Yet some, from subtle hints, have got
Mysterious light it was a trot;
But let that pass: they now begun
To spur their living engines on:
For as whipp'd tops and bandy'd balls,
The learned hold, are animals;
So horses they affirm to be
Mere engines made by Geometry,
And were invented first from engines,
As Indian Britains were from Penguins.
So let them be, and, as I was saying,
They their live engines ply'd, not staying
Until they reach'd the fatal champain
Which th' enemy did then encamp on;
The dire Pharsalian plain, where battle
Was to be wag'd 'twixt puissant cattle,
And fierce, auxiliary men,
That came to aid their brethren,
Who now began to take the field,
As Knight from ridge of steed beheld.
For as our modern wits behold,
Mounted a pick-back on the old,
Much further off, much further he,
Rais'd on his aged beast, could see;
Yet not sufficient to descry

V. 74. Var. 'From off.'

All postures of the enemy,
Wherefore he bids the Squire ride further,
T' observe their numbers and their order,
That, when their motions he had known,
He might know how to fit his own.
Mean-while he stopp'd his willing steed,
To fit himself for martial deed:
Both kinds of metal he prepar'd,
Either to give blows or to ward;
Courage and steel, both of great force,
Prepar'd for better or for worse.
His death-charg'd pistols he did fit well,
Drawn out from life-preserving vittle;
These being prim'd, with force he labour'd
To free 's sword from retentive scabbard,
And after many a painful pluck,
From rusty durance he bail'd tuck:
Then shook himself, to see that prowess
In scabbard of his arms sat loose;
And, rais'd upon his desp'rate foot,
On stirrup-side he gaz'd about,
Portending blood, like blazing star,
The beacon of approaching war.
Ralpho rode on with no less speed
Than Hugo in the forest did;

V. 85, 86. Var. 'Courage within, and steel without,
To give and to receive a rout.'
V. 92. Var. 'He clear'd at length the rugged tuck.'
V. 99, 100. Var. 'The Squire advanc'd with greater speed
Than could b' expected from his steed:'

But far more in returning made,
For now the foe he had survey'd,
Rang'd, as to him they did appear,
With van, main-battle, wings and rear.
I' th' head of all this warlike rabble,
Crowdero march'd expert and able;
Instead of trumpet and of drum,
That makes the warrior's stomach come,
Whose noise whets valour sharp, like beer
By thunder turn'd to vinegar;
(For if a trumpet sound or drum beat
Who has not a month's mind to combat?)
A squeaking engine he apply'd
Unto his neck, on north-east side,
Just where the hangman does dispose
To special friends the knot of noose:
For 'tis great grace when statesmen straight
Dispatch a friend, let others wait.
His warped ear hung o'er the strings,
Which was but souse to chitterlings;
For guts, some write, ere they are sodden,

V. 101, 102. Var. But 'with a great deal' more 'return'd,'
For now the foe he had 'discern'd.'

V. 106. So called from 'croud,' a fiddle: This was one Jackson, a milliner, who lived in the New Exchange in the Strand. He had formerly been in the service of the Roundheads, and had lost a leg in it; this brought him to decay, so that he was obliged to scrape upon a fiddle, from one ale-house to another, for his bread. Mr. Butler very judiciously places him at the head of his catalogue: for country diversions are generally attended with a fiddler or bagpiper.

Are fit for music or for pudden ;
From whence men borrow ev'ry kind
Of minstrelsy by string or wind.
His grisly beard was long and thick,
With which he strung his fiddlestick,
For he to horse-tail scorn'd to owe
For what on his own chin did grow ;
Chiron, the four-legg'd bard, had both
A beard and tail of his own growth,
And yet by authors 'tis averr'd
He made use only of his beard.
In Staffordshire, where virtuous worth
Does raise the minstrelsy, not birth,
Where bulls do choose the boldest king
And ruler o'er the men of string
(As once in Persia, 'tis said,
Kings were proclaim'd by a horse that neigh'd),
He, bravely vent'ring at a crown,
By chance of war was beaten down,
And wounded sore ; his leg then broke
Had got a deputy of oak :
For when a shin in fight is cropt,
The knee with one of timber's propt,
Esteem'd more honourable than the other,
And takes place, though the younger brother.
Next march'd brave Orsin, famous for
Wise conduct and success in war ;

V. 147. Var. 'Next follow'd.' Joshua Gosling, who kept bears at Paris-garden, in Southwark. However, says Sir Roger, he stood hard and fast for the Rump Parliament.

A skilful leader, stout, severe,
Now Marshal to the champion Bear.
With truncheon tipp'd with iron head,
The warrior to the lists he led;
With solemn march and stately pace,
But far more grave and solemn face;
Grave as the emperor of Pegu,
Or Spanish potentate, Don Diego.
This leader was of knowledge great,
Either for charge or for retreat;
He knew when to fall on pell-mell,
To fall back and retreat as well:
So lawyers, lest the Bear defendant
And plaintiff Dog should make an end on't,
Do stave and tail with writs of Error,
Reverse of Judgment, and Demurrer,
To let them breathe awhile, and then
Cry Whoop and set them on agen.
As Romulus a wolf did rear,
So he was dry-nurs'd by a bear,
That fed him with the purchas'd prey
Of many a fierce and bloody fray;
Bred up, where discipline most rare is,
In military garden Paris:
For soldiers heretofore did grow
In gardens just as weeds do now,
Until some splay-foot politicians

V. 159, 160. Var. 'Knew when t' engage his bear pell-mell,
And when to bring him off as well.'

T' Apollo offer'd up petitions
For licensing a new invention
Th' had found out of an antique engine,
To root out all the weeds that grow
In public gardens, at a blow,
And leave th' herbs standing. Quoth Sir Sun,
My friends, that is not to be done.
Not done! quoth Statesman; Yes, an't please ye,
When 'tis once known you'll say 'tis easy.
Why then let's know it, quoth Apollo:
We'll beat a drum, and they'll all follow.
A drum! (quoth Phœbus) Troth, that's true,
A pretty invention, quaint and new:
But though of voice and instrument
We are th' undoubted president,
We such loud music do not profess,
The Devil's master of that office,
Where it must pass; if't be a drum,
He'll sign it with *Cler. Parl. Dom. Com.*;
To him apply yourselves, and he
Will soon dispatch you for his fee.
They did so, but it prov'd so ill
Th' had better let 'em grow there still.
But to resume what we discoursing
Were on before, that is, stout Orsin:
That which so oft by sundry writers

V. 194. The House of Commons, even before the Rump had murdered the King, and expelled the House of Lords, usurped many branches of the Royal prerogative, and particularly this for granting licenses for new inventions.

Has been apply'd t' almost all fighters,
More justly may b' ascrib'd to this
Than any other warrior, (viz.)
None ever acted both parts bolder,
Both of a chieftain and a soldier.
He was of great descent, and high
For splendour and antiquity,
And from celestial origine
Deriv'd himself in a right line:
Not as the ancient heroes did,
Who, that their base births might be hid
(Knowing they were of doubtful gender,
And that they came in at a windore),
Made Jupiter himself and others
O' th' gods gallants to their own mothers,
To get on them a race of champions,
(Of which old Homer first made lampoons).
Arctophylax, in northern sphere,
Was his undoubted ancestor;
From him his great forefathers came,
And in all ages bore his name.
Learned he was in med'c'nal lore,
For by his side a pouch he wore
Replete with strange hermetic powder,
That wounds nine miles point-blank would solder;
By skilful chemist with great cost
Extracted from a rotten post;

V. 211. This is one instance of the Author's making great things little, though his talent lay chiefly the other way.

But of a heav'nlier influence
Than that which mountebanks dispense,
Though by Promethean fire made;
As they do quack that drive that trade.
For as, when slovens do amiss
At others' doors, by stool or piss,
The learned write a red-hot spit
B'ing prudently apply'd to it
Will convey mischief from the dung
Unto the part that did the wrong,
So this did healing; and, as sure
As that did mischief, this would cure.
  Thus virtuous Orsin was endu'd
With learning, conduct, fortitude
Incomparable; and as the prince
Of poets, Homer, sung long since,
A skilful leech is better far
Than half a hundred men of war;
So he appear'd, and by his skill,
No less than dint of sword, could kill.
  The gallant Bruin march'd next him,
With visage formidably grim,
And rugged as a Saracen,
Or Turk of Mahomet's own kin;
Clad in a mantle *delle guerre*
Of rough impenetrable fur,
And in his nose, like Indian king,
He wore, for ornament, a ring;

V. 238. Var. Unto the 'breech.'

About his neck a threefold gorget,
As rough as trebled leathern target;
Armed, as heralds, cant and langued,
Or, as the vulgar say, sharp-fanged:
For as the teeth in beasts of prey
Are swords, with which they fight in fray,
So swords, in men of war, are teeth
Which they do eat their vittle with.
He was by birth, some authors write,
A Russian, some a Muscovite,
And 'mong the Cossacks had been bred,
Of whom we in Diurnals read,
That serve to fill up pages here,
As with their bodies ditches there.
Scrimansky was his cousin-german,
With whom he serv'd, and fed on vermin;
And when these fail'd he'd suck his claws,
And quarter himself upon his paws:
And though his countrymen, the Huns,
Did stew their meat between their bums
And th' horses' backs o'er which they straddle,
And ev'ry man ate up his saddle;
He was not half so nice as they,
But ate it raw when 't came in 's way.
H' had trac'd the countries far and near
More than Le Blanc the traveller,
Who writes, he spous'd in India,
Of noble house a lady gay,
And got on her a race of worthies
As stout as any upon earth is.

Full many a fight for him between
Talgol and Orsin oft had been,
Each striving to deserve the crown
Of a sav'd citizen; the one
To guard his Bear, the other fought
To aid his Dog; both made more stout
By sev'ral spurs of neighborhood,
Church-fellow-membership, and blood:
But Talgol, mortal foe to cows,
Never got aught from him but blows,
Blows hard and heavy, such as he
Had lent, repaid with usury.
 Yet Talgol was of courage stout,
And vanquish'd oft'ner than he fought;
Inur'd to labour, sweat and toil,
And, like a champion, shone with oil:
Right many a widow his keen blade,
And many fatherless, had made;
He many a boar and huge dun-cow
Did, like another Guy, o'erthrow:
But Guy with him in fight compar'd,
Had like the boar or dun-cow far'd
With greater troops of sheep h' had fought
Than Ajax or bold Don Quixote;
And many a serpent of fell kind,
With wings before and stings behind,
Subdu'd; as, poets say, long agone

V. 299. A butcher in Newgate-market, who afterwards obtained a captain's commission for his rebellious bravery at Naseby, as Sir R. L'Estrange observes.

Bold Sir George Saint George did the Dragon.
Nor engine, nor device polemic,
Disease, nor doctor epidemic,
Though stor'd with deletery med'cines,
(Which whosoever took is dead since)
E'er sent so vast a colony
To both the under worlds as he;
For he was of that noble trade
That demi-gods and heroes made,
Slaughter, and knocking on the head,
The trade to which they all were bred;
And is, like others, glorious when
'Tis great and large, but base, if mean:
The former rides in triumph for it,
The latter in a two-wheel'd chariot,
For daring to profane a thing
So sacred with vile bungling.
  Next these the brave Magnano came,
Magnano great in martial fame;
Yet when with Orsin he wag'd fight,
'Tis sung he got but little by 't:
Yet he was fierce as forest boar,
Whose spoils upon his back he wore,
As thick as Ajax' sevenfold shield,
Which o'er his brazen arms he held:
But brass was feeble to resist

V. 331. Simeon Wait, a tinker, as famous an Independent preacher as Burroughs, who, with equal blasphemy to his Lord of Hosts, would style Oliver Cromwell the Archangel giving battle to the Devil.

The fury of his armed fist,
Nor could the hardest iron hold out
Against his blows, but they would through 't.
  In magic he was deeply read,
As he that made the brazen-head;
Profoundly skill'd in the black art,
As English Mèrlin for his heart;
But far more skilful in the spheres
Than he was at the sieve and shears.
He could transform himself in colour,
As like the Devil as a collier;
As like the hypocrites in show
Are to true saints, or crow to crow.
  Of warlike engines he was author,
Devis'd for quick dispatch of slaughter:
The cannon, blunderbuss, and saker,
He was th' inventor of, and maker:
The trumpet and the kettle-drum
Did both from his invention come.
He was the first that e'er did teach
To make, and how to stop a breach.
A lance he bore with iron pike,
Th' one half would thrust, the other strike;
And when their forces he had join'd,
He scorn'd to turn his parts behind.
  He Trulla lov'd, Trulla more bright

V. 365. The daughter of James Spenser, debauched by Magnano the tinker; so called because the tinker's wife or mistress was commonly called his 'trull.' See "The Coxcomb," a comedy.

Than burnish'd armour of her knight;
A bold virago, stout and tall,
As Joan of France, or English Mall:
Through perils both of wind and limb,
Through thick and thin she follow'd him,
In ev'ry adventure h' undertook,
And never him nor it forsook:
At breech of wall, or hedge surprize,
She shar'd i' th' hazard and the prize;
At beating quarters up, or forage,
Behav'd herself with matchless courage,
And laid about in fight more busily
Than th' Amazonian Dame Penthesile.
And though some critics here cry shame,
And say our authors are to blame,
That (spite of all philosophers,
Who hold no females stout but bears,
And heretofore did so abhor
That women should pretend to war,
They would not suffer the stout'st dame
To swear by Hercules's name)
Make feeble ladies, in their works,
To fight like termagants and Turks;
To lay their native arms aside,

V. 368. Alluding probably to Mary Carlton, called 'Kentish Moll,' but more commonly 'The German Princess;' a person notorious at the time this First Part of Hudibras was published. She was transported to Jamaica, 1671, but returning from transportation too soon, she was hanged at Tyburn, Jan. 22, 1672–3.

Their modesty, and ride astride;
To run a-tilt at men, and wield
Their naked tools in open field;
As stout Armida, bold Thalestris,
And she that would have been the mistress
Of Gundibert, but he had grace,
And rather took a country lass;
They say 'tis false without all sense,
But of pernicious consequence
To government, which they suppose
Can never be upheld in prose;
Strip Nature naked to the skin,
You'll find about her no such thing:
It may be so, yet what we tell
Of Trulla that's improbable,
Shall be depos'd by those have seen 't,
Or, what's as good, produc'd in print;
And if they will not take our word,
We'll prove it true upon record.
The upright Cerdon next advanc't,
Of all his race the valiant'st;
Cerdon the Great, renown'd in song,
Like Herc'les, for repair of wrong:

V. 409. 'Cerdon.' A one-eyed cobbler, like his brother Colonel Hewson. The poet observes that his chief talent lay in preaching. Is it not then indecent, and beyond the rules of decorum, to introduce him into such rough company? No: it is probable he had but newly set up the trade of a teacher, and we may conclude that the poet did not think that he had so much sanctity as to debar him the pleasure of his beloved diversion of bear-baiting.

He rais'd the low, and fortify'd
The weak against the strongest side:
Ill has he read that never hit
On him in Muses' deathless writ.
He had a weapon keen and fierce,
That through a bull-hide shield would pierce,
And cut it in a thousand pieces,
Though tougher than the Knight of Greece his,
With whom his black-thumb'd ancestor
Was comrade in the ten-years' war:
For when the restless Greeks sat down
So many years before Troy town,
And were renown'd, as Homer writes,
For well-sol'd boots no less than fights,
They ow'd that glory only to
His ancestor, that made them so.
Fast friend he was to reformation,
Until 'twas worn quite out of fashion;
Next rectifier of wry law,
And would make three to cure one flaw.
Learned he was, and could take note,
Transcribe, collect, translate, and quote:
But preaching was his chiefest talent,

V. 435. Mechanics of all sorts were then preachers, and some of them much followed and admired by the mob. "I am to tell thee, Christian Reader," says Dr. Featley, Preface to his "Dipper Dipped," wrote 1645, and published 1647, p. 1, "this new year of new changes, never heard of in former ages, namely, of stables turned into temples, and, I will beg leave to add, temples turned into stables (as was that of St. Paul's, and many more), stalls into quires, shop-boards into

Or argument, in which being valiant,
He us'd to lay about and stickle,
Like ram or bull, at Conventicle:
For disputants, like rams and bulls,
Do fight with arms that spring from sculls.
  Last Colon came, bold man of war,

communion-tables, tubs into pulpits, aprons into linen ephods, and mechanics of the lowest rank into priests of the high places. — I wonder that our door-posts and walls sweat not, upon which such notes as these have been lately affixed; on such a day such a brewer's clerk exerciseth, such a tailor expoundeth, such a waterman teacheth. — If cooks, instead of mincing their meat, fall upon dividing of the Word; if tailors leap up from the shop-board into the pulpit, and patch up sermons out of stolen shreds; if not only of the lowest of the people, as in Jeroboam's time, priests are consecrated to the Most High God — do we marvel to see such confusion in the Church as there is?" They are humorously girded in a tract entitled, 'The Reformado precisely character'd, by a modern Churchwarden,' p. 11. "Here are felt-makers," says he, "who can roundly deal with the blockheads and neutral dimicasters of the world; cobblers who can give good rules for upright walking, and handle Scripture to a bristle; coachmen who know how to lash the beastly enormities, and curb the head-strong insolences of this brutish age, stoutly exhorting us to stand up for the truth, lest the wheel of destruction roundly overrun us. We have weavers that can sweetly inform us of the shuttle swiftness of the times, and practically tread out the vicissitude of all sublunary things, till the web of our life be cut off: and here are mechanics of my profession who can separate the pieces of salvation from those of damnation, measure out every man's portion, and cut it out by a thread, substantially pressing the points, till they have fashionably filled up their work with a well-bottomed conclusion."

V. 441. 'Colon.' Ned Perry, an hostler.

Destin'd to blows by fatal star,
Right expert in command of horse,
But cruel, and without remorse.
That which of Centaur long ago
Was said, and has been wrested to
Some other knights, was true of this;
He and his horse were of a piece.
One spirit did inform them both,
The self-same vigour, fury, wroth;
Yet he was much the rougher part,
And always had a harder heart,
Although his horse had been of those
That fed on man's flesh, as fame goes:
Strange food for horse! and yet, alas!
It may be true, for flesh is grass.
Sturdy he was, and no less able
Than Hercules to clean a stable;
As great a drover, and as great
A critic too, in hog or neat.
He ripp'd the womb up of his mother,
Dame Tellus, 'cause she wanted fother
And provender, wherewith to feed
Himself and his less cruel steed.
It was a question whether he
Or 's horse were of a family
More worshipful; till antiquaries
(After they'd almost por'd out their eyes)
Did very learnedly decide
The bus'ness on the horse's side,
And prov'd not only horse, but cows,

Nay pigs, were of the elder house:
For beasts, when man was but a piece
Of earth himself, did th' earth possess.
These worthies were the chief that led
The combatants, each in the head
Of his command, with arms and rage
Ready and longing to engage.
The num'rous rabble was drawn out
Of sev'ral Counties round about,
From villages remote, and shires
Of east and western hemispheres.
From foreign parishes and regions,
Of different manners, speech, religions,
Came men and mastiffs; some to fight
For fame and honour, some for sight.
And now the field of death, the lists,
Were enter'd by antagonists,
And blood was ready to be broach'd,
When Hudibras in haste approach'd,
With Squire and weapons to attack 'em;
But first thus from his horse bespake 'em.
What rage, O Citizens! what fury,
Doth you to these dire actions hurry?
What oestrum, what phrenetic mood,
Makes you thus lavish of your blood,
While the proud Vies your trophies boast,
And unreveng'd walks Waller's ghost?

V. 495. 'Oestrum' signifies the gad-bee or horse-fly.
V. 497. Sir W. Waller was defeated at the Devises.

What towns, what garrisons, might you
With hazard of this blood subdue,
Which now y' are bent to throw away
In vain untriumphable fray?
Shall saints in civil bloodshed wallow
Of saints, and let the cause lie fallow?
The cause, for which we fought and swore
So boldly, shall we now give o'er?
Then, because quarrels still are seen
With oaths and swearings to begin,
The Solemn League and Covenant
Will seem a mere God-dam-me rant,
And we that took it, and have fought,
As lewd as drunkards that fall out:
For as we make war for the King
Against himself, the self-same thing,
Some will not stick to swear, we do
For God and for Religion too:
For, if Bear-baiting we allow,
What good can Reformation do?
The blood and treasure that's laid out

V. 503, 504. Mr. Walker observes, "That all the cheating, covetous, ambitious persons of the land were united together under the title of the Godly, the Saints, and shared the fat of the land between them;" and he calls them the Saints who were canonized no-where but in the Devil's Calendar.

V. 513, 514. The Presbyterians, in all their wars against the king, maintained still that they fought for him; for they pretended to distinguish his political person from his natural one: his political person, they said, must be and was with the Parliament, though his natural person was at war with them.

Is thrown away, and goes for nought.
Are these the fruits o' th' Protestation,
The prototype of Reformation,
Which all the saints, and some, since martyrs,
Wore in their hats like wedding-garters,
When 'twas resolved by either House
Six Members' quarrel to espouse?
Did they for this draw down the rabble,
With zeal and noises formidable,
And make all cries about the town
Join throats to cry the Bishops down?
Who having round begirt the palace,
(As once a month they do the gallows),
As Members gave the sign about,
Set up their throats with hideous shout.
When tinkers bawl'd aloud to settle
Church-Discipline, for patching kettle;
No sow-gelder did blow his horn
To geld a cat, but cry'd Reform;
The oyster-women lock'd their fish up,
And trudg'd away to cry No Bishop;
The mouse-trap men laid save-alls by,
And 'gainst Ev'l Counsellors did cry;
Botchers left old clothes in the lurch,
And fell to turn and patch the Church;

V. 530. "Good Lord!" (says the 'True Informer,' p. 12,) "what a deal of dirt was thrown in the Bishops' faces! — what infamous ballads were sung! — what a thick cloud of epidemical hatred hung suddenly over them! so far, that a dog with a black and white face was called a 'Bishop.'"

Some cry'd the Covenant, instead
Of pudding-pies and gingerbread;
And some for brooms, old boots and shoes,
Bawl'd out to purge the Common-House;
Instead of kitchen-stuff, some cry
A Gospel-preaching ministry;
And some for old suits, coats, or cloak,
No Surplices nor Service-book:
A strange harmonious inclination
Of all degrees to Reformation.
And is this all? Is this the end
To which these carr'ings on did tend?
Hath Public faith, like a young heir,
For this tak'n up all sorts of ware,
And run int' ev'ry tradesman's book,
Till both turn'd bankrupts and are broke?
Did Saints for this bring in their plate,
And crowd as if they came too late?
For, when they thought the cause had need on't,
Happy was he that could be rid on't.
Did they coin piss-pots, bowls, and flaggons,
Int' officers of horse and dragoons?
And into pikes and musqueteers
Stamp beakers, cups, and porringers?

V. 553, 554. Those flights, which seem most extravagant in our Poet, were really excelled by matter of fact. The Scots (in their 'Large Declaration,' 1637, p. 41) begin their petition against the Common Prayer-Book thus:—"We men, women, and children, and servants, having considered," &c. 'Foulis's Hist. of Wicked Plots.'

A thimble, bodkin, and a spoon,
Did start up living men as soon
As in the furnace they were thrown,
Just like the dragon's teeth being sown.
Then was the Cause of gold and plate,
The Brethren's off'rings, consecrate,
Like th' Hebrew calf, and down before it
The Saints fell prostrate, to adore it:
So say the Wicked — and will you
Make that sarcasmus scandal true
By running after Dogs and Bears,
Beasts more unclean than calves or steers?
Have pow'rful Preachers ply'd their tongues,
And laid themselves out and their lungs;
Us'd all means, both direct and sinister,
I' th' pow'r of Gospel-preaching Minister?
Have they invented tones to win
The women and make them draw in
The men, as Indians with a female
Tame elephant inveigle the male?
Have they told Prov'dence what it must do,

V. 589. It was a common practice to inform God of the transactions of the times. "Oh! my Good Lord God," says Mr. G. Swathe, 'Prayers,' p. 12, "I hear the King hath set up his standard at York against the Parliament and city of London. — Look thou upon them, take their cause into thine own hand; appear thou in the cause of thy Saints, the cause in hand. — It is thy cause, Lord. We know that the King is misled, deluded, and deceived by his Popish, Arminian, and temporising, rebellious, malignant faction and party," &c. "They would," says Dr. Echard, "in their prayers and sermons, tell God, that they would be willing to be at any

Whom to avoid, and whom to trust to?
Discover'd th' Enemy's design,
And which way best to countermine?
Prescrib'd what ways it hath to work,
Or it will ne'er advance the Kirk?
Told it the news o' th' last express,
And after good or bad success
Made prayers, not so like petitions

charge and trouble for him, and to do as it were any kindness for the Lord; the Lord might now trust them, and rely upon them, they should not fail him; they should not be unmindful of his business; his works should not stand still, nor his designs be neglected. They must needs say that they had formerly received some favours from God, and have been as it were beholden to the Almighty; but they did not much question but they should find some opportunity of making some amends for the many good things, and (as I may so say) civilities which they had received from him. Indeed, as for those that are weak in the Faith, and are yet but babes in Christ, it is fit that they should keep at some distance from God, should kneel before him, and stand (as I may say) cap in hand to the Almighty: but as for those that are strong in all Gifts, and grown up in all Grace, and are come to a fulness and ripeness in the Lord Jesus, it is comely enough to take a great chair, and sit at the end of the table, and, with their cock'd hats on their heads, to say, God, we thought it not amiss to call upon thee this evening, and let thee know how affairs stand. We have been very watchful since we were last with thee, and they are in a very hopeful condition. We hope that thou wilt not forget us; for we are very thoughtful of thy concerns. We do somewhat long to hear from thee; and if thou pleasest to give us such a thing ('Victory'), we shall be (as I may so say) good to thee in something else when it lies in our way." See a remarkable Scotch Prayer much to the same purpose, 'Scourge,' by Mr. Lewis, No. XVI. p. 130, edit. 1717.

As overtures and propositions
(Such as the Army did present
To their Creator, th' Parl'ament),
In which they freely will confess
They will not, cannot acquiesce,
Unless the Work be carry'd on
In the same way they have begun,
By setting Church and Commonweal
All on a flame, bright as their zeal,
On which the Saints were all agog,
And all this for a Bear and Dog?
The Parl'ament drew up petitions
To 'tself, and sent them, like commissions,
To well-affected persons down,

V. 602. Alluding probably to their profane expostulations with God from the pulpit. Mr. Vines, in St. Clement's Church, near Temple-bar, used the following words: "O Lord, thou hast never given us a victory this long while, for all our frequent fasting. What dost thou mean, O Lord, to fling into a ditch, and there to leave us?" And one Robinson, in his prayer at Southampton, Aug. 25, 1642, expressed himself in the following manner: "O God, O God, many are the hands that are lift up against us, but there is one God, it is thou thyself, O Father, who does us more mischief than they all." They seemed to encourage this profanity in their public sermons. "Gather upon God," says Mr. R. Harris, 'Fast Sermons before the Commons,' "and hold him to it, as Jacob did: press him with his precepts, with his promises, with his hand, with his seal, with his oath, till we do δυσωπεῖν, as some Greek Fathers boldly speak; that is, if I may speak it reverently enough, put the Lord out of countenance; put him, as you would say, to the blush, unless we be masters of our requests."

In every city and great town,
With pow'r to levy horse and men,
Only to bring them back agen?
For this did many, many a mile,
Ride manfully in rank and file,
With papers in their hats, that show'd
As if they to the pill'ry rode?
Have all these courses, these efforts,
Been try'd by people of all sorts,
Velis et remis, omnibus nervis,
And all t' advance the Cause's service;
And shall all now be thrown away
In petulent intestine fray?
Shall we, that in the Cov'nant swore
Each man of us to run before
Another, still in Reformation
Give Dogs and Bears a dispensation?
How will Dissenting Brethren relish it?
What will Malignants say? *Videlicet,*
That each man swore to do his best
To damn and perjure all the rest;
And bid the devil take the hin'most,
Which at this race is like to win most.
They'll say our bus'ness to Reform
The Church and State, is but a worm;
For to subscribe, unsight unseen,
To an unknown Church discipline,
What is it else but beforehand
T' engage and after understand?
For when we swore to carry on

The present Reformation,
According to the purest mode
Of churches best reform'd abroad,
What did we else but make a vow
To do we know not what, nor how?
For no three of us will agree
Where, or what churches these should be:
And is indeed the self-same case
With those that swore *et cæteras ;*
Or the French League, in which men vow'd
To fight the last drop of blood.
These slanders will be thrown upon
The cause and work we carry on,
If we permit men to run headlong
T' exorbitances fit for Bedlam,
Rather than gospel-walking times,
When slightest sins are greatest crimes.
But we the matter so shall handle
As to remove that odious scandal:
In name of King and Parl'ament,
I charge ye all, no more foment

V. 651. The Holy League in France, designed and made for extirpation of the Protestant religion, was the original out of which the Solemn League and Covenant here was (with difference only of circumstances) most faithfully transcribed. Nor did the success of both differ more than the intent and purpose; for, after the destruction of vast numbers of people of all sorts, both ended with the murder of two kings, whom they had both sworn to defend. And as our Covenanters swore every man to run one before another in the way of Reformation, so did the French, in the Holy League, to fight to the last drop of blood.

This feud, but keep the peace between
Your brethren and your countrymen,
And to those places straight repair
Where your respective dwellings are.
But to that purpose first surrender
The Fiddler, as the prime offender,
Th' incendiary vile, that is chief
Author and engineer of mischief;
That makes division between friends,
For profane and malignant ends.
He, and that engine of vile noise
On which illegally he plays,
Shall (*dictum factum*) both be brought
To condign pun'shment, as they ought:
This must be done, and I would fain see
Mortal so sturdy as to gainsay;

V. 673 - 676. The threatening punishment to the Fiddle was much like the threats of the pragmatical troopers to punish Ralph Dobbin's waggon, 'Plain Dealer,' vol. i. "I was driving," says he, "into a town upon the 29th of May, where my waggon was to dine. There came up in a great rage seven or eight of the troopers that were quartered there, and asked, 'What I bushed out my horses for?' I told them, 'To drive flies away.' But they said, I was a Jacobite rascal, that my horses were guilty of high treason, and my waggon ought to be hanged. I answered, 'it was already drawn, and within a yard or two of being quartered; but as to being hanged, it was a compliment we had no occasion for, and therefore desired them to take it back again, and keep it in their own hands, till they had an opportunity to make use of it.' I had no sooner spoke these words, but they fell upon me like thunder, stript my cattle in a twinkling, and beat me black and blue with my own oak branches."

For then I'll take another course,
And soon reduce you all by force.
This said, he clapt his hand on sword,
To show he meant to keep his word.
But Talgol, who had long supprest
Inflamed wrath in glowing breast,
Which now began to rage and burn as
Implacably as flame in furnace,
Thus answer'd him: Thou vermin wretched,
As e'er in measled pork was hatched;
Thou tail of worship, that dost grow
On rump of justice as of cow;
How dar'st thou with that sullen luggage
O' th' self, old ir'n, and other baggage,
With which thy steed of bones and leather
Has broke his wind in halting hither,
How durst th', I say, adventure thus
T' oppose thy lumber against us?
Could thine impertinence find out
No work t' employ itself about,
Where thou, secure from wooden blow,
Thy busy vanity might'st show?
Was no dispute a-foot between
The caterwauling Bretheren?

V. 683, 684. It may be asked, Why Talgol was the first in answering the Knight, when it seems more incumbent upon the Bearward to make a defence? Probably Talgol might then be a Cavalier; for the character the Poet has given him doth not infer the contrary, and his answer carries strong indications to justify the conjecture.

V. 694. Var. 'Is lam'd, and tir'd in halting hither.'

No subtle question rais'd among
Those out-o'-their wits and those i' th' wrong?
No prize between those combatants
O' th' times, the land and water saints,
Where thou might'st stickle, without hazard
Of outrage to thy hide and mazzard,
And not for want of bus'ness come
To us to be thus troublesome,
To interrupt our better sort
Of disputants, and spoil our sport?
Was there no felony, no bawd,
Cut-purse, or burglary abroad?
No stolen pig, nor plunder'd goose,
To tie thee up from breaking loose?
No ale unlicens'd, broken hedge,
For which thou statute might'st allege,
To keep thee busy from foul evil
And shame due to thee from the devil?
Did no Committee sit, where he
Might cut out journey-work for thee,
And set th' a task, with subornation,
To stitch up sale and sequestration;
To cheat, with holiness and zeal,
All parties and the commonweal?
Much better had it been for thee
He 'ad kept thee where th' art us'd to be,
Or sent th' on bus'ness any whither,
So he had never brought thee hither:
But if th' hast brain enough in scull

To keep itself in lodging whole,
And not provoke the rage of stones
And cudgels to thy hide and bones,
Tremble, and vanish while thou may'st,
Which I'll not promise if thou stay'st.
At this the knight grew high in wroth,
And, lifting hands and eyes up both,
Three times he smote on stomach stout,
From whence, at length, these words broke out:
Was I for this entitled Sir,
And girt with trusty sword and spur,
For fame and honour to wage battle,
Thus to be brav'd by foe to cattle?
Not all that pride that makes thee swell
As big as thou dost blown-up veal;
Nor all thy tricks and sleights to cheat,
And sell thy carrion for good meat;
Nor all thy magic to repair
Decay'd old age in tough lean ware,
Make nat'ral death appear thy work,

V. 732. Var. 'To keep within its lodging.'

V. 741. Hudibras shewed less patience upon this than Don Quixote did upon a like occasion, where he calmly distinguishes betwixt an affront and an injury. The Knight is irritated at the satirical answer of Talgol, and vents his rage in a manner exactly suited to his character; and when his passion was worked up to a height too great to be expressed in words, he immediately falls into action; but, alas! at this first entrance into it, he meets with an unlucky disappointment; an omen that the success would be as indifferent as the cause in which he was engaged.

V. 751. Var. 'Turn death of nature to thy work.

And stop the gangrene in stale pork ;
Not all the force that makes thee proud,
Because by bullock ne'er withstood ;
Though arm'd with all thy cleavers, knives,
And axes, made to hew down lives ;
Shall save or help thee to evade
The hand of Justice, or this blade,
Which I, her sword-bearer, do carry,
For civil deed and military.
Nor shall these words of venom base,
Which thou hast from their native place,
Thy stomach, pump'd to fling on me,
Go unreveng'd, though I am free ;
Thou down the same throat shalt devour 'em,
Like tainted beef, and pay dear for 'em :
Nor shall it e'er be said that wight
With gauntlet blue and bases white,
And round blunt truncheon by his side,
So great a man at arms defy'd
With words far bitterer than wormwood,
That would in Job or Grizel stir mood.
Dogs with their tongues their wounds do heal,
But men with hands, as thou shalt feel.
  This said, with hasty rage he snatch'd
His gun-shot that in holsters watch'd,
And, bending cock, he levell'd full
Against th' outside of Talgol's scull,
Vowing that he should ne'er stir further,
Nor henceforth cow or bullock murther :

But Pallas came in shape of Rust,
And 'twixt the spring and hammer thrust
Her Gorgon shield, which made the cock
Stand stiff, as 'twere transform'd to stock.
Meanwhile fierce Talgol, gath'ring might,
With rugged truncheon charg'd the Knight:
But he, with petronel upheav'd
Instead of shield, the blow receiv'd;
The gun recoil'd, as well it might,
Not us'd to such a kind of fight,
And shrunk from its great master's gripe,
Knock'd down and stunn'd with mortal stripe.
Then Hudibras, with furious haste,
Drew out his sword; yet not so fast
But Talgol first, with hardy thwack,

V. 781-783. This, and another passage in this Canto, are the only places where Deities are introduced in this poem. As it was not intended for an Epic Poem, consequently none of the heroes in it needed supernatural assistance; how then comes Pallas to be ushered in here, and Mars afterwards? Probably to ridicule Homer and Virgil, whose heroes scarce perform any action (even the most feasible) without the sensible aid of a Deity; and to manifest that it was not the want of abilities, but choice, that made our Poet avoid such subterfuges, he has given us a sample of his judgment in this way of writing in the passage before us, which, taken in its naked meaning, is only — that the Knight's pistol was, for want of use, grown so rusty, that it would not fire; or, in other words, that the rust was the cause of his disappointment.

V. 784. Var. 'Stand stiff, as if 'twere turn'd t' a stock.'

V. 786. Var. 'smote the Knight.'

V. 787, 788. Var. 'And he with rusty pistol held...
To take the blow on like a shield.'

Twice bruis'd his head, and twice his back.
But when his nut-brown sword was out,
With stomach huge he laid about,
Imprinting many a wound upon
His mortal foe, the truncheon:
The trusty cudgel did oppose
Itself against dead-doing blows,
To guard his leader from fell bane,
And then reveng'd itself again.
And though the sword (some understood)
In force had much the odds of wood,
'Twas nothing so; both sides were balanc't
So equal, none knew which was valiant'st:
For wood, with honour b'ing engag'd,
Is so implacably enrag'd,
Though iron hew and mangle sore,
Wood wounds and bruises honour more.
And now both knights were out of breath,
Tir'd in the hot pursuits of death,
Whilst all the rest amaz'd stood still,
Expecting which should take, or kill.
This Hudibras observ'd; and fretting
Conquest should be so long a-getting,
He drew up all his force into
One body, and that into one blow:
But Talgol wisely avoided it
By cunning sleight; for, had it hit,

V. 797. Var. 'But when his rugged sword was out.'
V. 798. Var. 'Courageously he laid about.'

The upper part of him the blow
Had slit, as sure as that below.
  Meanwhile th' incomparable Colon,
To aid his friend, began to fall on:
Him Ralph encounter'd, and straight grew
A dismal combat 'twixt them two;
Th' one arm'd with metal, th' other with wood,
This fit for bruise, and that for blood.
With many a stiff thwack, many a bang,
Hard crab-tree and old iron rang,
While none that saw them could divine
To which side conquest would incline:
Until Magnano, who did envy
That two should with so many men vie,
By subtle stratagem of brain
Perform'd what force could ne'er attain;
For he, by foul hap, having found
Where thistles grew on barren ground,
In haste he drew his weapon out,
And, having cropt them from the root,
He clapt them underneath the tail
Of steed, with pricks as sharp as nail.
The angry beast did straight resent
The wrong done to his fundament,
Began to kick, and fling, and wince,

V. 825. Var. 'But now fierce Colon 'gan draw on,
To aid the distress'd champion;'
V. 828. Var. 'A fierce dispute.'
V. 844. Var. 'With prickles sharper than a nail.'
V. 846. Var. 'And feel regret on fundament.'

As if h' had been beside his sense,
Striving to disengage from thistle,
That gall'd him sorely under his tail;
Instead of which, he threw the pack
Of Squire and baggage from his back,
And blund'ring still, with smarting rump,
He gave the Knight's steed such a thump
As made him reel. The Knight did stoop,
And sat on further side aslope.
This Talgol viewing, who had now
By sleight escap'd the fatal blow,
He rally'd, and again fell to 't;
For catching foe by nearer foot,
He lifted with such might and strength
As would have hurl'd him thrice his length,
And dash'd his brains (if any) out:
But Mars, that still protects the stout,
In pudding-time came to his aid,
And under him the Bear convey'd,
The Bear, upon whose soft fur-gown

V. 855. Var. 'That stagger'd him.'

V. 864, 865. I would here observe the judgment of the Poet: Mars is introduced to the Knight's advantage, as Pallas had been before to his disappointment. It was reasonable that the God of War should come in to his assistance, since a goddess had interested herself on the side of his enemies (agreeably to Homer and Virgil). Had the Knight directly fallen to the ground, he had been probably disabled from future action, and consequently the battle would too soon have been determined. Besides, we may observe a beautiful gradation to the honour of the hero: he falls upon the Bear, the Bear breaks loose, and the spectators run; so

The Knight with all his weight fell down.
The friendly rug preserv'd the ground,
And headlong Knight, from bruise or wound;
Like feather-bed betwixt a wall
And heavy brunt of cannon-ball.
As Sancho on a blanket fell,
And had no hurt, ours far'd as well
In body, though his mighty spirit,
B'ing heavy, did not so well bear it.
The Bear was in a greater fright,
Beat down and worsted by the Knight;
He roar'd, and rag'd, and flung about,
To shake off bondage from his snout:
His wrath inflam'd, boil'd o'er, and from
His jaws of death he threw the foam;
Fury in stranger postures threw him,
And more than ever herald drew him.
He tore the earth, which he had sav'd
From squelch of Knight, and storm'd and rav'd,
And vex'd the more because the harms
He felt were 'gainst the law of arms:
For men he always took to be
His friends, and dogs the enemy;
Who never so much hurt had done him,
As his own side did falling on him.
It griev'd him to the guts that they,
For whom he 'ad fought so many a fray,

that the Knight's fall is the primary cause of this rout, and he might justly, as he afterwards did, ascribe the honour of the victory to himself.

And serv'd with loss of blood so long,
Should offer such inhuman wrong;
Wrong of unsoldier-like condition,
For which he flung down his commission,
And laid about him, till his nose
From thrall of ring and cord broke loose.
Soon as he felt himself enlarg'd,
Through thickest of his foes he charg'd,
And made way through th' amazed crew;
Some he o'erran and some o'erthrew,
But took none; for by hasty flight
He strove t' escape pursuit of Knight,
From whom he fled with as much haste
And dread as he the rabble chas'd:
In haste he fled, and so did they,
Each and his fear a sev'ral way.
   Crowdero only kept the field,
Not stirring from the place he held,
Though beaten down, and wounded sore
I' th' Fiddle, and a leg that bore
One side of him; not that of bone,
But much its better, th' wooden one.
He spying Hudibras lie strow'd
Upon the ground, like log of wood,
With fright of fall, supposed wound,
And loss of urine, in a swound,
In haste he snatch'd the wooden limb

V. 906. Var. 'avoid the conqu'ring Knight.'
V. 920. Var. 'cast in swound.'

That hurt i' th' ankle lay by him,
And, fitting it for sudden fight,
Straight drew it up, t' attack the Knight;
For getting up on stump and huckle,
He with the foe began to buckle,
Vowing to be reveng'd, for breach
Of Crowd and shin, upon the wretch
Sole author of all detriment
He and his fiddle underwent.
But Ralpho (who had now begun
T' adventure resurrection
From heavy squelch, and had got up
Upon his legs, with sprained crup),
Looking about, beheld pernicion
Approaching Knight from fell musician:
He snatch'd his whinyard up, that fled
When he was falling off his steed
(As rats do from a falling house)
To hide itself from rage of blows,
And, wing'd with speed and fury, flew
To rescue Knight from black and blue;
Which ere he could achieve, his sconce
The leg encounter'd twice and once.
And now 'twas rais'd to smite agen
When Ralpho thrust himself between;

V. 923. Var. 'And listing it.'
V. 924. Var. 'to fall on Knight.'
V. 935, 936. Var. 'Looking about, beheld the Bard
To charge the Knight entranc'd prepar'd.'
V. 944. Var. 'The skin encounter'd,' &c.

He took the blow upon his arm,
To shield the Knight from further harm,
And, joining wrath with force, bestow'd
On th' wooden member such a load,
That down it fell, and with it bore
Crowdero, whom it propp'd before.
To him the Squire right nimbly run,
And setting conqu'ring foot upon
His trunk, thus spoke: What desp'rate frenzy
Made thee (thou whelp of Sin) to fancy
Thyself and all that coward rabble
T' encounter us in battle able?
How durst th', I say, oppose thy Curship
'Gainst arms, authority, and worship,
And Hudibras or me provoke,
Though all thy limbs were heart of oak,
And th' other half of thee as good
To bear out blows as that of wood?
Could not the whipping-post prevail,
With all its rhet'rick, nor the jail,
To keep from flaying scourge thy skin,
And ankle free from iron gin?
Which now thou shalt — but first our care
Must see how Hudibras does fare.
This said, he gently rais'd the Knight,
And set him on his bum upright.
To rouse him from lethargic dump,

V. 947. Var. 'on side and arm.'
V. 948. Var. 'To shield the Knight entranc'd from harm.'

He tweak'd his nose, with gentle thump
Knock'd on his breast, as if't had been
To raise the spirits lodg'd within:
They, waken'd with the noise, did fly
From inward room to window eye,
And gently op'ning lid, the casement,
Look'd out, but yet with some amazement.
This gladded Ralpho much to see,
Who thus bespoke the Knight. Quoth he,
Tweaking his nose, You are, great Sir,
A self-denying conqueror;
As high, victorious, and great,
As e'er fought for the Churches yet,
If you will give yourself but leave
To make out what y' already have;
That's victory. The foe, for dread
Of your nine-worthiness, is fled,
All save Crowdero, for whose sake
You did th' espous'd Cause undertake;
And he lies pris'ner at your feet,
To be dispos'd as you think meet,
Either for life, or death, or sale,
The gallows, or perpetual jail:
For one wink of your pow'rful eye
Must sentence him to live or die.
His Fiddle is your proper purchase,
Won in the service of the Churches;
And by your doom must be allow'd
To be, or be no more, a Crowd:
For though success did not confer

Just title on the conqueror;
Though dispensations were not strong
Conclusions whether right or wrong;
Although Outgoings did confirm,
And Owning were but a mere term;
Yet as the wicked have no right
To th' creature, though usurp'd by might,
The property is in the Saint,
From whom th' injuriously detain 't:
Of him they hold their luxuries,
Their dogs, their horses, whores, and dice,
Their riots, revels, masks, delights,
Pimps, buffoons, fiddlers, parasites;
All which the Saints have title to,
And ought t' enjoy, if th' had their due.
What we take from 'em is no more
Than what was ours by right before:
For we are their true landlords still,
And they our tenants but at will.
At this the Knight began to rouse,
And by degrees grow valorous:
He star'd about, and seeing none
Of all his foes remain but one,
He snatch'd his weapon that lay near him,

V. 1009. It was a principle maintained by the Rebels of those days, that dominion is founded on grace; and therefore if a man wanted grace (in their opinion), if he was not a saint or a godly man, he had no right to any lands, goods, or chattels. The saints, as the Squire says, had a right to all, and might take it, wherever they had a power to do it.

And from the ground began to rear him,
Vowing to make Crowdero pay
For all the rest that ran away.
But Ralpho now, in colder blood,
His fury mildly thus withstood:
Great Sir, quoth he, your mighty spirit
Is rais'd too high; this slave does merit
To be the hangman's bus'ness sooner
Than from your hand to have the honour
Of his destruction; I that am
A Nothingness in deed and name,
Did scorn to hurt his forfeit carcase,
Or ill entreat his Fiddle or case:
Will you, great Sir, that glory blot
In cold blood, which you gain'd in hot?
Will you employ your conqu'ring sword
To break a fiddle, and your word?
For though I fought and overcame,
And quarter gave, 'twas in your name:
For great commanders always own
What's prosp'rous by the soldier done.
To save, where you have pow'r to kill,
Argues your pow'r above your will;
And that your will and pow'r have less
Than both might have of selfishness.
This pow'r, which now alive, with dread
He trembles at, if he were dead
Would no more keep the slave in awe,
Than if you were a Knight of straw;
For Death would then be his conqueror,

Not you, and free him from that terror.
If danger from his life accrue,
Or honour from his death, to you,
'Twere policy and honour too
To do as you resolv'd to do:
But, Sir, 'twould wrong your valour much,
To say it needs or fears a crutch.
Great conqu'rors greater glory gain
By foes in triumph led, than slain:
The laurels that adorn their brows
Are pull'd from living, not dead boughs,
And living foes: the greatest fame
Of cripple slain can be but lame;
One half of him 's already slain,
The other is not worth your pain;
Th' honour can but on one side light,
As worship did, when y' were dubb'd Knight;
Wherefore I think it better far
To keep him prisoner of war,
And let him fast in bonds abide,
At court of justice to be try'd;
Where if h' appear so bold or crafty
There may be danger in his safety,
If any member there dislike
His face, or to his beard have pique,
Or if his death will save or yield,
Revenge or fright, it is reveal'd;

V. 1084. When the Rebels had taken a prisoner, though they gave him quarter, and promised to save his life, yet if any of them afterwards thought it not proper that he should

Though he has quarter, ne'ertheless
Y' have pow'r to hang him when you please
This has been often done by some
Of our great conqu'rors, you know whom;
And has by most of us been held
Wise justice, and to some reveal'd:
For words and promises, that yoke
The conqueror, are quickly broke;
Like Samson's cuffs, though by his own
Direction and advice put on.
For if we should fight for the Cause
By rules of military laws,
And only do what they call just,
The Cause would quickly fall to dust.
This we among ourselves may speak;
But to the wicked or the weak
We must be cautious to declare
Perfection-truths, such as these are.
This said, the high outrageous mettle
Of Knight began to cool and settle.
He lik'd the Squire's advice, and soon
Resolv'd to see the bus'ness done;
And therefore charg'd him first to bind

be saved, it was only saying it was revealed to him that such a one should die, and they hanged him up, notwithstanding the promises before made. Dr. South observes of Harrison the Regicide, a butcher by profession, and preaching Colonel in the Parliament army, "That he was notable for having killed several after quarter given by others, using these words in doing it: 'Cursed be he who doth the work of the Lord negligently.'"

Crowdero's hands on rump behind,
And to its former place and use
The wooden member to reduce;
But force it take an oath before,
Ne'er to bear arms against him more.
  Ralpho dispatch'd with speedy haste,
And, having ty'd Crowdero fast,
He gave Sir Knight the end of cord,
To lead the captive of his sword
In triumph, whilst the steeds he caught,
And them to further service brought.
The Squire in state rode on before,
And on his nut-brown whinyard bore
The trophy Fiddle and the case,
Leaning on shoulder like a mace.
The Knight himself did after ride,
Leading Crowdero by his side;
And tow'd him if he lagg'd behind,
Like boat against the tide and wind.
Thus grave and solemn they march on,
Until quite through the town they 'ad gone,
At further end of which there stands
An ancient castle, that commands
Th' adjacent parts; in all the fabric
You shall not see one stone nor a brick,

V. 1122. Var. 'Plac'd on his shoulder.'

V. 1130. This is an enigmatical description of a pair of stocks and a whipping-post; it is so pompous and sublime, that we are surprised so noble a structure could be raised from so ludicrous a subject.

But all of wood, by pow'rful spell
Of magic made impregnable:
There's neither iron-bar nor gate,
Portcullis, chain, nor bolt, nor grate,
And yet men durance there abide,
In dungeon scarce three inches wide:
With roof so low, that under it
They never stand, but lie or sit;
And yet so foul, that whoso is in
Is to the middle-leg in prison;
In circle magical confin'd
With walls of subtle air and wind,
Which none are able to break thorough
Until they're freed by head of borough.
Thither arriv'd, th' advent'rous Knight
And bold Squire from their steeds alight
At th' outward wall, near which there stands
A Bastile, built t' imprison hands;
By strange enchantment made to fetter
The lesser parts, and free the greater.
For though the body may creep through,
The hands in grate are fast enough;
And when a circle 'bout the wrist
Is made by beadle exorcist,
The body feels the spur and switch,
As if 'twere ridden post by witch
At twenty miles an hour pace,
And yet ne'er stirs out of the place.
On top of this there is a spire,
On which Sir Knight first bids the Squire

The Fiddle, and its spoils, the case,
In manner of a trophy place;
That done, they ope the trap-door gate,
And let Crowdero down thereat.
Crowdero making doleful face,
Like hermit poor in pensive place,
To dungeon they the wretch commit,
And the survivor of his feet;
But th' other that had broke the peace,
And head of Knighthood, they release,
Though a delinquent false and forged,
Yet b'ing a stranger he's enlarged,
While his comrade, that did no hurt,
Is clapp'd up fast in prison for't:
So justice, while she winks at crimes,
Stumbles on innocence sometimes.

PART I. CANTO III.

THE ARGUMENT.

The scatter'd rout return and rally,
Surround the place: the Knight does sally,
And is made pris'ner: then they seize
Th' enchanted fort by storm, release
Crowdero, and put the Squire in 's place;
I should have first said Hudibras.

Ay me! what perils do environ
The man that meddles with cold iron!
What plaguy mischiefs and mishaps
Do dog him still with after-claps!
For though Dame Fortune seem to smile,
And leer upon him for a while,
She'll after shew him, in the nick
Of all his glories, a dog-trick.
This any man may sing or say
I' th' ditty call'd, What if a Day?
For Hudibras, who thought he 'ad won
The field, as certain as a gun,
And having routed the whole troop,
With victory was cock-a-hoop,
Thinking he 'ad done enough to purchase
Thanksgiving-day among the Churches,
Wherein his mettle and brave worth
Might be explain'd by holder-forth

And register'd by fame eternal
In deathless pages of Diurnal,
Found in few minutes, to his cost,
He did but count without his host,
And that a turnstile is more certain
Than, in events of war, Dame Fortune.
  For now the late faint-hearted rout,
O'erthrown and scatter'd round about,
Chas'd by the horror of their fear
From bloody fray of Knight and Bear
(All but the Dogs, who in pursuit
Of the Knight's victory stood to 't,
And most ignobly fought to get
The honour of his blood and sweat),
Seeing the coast was free and clear
O' the conquer'd and the conqueror,
Took heart again, and fac'd about
As if they meant to stand it out:
For by this time the routed Bear,
Attack'd by th' enemy i' th' rear,
Finding their number grew too great
For him to make a safe retreat,
Like a bold chieftain fac'd about;
But wisely doubting to hold out,
Gave way to fortune, and with haste
Fac'd the proud foe, and fled, and fac'd,
Retiring still, until he found

V. 35. Var. 'Took heart of grace.'
V. 37. Var. 'For now the half-defeated Bear.'

He 'ad got the advantage of the ground,
And then as val'antly made head
To check the foe, and forthwith fled,
Leaving no art untry'd, nor trick
Of warrior stout and politic,
Until, in spite of hot pursuit,
He gain'd a pass, to hold dispute
On better terms, and stop the course
Of the proud foe. With all his force
He bravely charg'd, and for a while
Forc'd their whole body to recoil;
But still their numbers so increas'd,
He found himself at length oppress'd,
And all evasions so uncertain,
To save himself for better fortune,
That he resolv'd, rather than yield,
To die with honour in the field,
And sell his hide and carcase at
A price as high and desperate
As e'er he could. This resolution
He forthwith put in execution,
And bravely threw himself among
The enemy, i' th' greatest throng:
But what could single valour do
Against so numerous a foe?
Yet much he did, indeed too much
To be believ'd, where th' odds were such;
But one against a multitude,
Is more than mortal can make good:
For while one party he oppos'd,

His rear was suddenly inclos'd,
And no room left him for retreat
Or fight against a foe so great.
For now the Mastives, charging home,
To blows and handy-gripes were come;
While manfully himself he bore,
And setting his right foot before,
He rais'd himself, to shew how tall
His person was above them all.
This equal shame and envy stirr'd
In th' enemy, that one should beard
So many warriors, and so stout,
As he had done, and stav'd it out,
Disdaining to lay down his arms,
And yield on honourable terms.
Enraged thus, some in the rear
Attack'd him, and some ev'ry where,
Till down he fell; yet falling fought,
And, being down, still laid about:
As Widdrington, in doleful dumps,
Is said to fight upon his stumps.
 But all, alas! had been in vain,
And he inevitably slain,
If Trulla and Cerdon in the nick
To rescue him had not been quick:
For Trulla, who was light of foot
As shafts which long-field Parthians shoot

V. 102. 'As shafts which long-field Parthians shoot.' Mr. Warburton is of opinion that 'long-filed' would be more proper; as the Parthians were ranged in long files, a disposition

(But not so light as to be borne
Upon the ears of standing corn,
Or trip it o'er the water quicker
Than witches when their staves they liquor,
As some report), was got among
The foremost of the martial throng.
There pitying the vanquish'd Bear,
She call'd to Cerdon, who stood near,
Viewing the bloody fight; to whom,
Shall we (quoth she) stand still hum-drum,
And see stout Bruin, all alone,
By numbers basely overthrown?
Such feats already he 'as achiev'd
In story not to be believ'd,
And 'twould to us be shame enough
Not to attempt to fetch him off.
I would (quoth he) venture a limb
To second thee, and rescue him;
But then we must about it straight,
Or else our aid will come too late:
Quarter he scorns, he is so stout,
And therefore cannot long hold out.
This said, they wav'd their weapons round
About their heads to clear the ground,

proper for their manner of fighting, which was by sudden retreats and sudden charges. Mr. Smith of Harleston, in Norfolk, thinks that the following alteration of the line would be an improvement:

'As long-field shafts, which Parthians shoot.'

'Long-field Parthians' is right, i. e. Parthians who shoot from a distance. Ed.

And joining forces, laid about
So fiercely, that th' amaz'd rout
Turn'd tail again, and straight begun,
As if the devil drove, to run.
Meanwhile th' approach'd the place where Bruin
Was now engag'd to mortal ruin:
The conqu'ring foe they soon assail'd,
First Trulla stav'd, and Cerdon tail'd,
Until their Mastives loos'd their hold;
And yet, alas! do what they could,
The worsted Bear came off with store
Of bloody wounds, but all before.
For as Achilles, dipt in pond,
Was anabaptiz'd free from wound,
Made proof against dead-doing steel
All over, but the Pagan heel;
So did our champion's arms defend
All of him but the other end,
His head and ears, which in the martial
Encounter lost a leathern parcel.
For as an Austrian archduke once
Had one ear (which in ducatoons
Is half the coin) in battle par'd
Close to his head, so Bruin far'd;
But tugg'd and pull'd on th' other side
Like scriv'ner newly crucify'd,
Or like the late corrected leathern
Ears of the circumcised brethren.
But gentle Trulla into th' ring
He wore in 's nose convey'd a string,

With which she march'd before, and led
The warrior to a grassy bed,
As authors write, in a cool shade
Which eglantine and roses made,
Close by a softly murm'ring stream,
Where lovers us'd to loll and dream:
There leaving him to his repose,
Secured from pursuit of foes,
And wanting nothing but a song
And a well-tun'd theorbo hung
Upon a bough, to ease the pain
His tugg'd ears suffer'd, with a strain,
They both drew up, to march in quest
Of his great leader and the rest.
  For Orsin (who was more renown'd
For stout maintaining of his ground,
In standing fight, than for pursuit,
As being not so quick of foot)
Was not long able to keep pace
With others that pursu'd the chace,
But found himself left far behind,
Both out of heart and out of wind.
Griev'd to behold his Bear pursued
So basely by a multitude,
And like to fall, not by the prowess,
But numbers, of his coward foes,
He rag'd, and kept as heavy a coil as
Stout Hercules for loss of Hylas,
Forcing the valleys to repeat
The accents of his sad regret:

He beat his breast and tore his hair,
For loss of his dear crony Bear,
That Echo, from the hollow ground,
His doleful wailings did resound
More wistfully, by many times,
That in small poets' splayfoot rhymes,
That make her, in their ruthful stories,
To answer to int'rrogatories,
And most unconscionably depose
To things of which she nothing knows;
And when she has said all she can say,
'Tis wrested to the lover's fancy.
Quoth he, O whither, wicked Bruin!
Art thou fled to my—: Echo, Ruin.
I thought th' hadst scorn'd to budge a step
For fear: quoth Echo, Marry guep.
Am not I here to take thy part?
Then what has quail'd thy stubborn heart?
Have these bones rattled, and this head
So often in thy quarrel bled?
Nor did I ever winch or grudge it
For thy dear sake: Quoth she, Mum budget.
Think'st thou 'twill not be laid i' th' dish
Thou turn'dst thy back? Quoth Echo, Pish.
To run from those th' hadst overcome

V. 189, 190. This passage is beautiful, not only as it is a moving lamentation, and evidences our Poet to be master of the pathetic as well as the sublime style, but also as it comprehends a fine satire upon that false kind of wit of making an echo talk sensibly, and give rational answers.

Thus cowardly? Quoth, Echo, Mum.
But what a vengeance makes thee fly
From me too, as thine enemy?
Or, if thou hast no thought of me,
Nor what I have endured for thee,
Yet shame and honour might prevail
To keep thee thus from turning tail:
For who would grutch to spend his blood in
His honour's cause? Quoth she, A puddin.
This said, his grief to anger turn'd,
Which in his manly stomach burn'd;
Thirst of revenge, and wrath, in place
Of sorrow, now began to blaze:
He vow'd the authors of his woe
Should equal vengeance undergo,
And with their bones and flesh pay dear
For what he suffer'd, and his Bear.
This being resolv'd, with equal speed
And rage he hasted to proceed
To action straight, and, giving o'er
To search for Bruin any more,
He went in quest of Hudibras,
To find him out where'er he was;
And, if he were above ground, vow'd
He'd ferret him, lurk where he would.
But scarce had he a furlong on
This resolute adventure gone,
When he encounter'd with that crew
Whom Hudibras did late subdue.
Honour, revenge, contempt, and shame,

Did equally their breasts inflame.
'Mong these the fierce Magnano was,
And Talgol, foe to Hudibras,
Cerdon and Colon, warriors stout
And resolute, as ever fought;
Whom furious Orsin thus bespoke:
  Shall we (quoth he) thus basely brook
The vile affront that paltry ass,
And feeble scoundrel, Hudibras,
With that more paltry ragamuffin,
Ralpho, with vapouring and huffing,
Have put upon us, like tame cattle,
As if th' had routed us in battle?
For my part, it shall ne'er be said
I for the washing gave my head:
Nor did I turn my back for fear
O' th' rascals, but loss of my Bear,
Which now I'm like to undergo;
For whether these fell wounds, or no,
He has receiv'd in fight, are mortal,
Is more than all my skill can foretell;
Nor do I know what is become
Of him, more than the Pope of Rome.
But if I can but find them out
That caus'd it (as I shall, no doubt,
Where'er th' in hugger-mugger lurk)
I'll make them rue their handiwork,
And wish that they had rather dar'd

V. 258. Var. 'Of them, but losing of my Bear.'

To pull the devil by the beard.
  Quoth Cerdon, Noble Orsin, th' hast
Great reason to do as thou say'st,
And so has ev'ry body here,
As well as thou hast, or thy Bear:
Others may do as they see good;
But if this twig be made of wood
That will hold tack, I'll make the fur
Fly 'bout the ears of that old cur,
And th' other mungrel vermin, Ralph,
That brav'd us all in his behalf.
Thy Bear is safe and out of peril,
Though lugg'd indeed and wounded very ill;
Myself and Trulla made a shift
To help him out at a dead lift,
And having brought him bravely off,
Have left him where he's safe enough
There let him rest; for if we stay,
The slaves may hap to get away.
  This said, they all engag'd to join
Their forces in the same design,
And forthwith put themselves in search
Of Hudibras upon their march:
Where leave we them awhile, to tel
What the victorious Knight befell;
For such, Crowdero being fast
In dungeon shut, we left him last.
Triumphant laurels seem'd to grow
No-where so green as on his brow,
Laden with which, as well as tir'd

With conqu'ring toil, he now retir'd
Unto a neighb'ring castle by,
To rest his body, and apply
Fit med'cines to each glorious bruise
He got in fight, reds, blacks, and blues;
To mollify th' uneasy pang
Of ev'ry honourable bang;
Which b'ing by skilful midwife drest,
He laid him down to take his rest.
  But all in vain: h' had got a hurt,
O' th' inside, of a deadlier sort,
By Cupid made, who took his stand
Upon a widow's jointure-land
(For he, in all his am'rous battles,
No 'dvantage finds like goods and chattels),
Drew home his bow, and, aiming right,
Let fly an arrow at the Knight.
The shaft against a rib did glance,
And gall him in the purtenance;
But time had somewhat 'swag'd his pain,
After he found his suit in vain;
For that proud dame, for whom his soul
Was burnt in 's belly like a coal,
(That belly that so oft did ake
And suffer griping for her sake,
Till purging comfits and ants' eggs
Had almost brought him off his legs),

V. 315, 316. Var. 'As how he did, and aiming right,
An arrow he let fly at Knight.'

Us'd him so like a base rascallion
That old Pyg—(what d' ye call him)—malion,
That cut his mistress out of stone,
Had not so hard a hearted one.
She had a thousand jadish tricks,
Worse than a mule that flings and kicks;
'Mong which one cross-grain'd freak she had,
As insolent as strange and mad:
She could love none but only such
As scorn'd and hated her as much.
'Twas a strange riddle of a lady;
Not love, if any lov'd her: hey-day!
So cowards never use their might
But against such as will not fight;
So some diseases have been found
Only to seize upon the sound.
He that gets her by heart must say her
The back way, like a witch's prayer.
Meanwhile the Knight had no small task
To compass what he durst not ask:
He loves, but dares not make the motion;
Her ignorance is his devotion:
Like caitiff vile, that for misdeed
Rides with his face to rump of steed,
Or rowing scull, he's fain to love;
Look one way, and another move:
Or like a tumbler that does play
His game, and look another way

V. 338. Var. 'Ha-day!'

Until he seize upon the coney;
Just so does he by matrimony.
But all in vain; her subtle snout
Did quickly wind his meaning out,
Which she return'd with too much scorn
To be by man of honour borne:
Yet much he bore, until the distress
He suffer'd from his spightful mistress
Did stir his stomach, and the pain
He had endur'd from her disdain
Turn'd to regret so resolute
That he resolv'd to wave his suit,
And either to renounce her quite
Or for a while play least in sight.
This resolution b'ing put on,
He kept some months, and more had done,
But being brought so nigh by Fate,
The vict'ry he achiev'd so late
Did set his thoughts agog, and ope
A door to discontinu'd hope,
That seem'd to promise he might win
His dame too, now his hand was in;
And that his valour, and the honour
H' had newly gain'd, might work upon her.
These reasons made his mouth to water
With am'rous longings to be at her:
Quoth he, unto himself, Who knows
But this brave conquest o'er my foes
May reach her heart, and make that stoop,
As I but now have forc'd the troop?

If nothing can oppugn love,
And virtue invious ways can prove,
What may not he confide to do
That brings both love and virtue too?
But thou bring'st valour too, and wit,
Two things that seldom fail to hit.
Valour's a mouse-trap, wit a gin,
Which women oft are taken in:
Then, Hudibras, why should'st thou fear
To be, that art, a conqueror?
Fortune th' audacious doth *juvare*,
But lets the timidous miscarry:
Then, while the honour thou hast got
Is spick and span new, piping-hot,
Strike her up bravely thou hadst best,
And trust thy fortune with the rest.
Such thoughts as these the Knight did keep,
More than his bangs, or fleas, from sleep:
And as an owl, that in a barn
Sees a mouse creeping in the corn,
Sits still, and shuts his round blue eyes
As if he slept, until he spies
The little beast within his reach,
Then starts, and seizes on the wretch;
So from his couch the Knight did start,
To seize upon the widow's heart,
Crying, with hasty tone and hoarse,
Ralpho, dispatch, to horse, to horse.
And 'twas but time; for now the rout,
We left engag'd to seek him out,

By speedy marches were advanc'd
Up to the fort where he ensconc'd,
And all th' avenues had possest
About the place, from east to west.
  That done, awhile they made a halt
To view the ground, and where t' assault:
Then call'd a council, which was best,
By siege or onslaught, to invest
The enemy; and 'twas agreed
By storm and onslaught to proceed.
This b'ing resolv'd, in comely sort
They now drew up t'attack the fort;
When Hudibras, about to enter
Upon another-gates adventure,
To Ralpho call'd aloud to arm,
Not dreaming of approaching storm.
Whether Dame Fortune, or the care
Of angel bad, or tutelar,
Did arm, or thrust him on a danger
To which he was an utter stranger,
That foresight might, or might not, blot
The glory he had newly got,
Or to his shame it might be sed,
They took him napping in his bed;
To them we leave it to expound
That deal in sciences profound.
  His courser scarce he had bestrid,
And Ralpho that on which he rid,

V. 437. Var. 'Might be said.'

When, setting ope the postern gate,
Which they thought best to sally at,
The foe appear'd drawn up and drill'd,
Ready to charge them in the field.
This somewhat startled the bold Knight,
Surpris'd with th' unexpected sight:
The bruises of his bones and flesh
He thought began to smart afresh;
Till, recollecting wonted courage,
His fear was soon converted to rage;
And thus he spoke: The coward foe,
Whom we but now gave quarter to,
Look, yonder's rally'd, and appears
As if they had outrun their fears.
The glory we did lately get,
The Fates command us to repeat;
And to their wills we must succumb,
Quocunque trahunt, 'tis our doom.
This is the same numeric crew
Which we so lately did subdue;
The self-same individuals that
Did run, as mice do from a cat,
When we courageously did wield
Our martial weapons in the field,
To tug for victory: and when
We shall our shining blades agen
Brandish in terror o'er our heads,
They'll straight resume their wonted dreads.

V. 444. Var. 'To take the field, and sally at.'

Fear is an ague, that forsakes
And haunts, by fits, those whom it takes;
And they'll opine they feel the pain
And blows they felt, to-day again.
Then let us boldly charge them home,
And make no doubt to overcome.
  This said, his courage to inflame,
He call'd upon his mistress' name;
His pistol next he cock'd anew,
And out his nut-brown whinyard drew,
And, placing Ralpho in the front,
Reserv'd himself to bear the brunt,
As expert warriors use: then ply'd
With iron heel his courser's side,
Conveying sympathetic speed
From heel of Knight to heel of steed.
  Meanwhile the foe, with equal rage
And speed, advancing to engage,
Both parties now were drawn so close,
Almost to come to handy-blows:
When Orsin first let fly a stone
At Ralpho; not so huge a one
As that which Diomed did maul
Æneas on the bum withal,
Yet big enough, if rightly hurl'd,
T' have sent him to another world,
Whether above ground or below,
Which saints twice dipt are destin'd to.

V. 472. Var. 'Haunts by turns.'

The danger startled the bold Squire,
And made him some few steps retire;
But Hudibras advanc'd to 's aid,
And rous'd his spirits half-dismay'd.
He, wisely doubting lest the shot
Of th' enemy, now growing hot,
Might at a distance gall, press'd close
To come pell-mell to handy-blows,
And that he might their aim decline
Advanc'd still in an oblique line;
But prudently forbore to fire,
Till breast to breast he had got nigher,
As expert warriors use to do
When hand to hand they charge their foe.
This order the advent'rous Knight,
Most soldier-like, observ'd in fight;
When Fortune (as she's wont) turn'd fickle,
And for the foe began to stickle:
The more shame for her Goodyship,
To give so near a friend the slip.
For Colon, choosing out a stone,
Levell'd so right, it thump'd upon
His manly paunch with such a force
As almost beat him off his horse.
He loos'd his whinyard and the rein,
But, laying fast hold on the mane,
Preserv'd his seat: and as a goose

V. 523. Var. 'He loos'd his weapon'—and, 'He lost his whinyard.'

In death contracts his talons close,
So did the Knight, and with one claw
The tricker of his pistol draw.
The gun went off; and as it was
Still fatal to stout Hudibras,
In all his feats of arms, when least
He dreamt of it, to prosper best,
So now he far'd; the shot, let fly
At random 'mong the enemy,
Pierc'd Talgol's gabardine, and grazing
Upon his shoulder, in the passing
Lodg'd in Magnano's brass habergeon,
Who straight A surgeon, cry'd, A surgeon:
He tumbled down, and, as he fell,
Did Murder, Murder, Murder, yell.
This startled their whole body so,
That if the Knight had not let go
His arms, but been in warlike plight,
He'd won (the second time) the fight;
As, if the Squire had but fall'n on,
He had inevitably done.
But he, diverted with the care
Of Hudibras his hurt, forbare
To press th' advantage of his fortune,
While danger did the rest dishearten.
For he with Cerdon b'ing engag'd

V. 545-548. Var. 'As Ralpho might, but he with care
Of Hudibras his hurt forbare.'
V. 548. Var. 'Hudibras his wound.'
V. 551. Var. 'He had with Cerdon.'

In close encounter, they both wag'd
The fight so well 'twas hard to say
Which side was like to get the day.
And now the busy work of Death
Had tir'd them so, th' agreed to breathe,
Preparing to renew the fight,
When the disaster of the Knight,
And th' other party, did divert
Their fell intent, and forc'd them part.
Ralpho press'd up to Hudibras,
And Cerdon where Magnano was,
Each striving to confirm his party
With stout encouragements and hearty.
  Quoth Ralpho, Courage, valiant Sir,
And let revenge and honour stir
Your spirits up; once more fall on,
The shatter'd foe begins to run:
For if but half so well you knew
To use your vict'ry as subdue,
They durst not, after such a blow
As you have given them, face us now,
But from so formidable a soldier
Had fled like crows when they smell powder.
Thrice have they seen your sword aloft
Wav'd o'er their heads, and fled as oft;
But if you let them recollect
Their spirits, now dismay'd and checkt,

V. 553. Var. 'So desperately.'
V. 560. Var. 'And force their sullen rage to part.'

You'll have a harder game to play
Than yet y' have had, to get the day.
Thus spoke the stout Squire, but was heard
By Hudibras with small regard;
His thoughts were fuller of the bang
He lately took, than Ralph's harangue:
To which he answer'd, Cruel Fate
Tells me thy counsel comes too late.
The knotted blood within my hose,
That from my wounded body flows,
With mortal crisis doth portend
My days to appropinque an end.
I am for action now unfit
Either of fortitude or wit,
Fortune, my foe, begins to frown,
Rosolv'd to pull my stomach down.
I am not apt upon a wound,
Or trivial basting, to despond,
Yet I'd be loth my days to curtal;
For if I thought my wounds not mortal,
Or that w' had time enough as yet
To make an honourable retreat,
'Twere the best course: but if they find
We fly, and leave our arms behind,
For them to seize on, the dishonour
And danger too is such, I'll sooner
Stand to it boldly and take quarter,
To let them see I am no starter.

V. 587. Var. 'The clotted blood.'

In all the trade of war no feat
Is nobler than a brave retreat:
For those that run away and fly
Take place at least o' th' enemy.
  This said, the Squire, with active speed,
Dismounted from his bony steed,
To seize the arms which, by mischance,
Fell from the bold Knight in a trance:
These being found out, and restor'd
To Hudibras, their nat'ral lord,
As a man may say, with might and main
He hasted to get up again.
Thrice he essay'd to mount aloft,
But by his weighty bum as oft
He was pull'd back, till, having found
Th' advantage of the rising ground,
Thither he led his warlike steed,
And, having plac'd him right, with speed
Prepar'd again to scale the beast;
When Orsin, who had newly drest
The bloody scar upon the shoulder
Of Talgol with Promethean powder,
And now was searching for the shot
That laid Magnano on the spot,
Beheld the sturdy Squire aforesaid,
Preparing to climb up his horse-side:
He left his cure, and, laying hold

V. 617. Var. 'The active Squire, with might and main,
Prepar'd in haste to mount again.'

Upon his arms, with courage bold
Cry'd out, 'Tis now no time to dally,
The enemy begin to rally;
Let us that are unhurt and whole
Fall on, and happy man be 's dole.
  This said, like to a thunderbolt
He flew with fury to th' assault,
Striving th' enemy to attack
Before he reach'd his horse's back.
Ralpho was mounted now, and gotten
O'erthwart his beast with active vau'ting,
Wriggling his body to recover
His seat, and cast his right leg over:
When Orsin, rushing in, bestow'd
On horse and man so heavy a load,
The beast was startled, and begun
To kick and fling like mad, and run,
Bearing the tough Squire like a sack,
Or stout King Richard, on his back;
Till stumbling, he threw him down,
Sore bruis'd and cast into a swoon.
Meanwhile the Knight began to rouse
The sparkles of his wonted prowess:
He thrust his hand into his hose,
And found, both by his eyes and nose,
'Twas only choler, and not blood,
That from his wounded body flow'd.
This, with the hazard of the Squire,
Inflam'd him with despiteful ire:
Courageously he fac'd about,

And drew his other pistol out,
And now had half-way bent the cock;
When Cerdon gave so fierce a shock
With sturdy truncheon, thwart his arm,
That down it fell and did no harm;
Then, stoutly pressing on with speed,
Assay'd to pull him off his steed.
The Knight his sword had only left,
With which he Cerdon's head had cleft,
Or at the least cropp'd off a limb,
But Orsin came, and rescu'd him.
He with his lance attack'd the Knight
Upon his quarters opposite:
But as a barque, that in foul weather,
Toss'd by two adverse winds together,
Is bruis'd and beaten to and fro,
And knows not which to turn him to;
So far'd the Knight between two foes,
And knew not which of them t' oppose:
Till Orsin, charging with his lance
At Hudibras, by spiteful chance
Hit Cerdon such a bang, as stunn'd
And laid him flat upon the ground.
At this the Knight began to cheer up,
And, raising up himself on stirrup,
Cry'd out, *Victoria*, lie thou there,
And I shall straight dispatch another
To bear thee company in death;
But first I'll halt awhile, and breathe:
As well he might; for Orsin, griev'd

At th' wound that Cerdon had receiv'd,
Ran to relieve him with his lore,
And cure the hurt he gave before.
Meanwhile the Knight had wheel'd about
To breathe himself, and next find out
Th' advantage of the ground, where best
He might the ruffled foe infest.
This b'ing resolv'd, he spurr'd his steed,
To run at Orsin with full speed,
While he was busy in the care
Of Cerdon's wound, and unaware:
But he was quick, and had already
Unto the part apply'd remedy;
And seeing th' enemy prepar'd,
Drew up and stood upon his guard.
Then like a warrior right expert
And skilful in the martial art,
The subtle Knight straight made a halt,
And judg'd it best to stay th' assault,
Until he had reliev'd the Squire,
And then (in order) to retire,
Or, as occasion should invite,
With forces join'd renew the fight.
Ralpho, by this time disentranc'd,
Upon his bum himself advanc'd,
Though sorely bruis'd; his limbs all o'er
With ruthless bangs were stiff and sore:
Right fain he would have got upon
His feet again, to get him gone,
When Hudibras to aid him came:

Quoth he (and call'd him by his name),
Courage, the day at length is ours,
And we once more, as conquerors,
Have both the field and honour won;
The foe is profligate and run:
I mean all such as can, for some
This hand hath sent to their long home;
And some lie sprawling on the ground,
With many a gash and bloody wound.
Cæsar himself could never say
He got two vict'ries in a day
As I have done, that can say, twice I
In one day *veni, vidi, vici.*
The foe's so numerous, that we
Cannot so often *vincere*,
And they *perire*, and yet enow
Be left to strike an after-blow:
Then lest they rally, and once more
Put us to fight the bus'ness o'er,
Get up and mount thy steed; dispatch,
And let us both their motions watch.
Quoth Ralph, I should not, if I were
In case for action, now be here;
Nor have I turn'd my back, or hang'd
An arse, for fear of being bang'd.
It was for you I got these harms,
Advent'ring to fetch off your arms.
The blows and drubs I have receiv'd
Have bruis'd my body, and bereav'd
My limbs of strength: unless you stoop

And reach your hands to pull me up,
I shall lie here, and be a prey
To those who now are run away.
  That thou shalt not (quoth Hudibras):
We read the ancients held it was
More honourable far *servare*
Civem than slay an adversary:
The one we oft to-day have done,
The other shall dispatch anon;
And, though thou'rt of a diff'rent church,
I will not leave thee in the lurch.
This said, he jogg'd his good steed nigher,
And steer'd him gently t'wards the Squire,
Then, bowing down his body, stretch'd
His hand out, and at Ralpho reach'd;
When Trulla, whom he did not mind,
Charg'd him like lightening behind.
She had been long in search about
Magnano's wound, to find it out,
But could find none, nor where the shot
That had so startled him was got;
But, having found the worst was past,
She fell to her own work at last,
The pillage of the prisoners,
Which in all feats of arms was hers:
And now to plunder Ralph she flew,
When Hudibras his hard fate drew
To succour him; for as he bow'd
To help him up, she laid a load
Of blows so heavy, and plac'd so well,

On th' other side, that down he fell.
Yield, scoundrel base (quoth she), or die;
Thy life is mine, and liberty:
But if thou think'st I took thee tardy,
And dar'st presume to be so hardy
To try thy fortune o'er afresh,
I'll wave my title to thy flesh,
Thy arms and baggage, now my right,
And, if thou hast the heart to try 't,
I'll lend thee back thyself awhile,
And once more, for that carcase vile,
Fight upon tick. — Quoth Hudibras,
Thou off'rest nobly, valiant lass,
And I shall take thee at thy word:
First let me rise and take my sword.
That sword which has so oft this day
Through squadrons of my foes made way,
And some to other worlds dispatcht,
Now, with a feeble spinster matcht,
Will blush, with blood ignoble stain'd,
By which no honour's to be gain'd.
But if thou'lt take m' advice in this,
Consider, whilst thou may'st, what 'tis
To interrupt a victor's course
B' opposing such a trivial force:
For if with conquest I come off
(And that I shall do sure enough),
Quarter thou canst not have nor grace,
By law of arms, in such a case;
Both which I now do offer freely.

I scorn (quoth she), thou coxcomb silly
(Clapping her hand upon her breech,
To show how much she priz'd his speech),
Quarter or counsel from a foe;
If thou canst force me to it, do:
But lest it should again be said,
When I have once more won thy head,
I took thee napping, unprepar'd,
Arm, and betake thee to thy guard.
  This said, she to her tackle fell,
And on the Knight let fall a peal
Of blows so fierce, and press'd so home,
That he retir'd, and follow'd 's bum.
Stand to't, quoth she, or yield to mercy;
It is not fighting *arsie-versie*
Shall serve thy turn. — This stirr'd his spleen
More than the danger he was in,
The blows he felt or was to feel,
Although th' already made him reel.
Honour, despite, revenge, and shame,
At once into his stomach came;
Which fir'd it so, he rais'd his arm
Above his head and rain'd a storm
Of blows so terrible and thick,
As if he meant to hash her quick.
But she upon her truncheon took them,
And by oblique diversion broke them,
Waiting an opportunity
To pay all back with usury,
Which long she fail'd not of; for now

The Knight with one dead-doing blow
Resolving to decide the fight,
And she with quick and cunning sleight
Avoiding it, the force and weight
He charg'd upon it was so great
As almost sway'd him to the ground.
No sooner she th' advantage found,
But in she flew; and, seconding
With home-made thrust the heavy swing,
She laid him flat upon his side,
And, mounting on his trunk astride,
Quoth she, I told thee what would come
Of all thy vapouring, base scum:
Say, will the law of arms allow
I may have grace and quarter now?
Or wilt thou rather break thy word,
And stain thine honour than thy sword?
A man of war to damn his soul,
In basely breaking his parole!
And when before the fight th' hadst vow'd
To give no quarter in cold blood;
Now thou hast got me for a Tartar,
To make me 'gainst my will take quarter,
Why dost not put me to the sword,
But cowardly fly from thy word?

V. 857-866. Var.
'Shall I have quarter now, you ruffin?
Or wilt thou be worse than thy huffing?
Thou saidst th' would'st kill me, marry would'st thou?
Why dost thou not, thou Jack-a-nods thou?'

Quoth Hudibras, The day's thine own;
Thou and thy stars have cast me down:
My laurels are transplanted now,
And flourish on thy conqu'ring brow:
My loss of honour's great enough,
Thou need'st not brand it with a scoff:
Sarcasms may eclipse thine own,
But cannot blur my lost renown:
I am not now in Fortune's power;
He that is down can fall no lower.
The ancient heroes were illustr'ous
For being benign, and not blustrous
Against a vanquish'd foe: their swords
Were sharp and trenchant, not their words;
And did in fight but cut work out
T' employ their courtesies about.
Quoth she, Although thou hast deserv'd,
Base Slubberdegullion, to be serv'd
As thou didst vow to deal with me
If thou hadst got the victory,
Yet I shall rather act a part
That suits my fame than thy desert:
Thy arms, thy liberty, beside
All that's on th' outside of thy hide,
Are mine by military law,
Of which I will not bate one straw;
The rest, thy life and limbs, once more,
Though doubly forfeit, I restore.
Quoth Hudibras, It is too late
For me to treat or stipulate;

What thou command'st I must obey!
Yet those whom I expugn'd to-day,
Of thine own party, I let go,
And gave them life and freedom too,
Both Dogs and Bear, upon their parole,
Whom I took pris'ners in this quarrel.
Quoth Trulla, Whether thou or they
Let one another run away,
Concerns not me; but was 't not thou
That gave Crowdero quarter too?
Crowdero whom, in irons bound,
Thou basely threw'st into Lob's pound,
Where still he lies, and with regret
His gen'rous bowels rage and fret.
But now thy carcase shall redeem,
And serve to be exchang'd for him.
  This said, the Knight did straight submit,
And laid his weapons at her feet.
Next he disrob'd his gabardine,
And with it did himself resign.
She took it, and forthwith divesting
The mantle that she wore, said jesting,
Take that and wear it for my sake;
Then threw it o'er his sturdy back.
And as the French we conquer'd once
Now give us laws for pantaloons,
The length of breeches and the gathers,
Port-cannons, periwigs, and feathers;
Just so the proud insulting lass
Array'd and dighted Hudibras.

Meanwhile the other champions, yerst
In hurry of the fight disperst,
Arriv'd, when Trulla won the day,
To share i' th' honour and the prey,
And out of Hudibras his hide
With vengeance to be satisfy'd;
Which now they were about to pour
Upon him in a wooden show'r,
But Trulla thrust herself between,
And, striding o'er his back agen,
She brandish'd o'er her head his sword,
And vow'd they should not break her word:
She 'ad given him quarter, and her blood,
Or theirs, should make that quarter good;
For she was bound by law of arms
To see him safe from further harms.
In dungeon deep Crowdero, cast
By Hudibras, as yet lay fast,
Where, to the hard and ruthless stones,
His great heart made perpetual moans;
Him she resolv'd that Hudibras
Should ransom, and supply his place.
This stopp'd their fury, and the basting
Which towards Hudibras was hasting;
They thought it was but just and right
That what she had achiev'd in fight
She should dispose of how she pleas'd;
Crowdero ought to be releas'd,
Nor could that any way be done
So well as this she pitch'd upon:

For who a better could imagine?
This therefore they resolv'd t' engage in.
The Knight and Squire first they made
Rise from the ground where they were laid,
Then mounted both upon their horses,
But with their faces to the arses.
Orsin led Hudibras's beast,
And Talgol that which Ralpho prest;
Whom stout Magnano, valiant Cerdon,
And Colon, waited as a guard on;
All ush'ring Trulla in the rear,
With th' arms of either prisoner.
In this proud order and array
They put themselves upon their way,
Striving to reach th' enchanted Castle,
Where stout Crowdero' in durance lay still.
Thither with greater speed than shows
And triumph over conquer'd foes
Do use t' allow, or than the Bears,
Or pageants borne before lord-mayors,
Are wont to use, they soon arriv'd,
In order soldier-like contriv'd,
Still marching in a warlike posture,
As fit for battle as for muster.
The Knight and Squire they first unhorse,
And, bending 'gainst the fort their force,
They all advanc'd, and round about
Begirt the magical redoubt.
Magnan' led up in this adventure,
And made way for the rest to enter:

For he was skilful in Black Art
No less than he that built the fort,
And with an iron mace laid flat
A breach, which straight all enter'd at,
And in the wooden dungeon found
Crowdero laid upon the ground:
Him they release from durance base,
Restor'd t' his Fiddle and his case,
And liberty, his thirsty rage
With luscious vengeance to assuage:
For he no sooner was at large,
But Trulla straight brought on the charge,
And in the self-same limbo put
The Knight and Squire where he was shut;.
Where leaving them in Hockley-i'-th'-hole,
Their bangs and durance to condole,
Confin'd and conjur'd into narrow
Enchanted mansion to know sorrow,
In the same order and array
Which they advanc'd, they march'd away.
But Hudibras, who scorn'd to stoop
To Fortune, or be said to droop,
Cheer'd up himself with ends of verse
And sayings of philosophers.
  Quoth he, Th' one half of man, his mind,
Is, *sui juris*, unconfin'd,
And cannot be laid by the heels,
Whate'er the other moiety feels.

V. 1003. Var. 't' the wretched hole.'

'Tis not restraint or liberty
That makes men prisoners or free;
But perturbations that possess
The mind or equanimities.
The whole world was not half so wide
To Alexander, when he cry'd
Because he had but one to subdue,
As was a paltry narrow tub to
Diogenes; who is not said
(For aught that ever I could read)
To whine, put finger i' th' eye, and sob,
Because h' had ne'er another tub.
The Ancients make two sev'ral kinds
Of prowess in heroic minds,
The active and the passive val'ant,
Both which are *pari libra* gallant;
For both to give blows, and to carry,
In fights are equi-necessary:
But in defeats the passive stout
Are always found to stand it out
Most desp'rately, and to outdo
The active 'gainst a conqu'ring foe.
Though we with blacks and blues are suggil'd,
Or, as the vulgar say, are cudgel'd,
He that is valiant and dares fight,
Though drubb'd, can lose no honour by 't.
Honour's a lease for lives to come,
And cannot be extended from
The legal tenant: 'tis a chattel
Not to be forfeited in battle.

If he that in the field is slain
Be in the bed of honour lain,
He that is beaten may be said
To lie in Honour's truckle-bed.
For as we see th' eclipsed sun
By mortals is more gaz'd upon
Than when, adorn'd with all his light,
He shines in serene sky most bright;
So valour in a low estate
Is most admir'd and wonder'd at.
  Quoth Ralph, How great I do not know
We may by being beaten grow;
But none that see how here we sit
Will judge us overgrown with wit.
As Gifted Brethren, preaching by
A carnal hour-glass, do imply
Illumination can convey
Into them what they have to say,
But not how much; so well enough
Know you to charge, but not draw off:

V. 1061, 1062. In those days there was always an hour-glass stood by the pulpit, in a frame of iron made on purpose for it, and fastened to the board on which the cushion lay, that it might be visible to the whole congregation; who, if the sermon did not hold till the glass was out (which was turned up as soon as the text was taken), would say that the preacher was lazy; and, if he held out much longer, would yawn and stretch, and by those signs signify to the preacher that they began to be weary of his discourse, and wanted to be dismissed. These hour-glasses remained in some churches till within these forty years. If they liked his discourse, they would sometimes ask him for 'another glass.' Ed.

For who, without a cap and bawble,
Having subdued a Bear and rabble,
And might with honour have come off,
Would put it to a second proof?
A politic exploit, right fit
For Presbyterian zeal and wit.
  Quoth Hudibras, That cuckoo's tone,
Ralpho, thou always harp'st upon:
When thou at any thing would'st rail,
Thou mak'st Presbytery thy scale
To take the height on't, and explain
To what degree it is profane.
Whats'ever will not with (thy what-d'-ye-call)
Thy Light jump right, thou call'st Synodical;
As if Presbyt'ry were a standard
To size whats'ever's to be slander'd.
Dost not remember how this day
Thou to my beard wast bold to say
That thou could'st prove Bear-baiting, equal
With Synods, orthodox and legal?
Do, if thou can'st; for I deny't,
And dare thee to't with all thy light.
  Quoth Ralpho, Truly that is no
Hard matter for a man to do

V. 1072. Ralpho looked upon their ill plight to be owing to his master's bad conduct; and, to vent his resentment, he satirises him in the most affecting part of his character, his religion. This by degrees brings on the old arguments about Synods. The Poet, who thought he had not sufficiently lashed classical assemblies, very judiciously completes it, now there is full leisure for it.

That has but any guts in's brains,
And could believe it worth his pains:
But since you dare and urge me to it,
You'll find I've light enough to do it.
Synods are mystical Bear-gardens,
Where Elders, Deputies, Church-wardens,
And other Members of the Court,
Manage the Babylonish sport;
For Prolocutor, Scribe, and Bear-ward,
Do differ only in a mere word.
Both are but sev'ral synagogues
Of carnal men, and Bears and Dogs:
Both antichristian assemblies,
To mischief bent as far 's in them lies:
Both stave and tail, with fierce contests,
The one with men, the other beasts.
The diff'rence is, the one fights with
The tongue, the other with the teeth;
And that they bait but Bears in this,
In th' other Souls and Consciences:
Where Saints themselves are brought to stake
For Gospel-light and Conscience' sake;
Expos'd to Scribes and Presbyters,
Instead of Mastive Dogs and Curs;
Than whom they've less humanity,
For these at souls of men will fly.
This to the prophet did appear,
Who in a vision saw a Bear,
Prefiguring the beastly rage
Of Church-rule in this latter age;

As is demonstrated at full
By him that baited the Pope's Bull.
Bears nat'rally are beasts of prey,
That live by rapine ; so do they.
What are their Orders, Constitutions,
Church-censures, Curses, Absolutions,
But sev'ral mystic chains they make,
To tie poor Christians to the stake?
And then set Heathen officers,
Instead of Dogs, about their ears.
For to prohibit and dispense,
To find out, or to make offence;
Of hell and heaven to dispose,
To play with souls at fast and loose;
To set what characters they please,
And mulcts on sin or godliness;
Reduce the Church to Gospel-order,
By rapine, sacrilege, and murder;
To make Presbytery supreme,
And Kings themselves submit to them;
And force all people, though against
Their consciences, to turn Saints;
Must prove a pretty thriving trade,
When Saints monopolists are made:
When pious frauds and holy shifts
Are Dispensations and Gifts,
There godliness becomes mere ware,
And ev'ry Synod but a fair.
Synods are whelps o' th' Inquisition,
A mongrel breed of like pernicion,

And, growing up, became the sires
Of Scribes, Commissioners, and Triers:
Whose bus'ness is, by cunning sleight
To cast a figure for men's light;
To find, in lines of beard and face,
The physiognomy of Grace;
And by the sound and twang of nose,
If all be sound within disclose,
Free from a crack or flaw of sinning,
As men try pipkins by the ringing;
By black caps underlaid with white
Give certain guess at inward light,
Which Sergeants at the Gospel wear,
To make the Sp'ritual Calling clear.
The handkerchief about the neck

V. 1156. These Triers pretended to great skill in this respect; and, if they disliked the beard or face of a man, they would, for that reason alone, refuse to admit him, when presented to a living, unless he had some powerful friend to support him. "The questions that these men put to the persons to be examined were not abilities and learning, but grace in their hearts, and that with so bold and saucy an inquisition, that some men's spirits trembled at the interrogatories; they phrasing it so, as if (as was said at the Council of Trent) they had the Holy Ghost in a cloke-bag."

Their questions generally were these, or such like: When were you converted? Where did you begin to feel the motions of the Spirit? In what year? in what month? in what day? about what hour of the day had you the secret call, or motion of the Spirit, to undertake and labour in the ministry? What work of grace has God wrought upon your soul? And a great many other questions about regeneration, predestination, and the like.

(Canonical cravat of Smeck,
From whom the institution came,
When Church and State they set on flame,
And worn by them as badges then
Of Spiritual Warfaring-men)
Judge rightly if Regeneration
Be of the newest cut in fashion.
Sure 'tis an orthodox opinion,
That grace is founded in dominion:
Great piety consists in pride;
To rule is to be sanctify'd:
To domineer, and to control,
Both o'er the body and the soul,
Is the most perfect discipline
Of Church-rule, and by right divine.
Bell and the Dragon's chaplains were
More moderate than these by far:
For they (poor knaves) were glad to cheat,
To get their wives and children meat;
But these will not be fobb'd off so,
They must have wealth and power too;
Or else with blood and desolation
They'll tear it out o' th' heart o' th' nation.
 Sure these themselves from primitive
And Heathen priesthood do derive,
When butchers were the only clerks,
Elders and Presbyters of Kirks;
Whose directory was to kill,

V. 1166. 'Smectymans' was a club of holders-forth.

And some believe it is so still.
The only diff'rence is that then
They slaughter'd only beasts, now men.
For then to sacrifice a bullock,
Or, now and then, a child to Moloch,
They count a vile abomination,
But not to slaughter a whole nation.
Presbytery does but translate
The papacy to a free state:
A commonwealth of Popery,
Where ev'ry village is a See
As well as Rome, and must maintain
A tithe-pig metropolitan;
Where ev'ry Presbyter and Deacon
Commands the keys for cheese and bacon,
And ev'ry hamlet's governed
By 's Holiness, the Church's head,
More haughty and severe in 's place
Than Gregory and Boniface.
Such Church must, surely, be a monster
With many heads: for if we conster
What in th' Apocalypse we find,
According to th' Apostle's mind,
'Tis that the whore of Babylon
With many heads did ride upon;
Which heads denote the sinful tribe
Of Deacon, Priest, Lay-elder, Scribe.
  Lay-elder, Simeon to Levi,
Whose little finger is as heavy
As loins of patriarchs, prince-prelate,

And bishop-secular. This zealot
Is of a mongrel diverse kind,
Clerick before and Lay behind;
A lawless linsey-woolsey brother,
Half of one order, half another;
A creature of amphibious nature,
On land a beast, a fish in water:
That always preys on grace or sin;
A sheep without, a wolf within.
This fierce inquisitor has chief
Dominion over men's belief
And manners; can pronounce a saint
Idolatrous, or ignorant,
When superciliously he sifts
Through coarsest boulter others' gifts:
For all men live and judge amiss
Whose talents jump not just with his;
He'll lay on Gifts with hands, and place
On dullest noddle Light and Grace,
The manufacture of the kirk.
Those pastors are but th' handywork
Of his mechanic paws, instilling
Divinity in them by feeling;
From whence they start up Chosen Vessels,
Made by contact, as men get measles.
So Cardinals, they say, do grope
At th' other end the new-made Pope.
  Hold, hold, quoth Hudibras, soft fire,
They say, does make sweet malt. Good Squire,
Festina lentè, not too fast,

For haste (the proverb says) makes waste.
The quirks and cavils thou dost make
Are false and built upon mistake:
And I shall bring you, with your pack
Of fallacies, t' Elenchi back;
And put your arguments in mood
And figure to be understood.
I'll force you by right ratiocination
To leave your vitilitigation,
And make you keep to th' question close
And argue *dialecticῶs.*
The question then, to state it first,
Is, which is better or which worst,
Synods or Bears? Bears I avow
To be the worst, and Synods thou;
But to make good th' assertion,
Thou say'st they're really all one.
If so, not worse; for if they're *idem,*
Why then *tantundem dat tantidem.*
For if they are the same, by course
Neither is better, neither worse.
But I deny they are the same,
More than a maggot and I am.
That both are *animalia*
I grant, but not *rationalia:*
For though they do agree in kind,
Specific difference we find;
And can no more make Bears of these,
Than prove my horse is Socrates.
That Synods are Bear-gardens, too,

Thou dost affirm; but I say No:
And thus I prove it, in a word;
Whats'ever Assembly 's not empow'r'd
To Censure, Curse, Absolve, and ordain,
Can be no Synod; but Bear-garden
Has no such pow'r; *ergo*, 'tis none:
And so thy sophistry 's o'erthrown.
But yet we are beside the quest'on
Which thou didst raise the first contest on:
For that was, Whether Bears are better
Than Synod-men? I say *Negatur.*
That Bears are beasts, and Synods men,
Is held by all: they're better then;
For Bears and Dogs on four legs go,
As beasts; but Synod-men on two.
'Tis true they all have teeth and nails;
But prove that Synod-men have tails;
Or that a rugged shaggy fur
Grows o'er the hide of Presbyter;
Or that his snout and spacious ears
Do hold proportion with a Bear's.
A Bear's a savage beast, of all
Most ugly and unnatural:
Whelp'd without form, until the dam
Has lickt it into shape and frame:
But all thy light can ne'er evict
That ever Synod-man was lickt,
Or brought to any other fashion
Than his own will and inclination.
But thou dost further yet in this

Oppugn thyself and sense; that is,
Thou would'st have Presbyters to go
For Bears and Dogs, and Bear-wards too:
A strange chimera of beasts and men,
Made up of pieces het'rogene;
Such as in Nature never met
In eodem subjecto yet.
  Thy other arguments are all
Supposures hypothetical,
That do but beg; and we may choose
Either to grant them or refuse.
Much thou hast said, which I know when
And where thou stol'st from other men
(Whereby 'tis plain thy Light and Gifts
Are all but plagiary shifts),
And is the same that Ranter said,
Who, arguing with me, broke my head,
And tore a handful of my beard:
The self-same cavils then I heard,
When, b'ing in hot dispute about
This controversy, we fell out;
And what thou know'st I answer'd then
Will serve to answer thee agen.

V. 1329. The Ranters were a vile sect that sprung up in those times. Alexander Ross observes, "That they held that God, devil, angels, heaven and hell, &c. were fictions and fables; that Moses, John Baptist, and Christ, were impostors; and what Christ and the Apostles acquainted the world with, as to matter of religion, perished with them; that preaching and praying are useless, and that preaching is but publick

Quoth Ralpho, Nothing but th' abuse
Of human learning you produce;
Learning, that cobweb of the brain,
Profane, erroneous, and vain;
A trade of knowledge as replete
As others are with fraud and cheat;
An art t' encumber Gifts and wit,

lying; that there is an end of all ministry and administrations, and people are to be taught immediately from God," &c.

V. 1339. Ralpho was as great an enemy to human learning as Jack Cade and his fellow rebels. Cade's words to Lord Say, before he ordered his head to be cut off: "I am the besom that must sweep the Court clean of such filth as thou art; thou hast most traitorously corrupted the youth of the realm in erecting a grammar-school; and whereas, before, our forefathers had no other books but the Score and the Tally, thou hast caused Printing to be used; and, contrary to the King, his crown and dignity, thou hast built a Paper-mill. It will be proved to thy face, that thou hast men about thee that usually talk of a noun and a verb, and such abominable words, as no Christian ear can endure to hear."

It was the opinion of those tinkers, tailors, &c. that governed Chelmsford at the beginning of the Rebellion, "That learning had always been an enemy to the Gospel, and that it were a happy thing if there were no universities, and that all books were burned except the Bible."

"I tell you (says a writer of those times) wicked books do as much wound us as the swords of our adversaries; for this manner of learning is superfluous and costly: many tongues and languages are only confusion, and only wit, reason, understanding, and scholarship, are the main means that oppose us, and hinder our cause; therefore, if ever we have the fortune to get the upperhand — we will down with all law and learning, and have no other rule but the Carpenter's, nor any writing or reading but the Score and the Tally."

And render both for nothing fit;
Makes Light unactive, dull and troubled,
Like little David in Saul's doublet:
A cheat that scholars put upon
Other men's reason and their own;
A fort of error, to ensconce
Absurdity and ignorance,
That renders all the avenues
To truth impervious and abstruse,
By making plain things, in debate,
By art perplext and intricate:
For nothing goes for Sense or Light,
That will not with old rules jump right;
As if rules were not in the schools
Deriv'd from truth, but truth from rules.
This Pagan, Heathenish invention
Is good for nothing but contention:
For as in sword and buckler fight
All blows do on the target light,
So, when men argue, the great'st part
O' th' contest falls on terms of art,
Until the fustian stuff be spent,
And then they fall to th' argument.
Quoth Hudibras, Friend Ralph, thou hast
Outrun the constable at last:
For thou art fallen on a new
Dispute, as senseless as untrue,
But to the former opposite,
And contrary as black to white:
Mere *disparata;* that concerning

Presbytery, this human learning;
Two things s' averse, they never yet
But in thy rambling fancy met.
But I shall take a fit occasion
T' evince thee by' ratiocination,
Some other time in place more proper
Than this we 're in; therefore let's stop here,
And rest our weary'd bones awhile,
Already tir'd with other toil.

PART II. CANTO I.

THE ARGUMENT.

The Knight, by damnable Magician,
Being cast illegally in prison,
Love brings his action on the case,
And lays it upon Hudibras.
How he receives the Lady's visit,
And cunningly solicits his suit,
Which she defers; yet, on parole,
Redeems him from th' enchanted hole.

BUT now, t' observe Romantique method,
Let bloody steel awhile be sheathed,
And all those harsh and rugged sounds
Of bastinadoes, cuts, and wounds,
Exchang'd to love's more gentle style,

Arg. V. 1, 2. Var.
'The Knight being clapp'd by th' heels in prison,
The last unhappy expedition.'

Arg. V. 5. Var. 'How he revi's,' &c.

V. 1. The beginning of this Second Part may perhaps seem strange and abrupt to those who do not know that it was written on purpose in imitation of Virgil, who begins the Fourth Book of his Æneid in the very same manner, 'At regina gravi,' &c. And this is enough to satisfy the curiosity of those who believe that invention and fancy ought to be measured, like cases in law, by precedents, or else they are in the power of the critic.

V. 2. Var. 'Let rusty steel,' and 'To trusty steel.'

To let our reader breathe awhile.
In which, that we may be as brief as
Is possible, by way of preface:
Is 't not enough to make one strange,
That some men's fancies should ne'er change,
But make all people do and say
The same things still the self-same way?
Some writers make all ladies purloin'd,
And knights pursuing like a whirlwind:
Others make all their knights, in fits
Of jealousy, to lose their wits;
Till drawing blood o' th' dames, like witches,
They're forthwith cur'd of their capriches.
Some always thrive in their amours,
By pulling plasters off their sores
As cripples do to get an alms,
Just so do they, and win their dames.
Some force whole regions, in despite
O' geography, to change their site;
Make former times shake hands with latter,
And that which was before come after.
But those that write in rhyme still make
The one verse for the other's sake;
For one for sense, and one for rhyme,
I think 's sufficient at one time.

V. 5–8. Var. 'And unto love turn we our style,
To let our readers breathe awhile,
By this time tir'd with th' horrid sounds
Of blows, and cuts, and blood, and wounds.'

V. 10. Var. 'That a man's fancy.'

But we forget in what sad plight
We whilom left the captiv'd Knight
And pensive Squire, both bruis'd in body,
And conjur'd into safe custody.
Tir'd with dispute, and speaking Latin,
As well as basting and Bear-baiting,
And desperate of any course
To free himself by wit or force,
His only solace was, that now
His dog-bolt fortune was so low,
That either it must quickly end,
Or turn about again, and mend;
In which he found th' event, no less
Than other times, beside his guess.
There is a tall long-sided dame,
(But wond'rous light) ycleped Fame,
That like a thin cameleon boards
Herself on air, and eats her words;
Upon her shoulders wings she wears
Like hanging sleeves, lin'd through with ears,
And eyes, and tongues, as poets list,
Made good by deep mythologist:
With these she through the welkin flies,
And sometimes carries truth, oft lies;
With letters hung, like eastern pigeons,

V. 32. Var. 'We lately.'

V. 48. The beauty of this consists in the double meaning. The first alludes to Fame's living on Report: the second is an insinuation, that if a report is narrowly enquired into, and traced up to the original author, it is made to contradict itself.

And Mercuries of furthest regions;
Diurnals writ for regulation
Of lying, to inform the nation,
And by their public use to bring down
The rate of whetstones in the kingdom.
About her neck a packet-mail,
Fraught with advice, some fresh, some stale:
Of men that walk'd when they were dead,
And cows of monsters brought to bed;
Of hailstones big as pullets' eggs,
And puppies whelp'd with twice two legs;
A blazing star seen in the west,
By six or seven men at least.
Two trumpets she does sound at once,
But both of clean contrary tones;
But whether both with the same wind,
Or one before and one behind,
We know not, only this can tell,
The one sounds vilely, th' other well;
And therefore vulgar authors name
Th' one Good, the other evil Fame.
This tattling gossip knew too well
What mischief Hudibras befell;
And straight the spiteful tidings bears
Of all, to th' unkind Widow's ears.
Democritus ne'er laugh'd so loud
To see bawds carted through the crowd,
Or funerals, with stately pomp,

V. 77. Var. 'Twattling gossip.'

March slowly on in solemn dump,
As she laugh'd out, until her back,
As well as sides, was like to crack.
She vow'd she would go see the sight,
And visit the distressed Knight;
To do the office of a neighbour,
And be a gossip at his labour;
And from his wooden jail the stocks
To set at large his fetter-locks;
And by exchange, parole, or ransom,
To free him from th' enchanted mansion.
This b'ing resolv'd, she call'd for hood
And usher, implements abroad
Which ladies wear, besides a slender
Young waiting damsel to attend her.
All which appearing, on she went
To find the Knight, in limbo pent;
And 'twas not long before she found
Him and his stout Squire in the pound,
Both coupled in enchanted tether
By further leg behind together.
For as he sat upon his rump,
His head, like one in doleful dump,
Between his knees, his hands apply'd
Unto his ears on either side,
And by him in another hole
Afflicted Ralpho, cheek by jowl;

V. 91. Var. 'That is to see him deliver'd safe
Of 's wooden burden, and Squire Raph.'

She came upon him in his wooden
Magician's circle on a sudden,
As spirits do t' a conjurer
When in their dreadful shapes th' appear.
No sooner did the Knight perceive her,
But straight he fell into a fever,
Inflam'd all over with disgrace
To be seen by her in such a place;
Which made him hang his head, and scowl,
And wink, and goggle like an owl:
He felt his brains begin to swim,
When thus the Dame accosted him.
This place (quoth she) they say 's enchanted,
And with delinquent spirits haunted,
That here are ty'd in chains and scourg'd
Until their guilty crimes be purg'd:
Look, there are two of them appear
Like persons I have seen somewhere.
Some have mistaken blocks and posts
For spectres, apparitions, ghosts,
With saucer eyes, and horns; and some
Have heard the devil beat a drum;
But, if our eyes are not false glasses
That give a wrong account of faces,

V. 111, 112. There was never certainly a pleasanter scene imagined than this before us; it is the most diverting incident in the whole Poem. The unlucky and unexpected visit of the Lady, the attitude and surprise of the Knight, the confusion and blushes of the lover, and the satirical raillery of a mistress, are represented in lively colours, and conspire to make this interview wonderfully pleasing.

That beard and I should be acquainted
Before 'twas conjur'd and enchanted;
For, though it be disfigur'd somewhat,
As if 't had lately been in combat,
It did belong to a worthy Knight,
Howe'er this goblin is come by 't.
When Hudibras the Lady heard
Discoursing thus upon his beard,
And speak with such respect and honour
Both of the beard and the beard's owner,
He thought it best to set as good
A face upon it as he could;
And thus he spoke: Lady, your bright
And radiant eyes are in the right;
The beard 's th' identique beard you knew,
The same numerically true;
Nor is it worn by fiend or elf,
But its proprietor himself.
O heavens! quoth she, can that be true?
I do begin to fear 'tis you;
Not by your individual whiskers,
But by your dialect and discourse,
That never spoke to man or beast
In notions vulgarly exprest:
But what malignant star, alas!
Has brought you both to this sad pass?
Quoth he, The fortune of the war,
Which I am less afflicted for

V. 142. Var. 'To take kind notice of his beard.'

Than to be seen with beard and face
By you in such a homely case.
Quoth she, Those need not be asham'd
For being honourably maim'd:
If he that is in battle conquer'd
Have any title to his own beard,
Though yours be sorely lugg'd and torn,
It does your visage more adorn
Than if 'twere prun'd and starch'd and lander'd,
And cut square by the Russian standard.
A torn beard 's like a tatter'd ensign;
That 's bravest which there are most rents in.
That petticoat about your shoulders
Does not so well become a soldier's;
And I'm afraid they are worse handled,
Although i' th' rear your beard the van led;
And those uneasy bruises make
My heart for company to ake,
To see so worshipful a friend
I' th' pillory set, at the wrong end.
Quoth Hudibras, This thing call'd Pain
Is (as the learned Stoics maintain)
Not bad *simpliciter*, nor good,
But merely as 'tis understood.
Sense is deceitful, and may feign
As well in counterfeiting pain
As other gross phenomenas,
In which it oft mistakes the case.

V. 164. Var. 'In such elenctique case.'

But since th' immortal intellect
(That 's free from error and defect,
Whose objects still persist the same)
Is free from outward bruise or maim,
Which nought external can expose
To gross material bangs or blows,
It follows we can ne'er be sure
Whether we pain or not endure;
And just so far are sore and griev'd
As by the fancy is believ'd.
Some have been wounded with conceit,
And dy'd of mere opinion straight;
Others, though wounded sore in reason,
Felt no contusion nor discretion.
A Saxon duke did grow so fat
That mice (as histories relate)
Ate grots and labyrinths to dwell in
His postique parts, without his feeling;
Then how is 't possible a kick
Should e'er reach that way to the quick?
   Quoth she, I grant it is in vain
For one that 's basted to feel pain,
Because the pangs his bones endure
Contribute nothing to the cure;
Yet honour hurt is wont to rage
With pain no med'cine can assuage.
   Quoth he, That honour 's very squeamish
That takes a basting for a blemish;
For what 's more hon'rable than scars,
Or skin to tatters rent in wars?

Some have been beaten till they know
What wood a cudgel 's of by th' blow:
Some kick'd until they can feel whether
A shoe be Spanish or neat's leather;
And yet have met, after long running,
With some whom they have taught that cunning.
The furthest way about t' o'ercome
In th' end does prove the nearest home.
By laws of learned duellists,
They that are bruis'd with wood or fists,
And think one beating may for once
Suffice, are cowards and pultroons;
But if they dare engage t' a second,
They 're stout and gallant fellows reckon'd.
Th' old Romans freedom did bestow,
Our princes worship, with a blow.
King Pyrrhus cur'd his splenetic
And testy courtiers with a kick.
The Negus, when some mighty lord
Or potentate 's to be restor'd,
And pardon'd for some great offence
With which he 's willing to dispense,
First has him laid upon his belly,
Then beaten back and side t' a jelly:
That done, he rises, humbly bows,
And gives thanks for the princely blows;

V. 232. Var. 'Poltroons.'
V. 239. A king of Ethiopia.
V. 241, 242. Var. 'To his good grace for some offence
Forfeit before, and pardon'd since.'

Departs not meanly proud, and boasting
Of his magnificent rib-roasting.
The beaten soldier proves most manful
That, like his sword, endures the anvil;
And justly 's held more formidable,
The more his valour 's malleable:
But he that fears a bastinado
Will run away from his own shadow.
And though I'm now in durance fast
By our own party basely cast,
Ransom, exchange, parole refus'd,
And worse than by the en'my us'd;
In close *catasta* shut, past hope
Of wit or valour to elope;
As beards, the nearer that they tend
To th' earth, still grow more reverend,
And cannons shoot the higher pitches
The lower we let down their breeches,
I'll make this low dejected fate
Advance me to a greater height.
  Quoth she, You 've almost made me' in love
With that which did my pity move.
Great wits and valours, like great states,
Do sometimes sink with their own weights:
Th' extremes of glory and of shame,
Like east and west, become the same:
No Indian prince has to his palace
More foll'wers than a thief to th' gallows,
But, if a beating seem so brave,
What glories must a whipping have?

Such great achievements cannot fail
To cast salt on a woman's tail:
For if I thought your nat'ral talent
Of passive courage were so gallant,
As you strain hard to have it thought,
I could grow amorous and dote.
  When Hudibras this language heard,
He prick'd up 's ears, and strok'd his beard;
Thought he, This is the lucky hour,
Wines work when vines are in the flow'r:
This crisis then I'll set my rest on,
And put her boldly to the quest'on.
  Madam, what you would seem to doubt
Shall be to all the world made out;
How I've been drubb'd, and with what spirit
And magnanimity I bear it:
And if you doubt it to be true,
I'll stake myself down against you;
And if I fail in love or truth,
Be you the winner and take both.
  Quoth she, I've heard old cunning stagers
Say, fools for arguments use wagers;
And, though I prais'd your valour, yet
I did not mean to baulk your wit;
Which if you have, you must needs know
What I have told you before now,
And you b' experiment have prov'd;
I cannot love where I'm belov'd.
  Quoth Hudibras, 'Tis a caprich
Beyond th' infliction of a witch;

So cheats to play with those still aim
That do not understand the game.
Love in your heart as idly burns
As fire in antique Roman urns
To warm the dead, and vainly light
Those only that see nothing by't.
Have you not power to entertain,
And render love for love again;
As no man can draw in his breath
At once, and force out air beneath?
Or do you love yourself so much,
To bear all rivals else a grutch?
What fate can lay a greater curse
Than you upon yourself would force?
For Wedlock without love, some say,
Is but a lock without a key.
It is a kind of rape to marry
One that neglects or cares not for ye:
For what does make it ravishment
But b'ing against the mind's consent?
A rape that is the more inhuman,
For being acted by a woman.
Why are you fair, but to entice us
To love you, that you may despise us?
But though you cannot love, you say,
Out of your own fanatic way,
Why should you not at least allow
Those that love you to do so too?

V. 332. Var. 'Fanatique.' Qy. 'Fantastic?'

For, as you fly me, and pursue
Love more averse, so I do you;
And am by your own doctrine taught
To practise what you call a fault.
Quoth she, If what you say is true,
You must fly me as I do you;
But 'tis not what we do, but say,
In love and preaching, that must sway.
Quoth he, To bid me not to love
Is to forbid my pulse to move,
My beard to grow, my ears to prick up,
Or (when I'm in a fit) to hiccup.
Command me to piss out the moon,
And 'twill as easily be done.
Love's pow'r 's too great to be withstood
By feeble human flesh and blood.
'Twas he that brought upon his knees
The hect'ring kill-cow Hercules,
Transform'd his leager-lion's skin
T' a petticoat, and made him spin;
Seiz'd on his club, and made it dwindle
T' a feeble distaff and a spindle:
'Twas he that made emp'rors gallants
To their own sisters and their aunts;
Set Popes and Cardinals agog,
To play with pages at leap-frog:
'Twas he that gave our Senate purges,
And fluxt the House of many a burgess;
Made those that represent the nation
Submit and suffer amputation;

And all the Grandees o' th' Cabal
Adjourn to tubs at spring and fall.
He mounted Synod-men and rode 'em
To Dirty-Lane and Little Sodom;
Made 'em curvet like Spanish Jenets,
And take the ring at Madam ——'s.
'Twas he that made Saint Francis do
More than the devil could tempt him to,
In cold and frosty weather grow
Enamour'd of a wife of snow;
And though she were of rigid temper,
With melting flames accost and tempt her;
Which after in enjoyment quenching,
He hung a garland on his engine.
Quoth she, If love have these effects,
Why is it not forbid our sex?
Why is 't not damn'd and interdicted
For diabolical and wicked?
And sung, as out of tune, against,
As Turk and Pope are by the Saints?
I find I've greater reason for it,
Than I believ'd before, t' abhor it.
Quoth Hudibras, These sad effects
Spring from your heathenish neglects

V. 370. "Stennet was the person whose name was dashed," says Sir Roger L'Estrange, 'Key to Hudibras.' "Her husband was by profession a broom-man and lay-elder. She followed the laudable employment of bawding, and managed several intrigues for those Brothers and Sisters whose purity consisted chiefly in the whiteness of their linen."

Of Love's great pow'r, which he returns
Upon yourselves with equal scorns,
And those who worthy lovers slight,
Plagues with prepost'rous appetite:
This made the beauteous Queen of Crete
To take a town-bull for her sweet;
And from her greatness stoop so low,
To be the rival of a cow:
Others to prostitute their great hearts
To be baboons' and monkeys' sweethearts:
Some with the devil himself in league grow,
By 's representative a Negro.
'Twas this made Vestal maid love-sick,
And venture to be bury'd quick:
Some by their fathers and their brothers
To be made mistresses and mothers.
'Tis this that proudest dames enamours
On lacquies and *valets des chambres;*
Their haughty stomachs overcomes,
And makes them stoop to dirty grooms;
To slight the world, and to disparage
Claps, issue, infamy, and marriage.
Quoth she, These judgments are severe,
Yet such as I should rather bear
Than trust men with their oaths, or prove
Their faith and secrecy in love.
Says he, There is as weighty reason
For secrecy in love as treason.

V. 406. Var. 'Varlets des chambres.'

Love is a burglarer, a felon,
That at the windore eye does steal in
To rob the heart, and with his prey
Steals out again a closer way,
Which whosoever can discover,
He 's sure (as he deserves) to suffer.
Love is a fire, that burns and sparkles
In men as nat'rally as in charcoals,
Which sooty chemists stop in holes
When out of wood they extract coals;
So lovers should their passions choke,
That though they burn, they may not smoke.
'Tis like that sturdy thief that stole
And dragg'd beasts backward into 's hole;
So love does lovers, and us men
Draws by the tails into his den,
That no impression may discover
And trace t' his cave the wary lover.
But if you doubt I should reveal
What you intrust me under seal,
I'll prove myself as close and virtuous
As your own secretary' Albertus.
  Quoth she, I grant you may be close
In hiding what your aims propose:
Love-passions are like parables,
By which men still mean something else:
Though love be all the world's pretence,
Money 's the mythologic sense,

V. 418. Var. 'Window eye.'

The real substance of the shadow,
Which all address and courtship 's made to.
  Thought he, I understand your play,
And how to quit you your own way:
He that will win his dame must do
As love does when he bends his bow;
With one hand thrust the lady from,
And with the other pull her home.
I grant, quoth he, wealth is a great
Provocative to am'rous heat:
It is all philtres and high diet
That makes love rampant and to fly out:
'Tis beauty always in the flower,
That buds and blossoms at fourscore:
'Tis that by which the sun and moon
At their own weapons are outdone:
That makes knights-errant fall in trances,
And lay about 'em in romances:
'Tis virtue, wit, and worth, and all
That men divine and sacred call;
For what is worth in any thing
But so much money as 'twill bring?
Or what but riches is there known
Which man can solely call his own,
In which no creature goes his half,
Unless it be to squint and laugh?
I do confess, with goods and land,
I'd have a wife at second-hand;
And such you are: nor is 't your person
My stomach 's set so sharp and fierce on,

But 'tis (your better part) your riches
That my enamour'd heart bewitches:
Let me your fortune but possess,
And settle your person how you please;
Or make it o'er in trust to th' devil,
You 'll find me reasonable and civil.
  Quoth she, I like this plainness better
Than false mock-passion, speech, or letter,
Or any feat of qualm or sowning,
But hanging of yourself or drowning;
Your only way with me to break
Your mind is breaking of your neck:
For as when merchants break, o'erthrown
Like nine-pins, they strike others down,
So that would break my heart; which done,
My tempting fortune is your own.
These are but trifles; ev'ry lover
Will damn himself over and over,
And greater matters undertake,
For a less worthy mistress' sake:
Yet they 're the only ways to prove
Th' unfeign'd realities of love;
For he that hangs, or beats out 's brains,
The devil 's in him if he feigns.
  Quoth Hudibras, This way 's too rough
For mere experiment and proof;
It is no jesting trivial matter
To swing i' th' air, or dive in water,

V. 483. Var. 'Swooning.'

And like a water-witch try love;
That 's to destroy, and not to prove:
As if a man should be dissected,
To find what part is disaffected;
Your better way is to make over,
In trust, your fortune to your lover.
Trust is a trial; if it break,
'Tis not so desp'rate as a neck:
Beside, th' experiment 's more certain;
Men venture necks to gain a fortune:
The soldier does it ev'ry day
(Eight to the week) for sixpence pay;
Your pettifoggers damn their souls,
To share with knaves in cheating fools;
And merchants, vent'ring through the main,
Slight pirates, rocks, and horns, for gain.
This is the way I advise you to;
Trust me, and see what I will do.
  Quoth she, I should be loth to run
Myself all th' hazard, and you none;
Which must be done, unless some deed
Of yours aforesaid do precede:
Give but yourself one gentle swing
For trial, and I'll cut the string;
Or give that rev'rend head a maul,
Or two or three, against a wall,
To show you are a man of mettle,
And I'll engage myself to settle.
  Quoth he, My head 's not made of brass,
As Friar Bacon's noddle was,

Nor (like the Indian's scull) so tough
That, authors say, 'twas musket-proof;
As it had need to be, to enter
As yet on any new adventure.
You see what bangs it has endur'd,
That would, before new feats, be cur'd:
But if that 's all you stand upon,
Here strike me, Luck, it shall be done.
  Quoth she, The matter 's not so far gone
As you suppose; two words t' a bargain:
That may be done, and time enough,
When you have given downright proof:
And yet 'tis no fantastic pique
I have to love, nor coy dislike;
'Tis no implicit nice aversion
T' your conversation, mien, or person;
But a just fear lest you should prove
False and perfidious in love:
For, if I thought you could be true,
I could love twice as much as you.
  Quoth he, My faith as adamantin
As chains of Destiny I'll maintain;
True as Apollo ever spoke,
Or oracle from heart of oak:
And if you 'll give my flame but vent,
Now in close hugger-mugger pent,
And shine upon me but benignly
With that one and that other pigsney,
The sun and day shall sooner part
Than love or you shake off my heart;

The sun, that shall no more dispense
His own, but your bright influence.
I'll carve your name on barks of trees
With true-love-knots and flourishes,
That shall infuse eternal spring
And everlasting flourishing;
Drink ev'ry letter on 't in stum,
And make it brisk Champaign become.
Where'er you tread, your foot shall set
The primrose and the violet;
All spices, perfumes, and sweet powders,
Shall borrow from your breath their odours;
Nature her charter shall renew,
And take all lives of things from you;
The world depend upon your eye,
And, when you frown upon it, die:
Only our loves shall still survive,
New worlds and Natures to outlive,
And like to heralds' moons remain
All crescents, without change or wane.
  Hold, hold, quoth she, no more of this;
Sir Knight, you take your aim amiss;
For you will find it a hard chapter
To catch me with poetic rapture,
In which your Mastery of Art
Doth shew itself, and not your heart;
Nor will you raise in mine combustion
By dint of high heroic fustian.
She that with poetry is won
Is but a desk to write upon;

And what men say of her they mean
No more than on the thing they lean.
Some with Arabian spices strive
T' embalm her cruelly alive;
Or season her, as French cooks use
Their *haut-gousts*, *bouilles*, or *ragousts;*
Use her so barbarously ill
To grind her lips upon a mill,
Until the *facet doublet* doth
Fit their rhymes rather than her mouth;
Her mouth, compar'd t' an oyster's, with
A row of pearl in 't 'stead of teeth.
Others make posies of her cheeks,
Where red and whitest colours mix;
In which the lily and the rose
For Indian lake and ceruse goes.
The sun and moon, by her bright eyes
Eclips'd and darken'd in the skies,
Are but black patches that she wears,
Cut into suns, and moons, and stars;
By which astrologers, as well
As those in heav'n above, can tell
What strange events they do foreshow
Unto her under-world below.
Her voice the music of the spheres,
So loud it deafens mortals' ears,
As wise philosophers have thought,
And that 's the cause we hear it not.
This has been done by some, who those
Th' ador'd in rhyme would kick in prose;

And in those ribands would have hung
Of which melodiously they sung.
That have the hard fate to write best
Of those still that deserve it least:
It matters not how false or forc'd,
So the best things be said o' th' worst;
It goes for nothing when 'tis said,
Only the arrow 's drawn to th' head,
Whether it be a swan or goose
They level at: so shepherds use
To set the same mark on the hip
Both of their sound and rotten sheep:
For wits that carry low or wide
Must be aim'd higher, or beside
The mark, which else they ne'er come nigh
But when they take their aim awry.
But I do wonder you should choose
This way t' attack me with your Muse,
As one cut out to pass your tricks on,
With Fulhams of poetic fiction.
I rather hop'd I should no more
Hear from you o' th' gallanting score;
For hard dry bastings us'd to prove
The readiest remedies of love
Next a dry diet: but if those fail,
Yet this uneasy loop-hol'd jail,
In which y' are hamper'd by the fetlock,
Cannot but put y' in mind of wedlock;

V. 642. A cant word for false dice.

Wedlock, that 's worse than any hole here,
If that may serve you for a cooler
T' allay your mettle, all agog
Upon a wife, the heavier clog:
Nor rather thank your gentler fate,
That for a bruis'd or broken pate
Has freed you from those knobs that grow
Much harder on the marry'd brow.
But if no dread can cool your courage
From vent'ring on that dragon, marriage;
Yet give me quarter, and advance
To nobler aims your puissance;
Level at beauty and at wit,
The fairest mark is easiest hit.
  Quoth Hudibras, I'm beforehand
In that already with your command;
For where does beauty and high wit
But in your Constellation meet?
  Quoth she, What does a match imply
But likeness and equality?
I know you cannot think me fit
To be th' yokefellow of your wit;
Nor take one of so mean deserts
To be the partner of your parts;
A grace which, if I could believe,
I've not the conscience to receive.
  That conscience, quoth Hudibras,
Is misinform'd: I'll state the case.
A man may be a legal doner
Of any thing whereof he 's owner,

And may confer it where he lists,
I' th' judgment of all casuists:
Then wit, and parts, and valour, may
Be ali'nated and made away
By those that are proprietors,
As I may give or sell my horse.
  Quoth she, I grant the case is true
And proper 'twixt your horse and you:
But whether I may take, as well
As you may give away or sell?
Buyers, you know, are bid beware;
And worse than thieves receivers are.
How shall I answer Hue and Cry
For a Roan-gelding, twelve hands high,
All spurr'd and switch'd, a lock on 's hoof,
A sorrel mane? Can I bring proof
Where, when, by whom, and what y' were sold for,
And in the open market told for?
Or, should I take you for a stray,
You must be kept a year and day
(Ere I can own you) here i' th' pound,
Where, if y' are sought, you may be found;
And in the mean time I must pay
For all your provender and hay.
  Quoth he, It stands me much upon
T' enervate this objection,
And prove myself, by topic clear,
No gelding, as you would infer.
Loss of virility 's averr'd
To be the cause of loss of beard,

That does (like embryo in the womb)
Abortive on the chin become:
This first a woman did invent
In envy of man's ornament,
Semiramis of Babylon,
Who first of all cut men o' th' stone
To mar their beards, and laid foundation
Of sow-geldering operation.
Look on this beard, and tell me whether
Eunuchs wear such, or geldings either?
Next it appears I am no horse,
That I can argue and discourse,
Have but two legs, and ne'er a tail.
  Quoth she, That nothing will avail;
For some philosophers of late here
Write men have four legs by Nature,
And that 'tis custom makes them go
Erroneously upon but two;
As 'twas in Germany made good
B' a boy that lost himself in a wood,
And growing down t' a man, was wont
With wolves upon all four to hunt.
As for your reasons drawn from tails,
We cannot say they're true or false,
Till you explain yourself and show
B' experiment 'tis so or no.
  Quoth he, If you'll join issue on't,
I'll give you sat'sfact'ry account;
So you will promise, if you lose,
To settle all and be my spouse.

That never shall be done (quoth she)
To one that wants a tail, by me;
For tails by Nature sure were meant,
As well as beards, for ornament;
And though the vulgar count them homely,
In men or beast they are so comely,
So gentee, alamode, and handsome,
I'll never marry man that wants one:
And till you can demonstrate plain
You have one equal to your mane,
I'll be torn piecemeal by a horse
Ere I'll take you for better or worse.
The Prince of Cambay's daily food
Is asp, and basilisk, and toad,
Which makes him have so strong a breath
Each night he stinks a queen to death;
Yet I shall rather lie in 's arms
Than yours on any other terms.
Quoth he, What Nature can afford
I shall produce, upon my word;
And if she ever gave that boon
To man, I'll prove that I have one;
I mean by postulate illation,
When you shall offer just occasion:
But since y' have yet deny'd to give
My heart, your pris'ner, a reprieve,
But made it sink down to my heel,
Let that at least your pity feel;
And, for the suff'rings of your martyr,
Give its poor entertainer quarter;

And, by discharge or mainprize, grant
Deliv'ry from this base restraint.
  Quoth she, I grieve to see your leg
Stuck in a hole here like a peg;
And if I knew which way to do't
(Your honour safe) I'd let you out.
That dames by jail-delivery
Of errant knights have been set free,
When by enchantment they have been,
And sometimes for it too, laid in;
Is that which knights are bound to do
By order, oath, and honour too.
For what are they renown'd and famous else,
But aiding of distressed damosels?
But for a lady, no ways errant,
To free a knight, we have no warrant
In any authentical romance,
Or classic author yet of France;
And I'd be loth to have you break
An ancient custom for a freak,
Or innovation introduce
In place of things of antique use,
To free your heels by any course
That might b' unwholesome to your spurs:
Which, if I should consent unto,
It is not in my pow'r to do;
For 'tis a service must be done ye
With solemn previous ceremony,
Which always has been us'd t' untie
The charms of those who here do lie.

For as the Ancients heretofore
To Honour's temple had no dore
But that which thorough Virtue's lay,
So from this dungeon there's no way
To honour'd freedom, but by passing
That other virtuous school of lashing;
Where knights are kept in narrow lists
With wooden lockets 'bout their wrists,
In which they for a while are tenants,
And for their ladies suffer penance.
Whipping, that 's Virtue's governess,
Tut'ress of arts and sciences,
That mends the gross mistakes of Nature,
And puts new life into dull matter,
That lays foundation for renown
And all the honours of the gown.
This suffer'd, they are set at large,
And freed with hon'rable discharge:
Then, in their robes, the penitentials
Are straight presented with credentials,
And in their way attended on
By magistrates of ev'ry town;
And, all respect and charges paid,
They 're to their ancient seats convey'd.
Now if you 'll venture, for my sake,
To try the toughness of your back,
And suffer (as the rest have done)
The laying of a whipping on
(And may you prosper in your suit,
As you with equal vigour do't).

I here engage myself to loose ye,
And free your heels from caperdewsie.
But since our sex's modesty
Will not allow I should be by,
Bring me on oath a fair account,
And honour too, when you have done 't;
And I'll admit you to the place
You claim as due in my good grace.
If matrimony and hanging go
By dest'ny, why not whipping too?
What med'cine else can cure the fits
Of lovers when they lose their wits?
Love is a boy by poets styl'd,
Then spare the rod, and spoil the child.
  A Persian emp'ror whipp'd his grannam,
The sea, his mother Venus came on;
And hence some rev'rend men approve
Of rosemary in making love.
As skilful coopers hoop their tubs
With Lydian and with Phrygian dubs,
Why may not whipping have as good
A grace, perform'd in time and mood,
With comely movement, and by art
Raise passion in a lady's heart?
It is an easier way to make
Love by, than that which many take.
Who would not rather suffer whippin,

V. 831. Var. 'I here engage to be your bayl,
And free you from the unknightly jayl.'

Than swallow toasts of bits of ribbin?
Make wicked verses, treats, and faces,
And spell names over with beer-glasses?
Be under vows to hang and die
Love's sacrifice, and all a lye?
With china-oranges and tarts,
And whining plays, lay baits for hearts?
Bribe chambermaids with love and money
To break no roguish jests upon ye?
For lilies limn'd on cheeks, and roses,
With painted perfumes hazard noses?
Or, vent'ring to be brisk and wanton,
Do penance in a paper lantern?
All this you may compound for now,
By suff'ring what I offer you;
Which is no more than has been done
By knights for ladies long agone.
Did not the great La Mancha do so
For the Infanta Del Toboso?
Did not th' illustrious Bassa make
Himself a slave for Misse's sake,
And with bull's pizzle, for her love,
Was taw'd as gentle as a glove?
Was not young Florio sent (to cool
His flame for Biancafiore) to school,
Where pedant made his pathic bum
For her sake suffer martyrdom?
Did not a certain lady whip,
Of late, her husband's own lordship?
And, though a grandee of the House,

Claw'd him with fundamental blows;
Ty'd him stark-naked to a bedpost,
And firk'd his hide as if sh' had rid post;
And after in the Sessions court,
Where whipping 's judg'd, had honour for 't?
This swear you will perform, and then
I'll set you from th' enchanted den,
And the Magician's circle, clear.
  Quoth he, I do profess and swear,
And will perform what you enjoin,
Or may I never see you mine.
  Amen (quoth she), then turn'd about,
And bid her Squire let him out.
But ere an artist could be found
T' undo the charms another bound,
The sun grew low and left the skies,
Put down (some write) by ladies' eyes.
The moon pull'd off her veil of light,
That hides her face by day from sight
(Mysterious veil, of brightness made,
That 's both her lustre and her shade),
And in the lantern of the night
With shining horns hung out her light;
For darkness is the proper sphere
Where all false glories use t' appear.
The twinkling stars began to muster,
And glitter with their borrow'd lustre,
While sleep the weary'd world reliev'd,

V. 894. Var. 'I'll free you.'

By counterfeiting death reviv'd.
His whipping penance, till the morn
Our vot'ry thought it best t' adjourn,
And not to carry on a work
Of such importance in the dark,
With erring haste, but rather stay,
And do 't in th' open face of day ;
And in the mean time go in quest
Of next retreat to take his rest.

PART II. CANTO II.

THE ARGUMENT.

The Knight and Squire in hot dispute,
Within an ace of falling out,
Are parted with a sudden fright
Of strange alarm, and stranger sight;
With which adventuring to stickle,
They 're sent away in nasty pickle.

'Tis strange how some men's tempers suit
(Like bawd and brandy) with dispute;
That for their own opinions stand fast,
Only to have them claw'd and canvast;
That keep their consciences in cases,
As fiddlers do their crowds and bases,
Ne'er to be us'd but when they 're bent
To play a fit for argument;
Make true and false, unjust and just,
Of no use but to be discust;
Dispute, and set a paradox
Like a straight boot upon the stocks,
And stretch it more unmercifully
Than Helmont, Montaigne, White, or Tully.
So th' ancient Stoics, in their porch,

V. 2. Var. 'Brandee.'
V. 14. Var. 'Montaign and Lully.'

With fierce dispute maintain'd their church,
Beat out their brains in fight and study
To prove that virtue is a body,
That *bonum* is an animal
Made good with stout polemic brawl;
In which some hundreds on the place
Were slain outright, and many a face
Retrench'd of nose, and eyes, and beard,
To maintain what their sect averr'd.
All which the Knight and Squire, in wrath,
Had like t' have suffer'd for their faith;
Each striving to make good his own,
As by the sequel shall be shown.
The sun had long since in the lap
Of Thetis taken out his nap,
And, like a lobster boil'd, the morn
From black to red began to turn;
When Hudibras, whom thoughts and aking
'Twixt sleeping kept all night and waking,
Began to rub his drowsy eyes,
And from his couch prepar'd to rise,
Resolving to dispatch the deed
He vow'd to do, with trusty speed.
But first with knocking loud, and bawling,
He rous'd the Squire in truckle lolling;
And after many circumstances,
Which vulgar authors in romances
Do use to spend their time and wits on,
To make impertinent description,
They got (with much ado) to horse,

And to the Castle bent their course,
In which he to the Dame before
To suffer whipping-duty swore.
Where now arriv'd, and half unharnest,
To carry on the work in earnest,
He stopp'd, and paus'd upon the sudden,
And with a serious forehead plodding,
Sprung a new scruple in his head,
Which first he scratch'd and after said,
Whether it be direct infringing
An oath, if I should wave this swinging,
And what I've sworn to bear forbear,
And so b' equivocation swear;
Or whether 't be a lesser sin
To be forsworn than act the thing,
Are deep and subtle points, which must,
T' inform my Conscience, be discust;

V. 48. Var. 'Whipping duly swore.'

V. 55, 56. This dialogue between Hudibras and Ralph sets before us the hypocrisy and villany of all parties of the Rebels with regard to oaths; what equivocations and evasions they made use of to account for the many perjuries they were daily guilty of, and the several oaths they readily took, and as readily broke, merely as they found it suited their interest, as appears from v. 107, &c. and v. 377, &c. of this Canto, and Part III. Canto III. v. 547, &c. Archbishop Bramhall says, "That the hypocrites of those times, though they magnified the obligation of an oath, yet in their own case dispensed with all oaths, civil, military, and religious. We are now told," says he, "that the oaths we have taken are not to be examined according to the interpretation of men: No! How then? — Surely according to the interpretation of devils."

In which to err a tittle may
To errors infinite make way:
And therefore I desire to know
Thy judgment ere we further go.
   Quoth Ralpho, Since you do enjoin it,
I shall enlarge upon the point;
And, for my own part, do not doubt
Th' affirmative may be made out.
But first, to state the case aright,
For best advantage of our light:
And thus 'tis: Whether 't be a sin
To claw and curry your own skin,
Greater or less than to forbear,
And that you are forsworn forswear.
But first o' th' first: The inward man,
And outward, like a clan and clan,
Have always been at daggers-drawing,
And one another clapper-clawing:
Not that they really cuff or fence,
But in a spiritual mystic sense;
Which to mistake, and make 'em squabble
In literal fray, 's abominable.
'Tis Heathenish, in frequent use
With Pagans and apostate Jews,
To offer sacrifice of Bridewells,
Like modern Indians to their idols;
And mongrel Christians of our times,
That expiate less with greater crimes,
And call the foul abomination
Contrition and mortification.

Is't not enough we're bruis'd and kicked
With sinful members of the Wicked;
Our vessels, that are sanctify'd,
Profan'd and curry'd back and side;
But we must claw ourselves with shameful
And Heathen stripes, by their example?
Which (were there nothing to forbid it)
Is impious, because they did it.
This, therefore, may be justly reckon'd
A heinous sin. Now to the second:
That saints may claim a dispensation
To swear and forswear on occasion,
I doubt not but it will appear
With pregnant light; the point is clear.
Oaths are but words, and words but wind;
Too feeble implements to bind;
And hold with deeds proportion, so
As shadows to a substance do.
Then when they strive for place, 'tis fit
The weaker vessel should submit.
Although your Church be opposite
To ours as Blackfriars are to White,
In rule and order, yet I grant
You are a Reformado saint;
And what the saints do claim as due,
You may pretend a title to.
But Saints, whom oaths and vows oblige,
Know little of their privilege;
Further (I mean) than carrying on
Some self-advantage of their own.

For if the devil, to serve his turn,
Can tell truth, why the saints should scorn,
When it serves theirs, to swear and lie,
I think there's little reason why:
Else he 'as a greater power than they
Which 'twere impiety to say.
We're not commanded to forbear,
Indefinitely, at all to swear;
But to swear idly, and in vain,
Without self-interest or gain.
For breaking of an oath, and lying,
Is but a kind of self-denying,
A saint-like virtue; and from hence
Some have broke oaths by Providence:
Some, to the Glory of the Lord,
Perjur'd themselves, and broke their word;
And this the constant rule and practice
Of all our late apostles' acts is.
Was not the cause at first begun
With perjury, and carried on?

V. 136. When it was first moved in the House of Commons to proceed capitally against the King, Cromwell stood up and told them, "That if any man moved this with design, he should think him the greatest traitor in the world; but since Providence and necessity had cast them upon it, he should pray to God to bless their counsels." And when he kept the King close prisoner in Carisbrook Castle, contrary to vows and protestations, he affirmed "The Spirit would not let him keep his word." And when, contrary to the public faith, they murdered him, they pretended they could not resist the motions of the Spirit.

Was there an oath the Godly took,
But in due time and place they broke?
Did we not bring our oaths in first,
Before our plate, to have them burst,
And cast in fitter models for
The present use of Church and War?
Did not our Worthies of the House,
Before they broke the peace, break vows?
For, having freed us first from both
Th' Allegiance and Suprem'cy oath,
Did they not next compel the nation
To take, and break the Protestation?
To swear, and after to recant,
The Solemn League and Covenant?
To take th' Engagement, and disclaim it;
Enforc'd by those who first did frame it?
Did they not swear, at first, to fight
For the King's safety, and his right;
And after march'd to find him out,
And charg'd him home with horse and foot;
But yet still had the confidence
To swear it was in his defence?
Did they not swear to live and die
With Essex, and straight laid him by?
If that were all, for some have swore
As false as they, if they did no more.
Did they not swear to maintain Law,
In which that swearing made a flaw?
For Protestant religion vow,
That did that vowing disallow?

For Privilege of Parliament,
In which that swearing made a rent ?
And since, of all the three, not one
Is left in being, 'tis well known.
Did they not swear, in express words,
To prop and back the House of Lords ;
And after turn'd out the whole houseful
Of Peers, as dang'rous and unuseful ?
So Cromwell, with deep oaths and vows,
Swore all the Commons out o' th' House ;
Vow'd that the Redcoats would disband,
Ay, marry would they, at their command ;
And troll'd them on, and swore, and swore,
Till th' Army turn'd them out of door.
This tells us plainly what they thought,
That oaths and swearing go for nought,
And that by them th' were only meant
To serve for an expedient.
What was the Public Faith found out for,
But to slur men of what they fought for?
The Public Faith, which ev'ry one
Is bound t' observe, yet kept by none;
And if that go for nothing, why
Should Private Faith have such a tie?
Oaths were not purpos'd, more than law,
To keep the Good and Just in awe,
But to confine the Bad and Sinful,
Like mortal cattle in a pinfold.
A Saint 's of th' heav'nly realm a Peer;
And as no Peer is bound to swear,

But on the Gospel of his Honour,
Of which he may dispose, as owner,
It follows, though the thing be forg'ry
And false, t' affirm it is no perj'ry,
But a mere ceremony, and a breach
Of nothing but a form of speech,
And goes for no more when 'tis took
Than mere saluting of the Book.
Suppose the Scriptures are of force,
They're but commissions of course;
And Saints have freedom to digress,
And vary from 'em, as they please;
Or misinterpret them by private
Instructions, to all aims they drive at.
Then why should we ourselves abridge,
And curtail our own privilege?
Quakers (that, like to lanterns, bear
Their light within 'em) will not swear;
Their Gospel is an Accidence,
By which they construe Conscience,
And hold no sin so deeply red,
As that of breaking Priscian's head
(The head and founder of their order,
That stirring hats held worse than murder).
These, thinking they're obliged to troth
In swearing, will not take an oath:
Like mules, who if they've not their will
To keep their own pace stand stock still:
But they are weak, and little know
What free-born Consciences may do.

'Tis the temptation of the devil
That makes all human actions evil:
For Saints may do the same things by
The Spirit, in sincerity,
Which other men are tempted to,
And at the devil's instance do;
And yet the actions be contrary,
Just as the Saints and Wicked vary.
For, as on land there is no beast
But in some fish at sea 's exprest,
So in the Wicked there's no vice
Of which the Saints have not a spice;
And yet that thing that's pious in
The one, in th' other is a sin.
Is't not ridiculous and nonsense
A saint should be a slave to Conscience;
That ought to be above such fancies,
As far as above Ordinances?
She's of the wicked, as I guess
B' her looks, her language, and her dress:
And though like constables we search
For false wares one another's Church;
Yet all of us hold this for true,
No faith is to the Wicked due.
For truth is precious and divine;
Too rich a pearl for carnal swine.
  Quoth Hudibras, All this is true:
Yet 'tis not fit that all men knew
Those mysteries and revelations;
And therefore topical evasions

Of subtle turns and shifts of sense,
Serve best with th' Wicked for pretence:
Such as the learned Jesuits use,
And Presbyterians, for excuse
Against the Protestants, when th' happen
To find their Churches taken napping.
As thus: A breach of Oath is duple,
And either way admits a scruple,
And may be *ex parte* of the maker
More criminal, than the injur'd taker;
For he that strains too far a vow
Will break it, like an o'erbent bow:
And he that made, and forc'd it, broke it;
Not he that for Convenience took it.
A broken oath is, *quatenus* oath,
As sound t' all purposes of troth;
As broken laws are ne'er the worse.
Nay, till they're broken have no force.
What's justice to a man, or laws,
That never comes within their claws?
They have no pow'r but to admonish;
Cannot control, coerce, or punish,
Until they're broken, and then touch
Those only that do make 'em such.
Beside, no engagement is allow'd
By men in prison made for good;
For when they're set at liberty
They're from th' engagement too set free.
The Rabbins write, When any Jew
Did make to God or man a vow

Which afterwards he found untoward
And stubborn to be kept, or too hard,
Any three other Jews o' th' nation
Might free him from the obligation:
And have not two Saints pow'r to use
A greater privilege than three Jews?
The court of Conscience, which in man
Should be supreme and soveran,
Is 't fit should be subordinate
To ev'ry petty court i' th' state,
And have less power than the lesser,
To deal with perjury at pleasure?
Have its proceedings disallow'd, or
Allow'd, at fancy of pie-powder?
Tell all it does, or does not know,
For swearing *ex officio*?
Be forc'd t' impeach a broken hedge,
And pigs unring'd, at *vis. franc.* pledge?
Discover thieves, and bawds, recusants,
Priests, witches, eaves-droppers, and nuisance?
Tell who did play at games unlawful,
And who fill'd pots of ale but half-full?
And have no pow'r at all, nor shift,
To help itself at a dead lift?
Why should not Conscience have vacation
As well as other Courts o' th' nation;
Have equal power to adjourn,
Appoint appearance and return;
And make as nice distinction serve
To split a case, as those that carve,

Invoking cuckolds' names, hit joints?
Why should not tricks as slight do points?
Is not th' High-court of Justice sworn
To just that law that serves their turn?
Make their own jealousies high treason,
And fix 'em whomsoe'er they please on?
Cannot the learned Counsel there
Make laws in any shape appear?
Mould 'em as witches do their clay,
When they make pictures to destroy;
And vex 'em into any form
That fits their purpose to do harm?
Rack 'em until they do confess,
Impeach of treason whom they please,
And most perfidiously condemn
Those that engage their lives for them;
And yet do nothing in their own sense,
But what they ought by Oath and Conscience?
Can they not juggle, and with slight
Conveyance play with wrong and right;
And sell their blasts of wind as dear,
As Lapland witches bottled air?
Will not Fear, Favour, Bribe, and Grudge,
The same case sev'ral ways adjudge;
As seamen with the self-same gale,
Will several diff'rent courses sail?
As when the sea breaks o'er its bounds,
And overflows the level grounds,

V. 345. Var. 'Grutch.'

Those banks and dams, that, like a screen,
Did keep it out, now keep it in;
So, when tyrannical usurpation
Invades the freedom of a nation,
The laws o' th' land, that were intended
To keep it out, are made defend it.
Does not in Chanc'ry ev'ry man swear
What makes best for him in his answer?
Is not the winding up witnesses,
And nicking, more than half the bus'ness?
For witnesses, like watches, go
Just as they're set, too fast or slow;
And, where in Conscience they're strait-lac'd,
'Tis ten to one that side is cast.
Do not your Juries give their verdict
As if they felt the cause, not heard it?
And, as they please, make matter o' fact
Run all on one side as they're packt?
Nature has made man's breast no windores,
To publish what he does within dores;
Nor what dark secrets there inhabit,
Unless his own rash folly blab it.
If Oaths can do a man no good
In his own bus'ness, why they should,
In other matters, do him hurt;
I think there's little reason for 't.
He that imposes an Oath, makes it;
Not he that for Convenience takes it:

V. 353. Var. 'tyrannic.'

Then how can any man be said
To break an oath he never made?
These reasons may perhaps look oddly
To th' Wicked, though they evince the Godly;
But if they will not serve to clear
My Honour, I am ne'er the near.
Honour is like that glassy bubble
That finds philosophers such trouble,
Whose least part crackt, the whole does fly,
And wits are crackt to find out why.
  Quoth Ralpho, Honour's but a word
To swear by only in a Lord:
In other men 'tis but a huff
To vapour with, instead of proof;
That, like a wen, looks big and swells,
Is senseless, and just nothing else.
Let it (quoth he) be what it will,
It has the world's opinion still.
But as men are not wise that run
The slightest hazard they may shun,
There may a medium be found out
To clear to all the world the doubt;
And that is, if a man may do 't,
By proxy whipt, or substitute.
  Though nice and dark the point appear
(Quoth Ralph), it may hold up and clear.
That Sinners may supply the place
Of suff'ring Saints, is a plain case.
Justice gives sentence many times
On one man for another's crimes.

Our Brethren of New England use
Choice Malefactors to excuse,
And hang the Guiltless in their stead,
Of whom the churches have less need;
As lately 't happen'd: In a town
There liv'd a Cobbler, and but one,
That out of Doctrine could cut Use,
And mend men's lives as well as shoes.
This precious Brother having slain
In times of peace an Indian,
Not out of malice, but mere zeal
(Because he was an Infidel),
The mighty Tottipottymoy
Sent to our Elders an Envoy,
Complaining sorely of the breach
Of league, held forth by Brother Patch,
Against the articles in force
Between both Churches, his and ours;
For which he crav'd the Saints to render
Into his hands, or hang, th' offender.
But they, maturely having weigh'd
They had no more but him o' th' trade
(A man that serv'd them in a double
Capacity, to teach and cobble),
Resolv'd to spare him; yet, to do
The Indian Hoghan Moghan too
Impartial justice, in his stead did
Hang an old Weaver that was bed-rid.
Then wherefore may not you be skipp'd,
And in your room another whipp'd?

For all philosophers, but the Sceptic,
Hold whipping may be sympathetic.
  It is enough, quoth Hudibras,
Thou hast resolv'd and clear'd the case;
And canst, in Conscience, not refuse
From thy own Doctrine to raise Use:
I know thou wilt not (for my sake)
Be tender-conscienc'd of thy back:
Then strip thee of thy carnal jerkin,
And give thy outward-fellow a ferking;
For when thy vessel is new hoop'd,
All leaks of sinning will be stopp'd.
  Quoth Ralpho, You mistake the matter;
For in all scruples of this nature
No man includes himself, nor turns
The point upon his own concerns.
As no man of his own self catches
The itch or amorous French aches;
So no man does himself convince,
By his own doctrine, of his sins:
And though all cry down self, none means
His own self in a literal sense.
Besides, it is not only foppish,
But vile, idolatrous, and Popish,
For one man out of his own skin
To firk and whip another's sin;
As pedants out of schoolboys' breeches
Do claw and curry their own itches.
But in this case it is profane,
And sinful too, because in vain;

For we must take our oaths upon it
You did the deed, when I have done it.
  Quoth Hudibras, That's answer'd soon;
Give us the whip, we'll lay it on.
  Quoth Ralpho, That we may swear true,
'Twere properer that I whipp'd you;
For when with your consent 'tis done,
The act is really your own.
  Quoth Hudibras, It is in vain
(I see) to argue 'gainst the grain;
Or, like the stars, incline men to
What they 're averse themselves to do:
For when disputes are weary'd out,
'Tis int'rest still resolves the doubt.
But since no reason can confute ye,
I'll try to force you to your duty;
For so it is, howe'er you mince it,
As, ere we part, I shall evince it;
And curry (if you stand out), whether
You will or no, your stubborn leather.
Canst thou refuse to bear thy part
I' th' public Work, base as thou art?
To higgle thus for a few blows,
To gain thy Knight an op'lent spouse,
Whose wealth his bowels yearn to purchase
Merely for th' int'rest of the Churches?
And when he has it in his claws
Will not be hide-bound to the Cause;
Nor shalt thou find him a curmudgin
If thou dispatch it without grudging:

If not, resolve, before we go,
That you and I must pull a crow.
Y' had best (quoth Ralpho), as the Ancients
Say wisely, Have a care o' th' main chance,
And Look before you ere you leap;
For As you sow, y' are like to reap:
And were y' as good as George-a-Green,
I should make bold to turn agen;
Nor am I doubtful of the issue
In a just quarrel, and mine is so.
Is 't fitting for a man of honour
To whip the Saints, like Bishop Bonner?
A Knight t' usurp the Beadle's office,
For which y' are like to raise brave trophies?
But I advise you (not for fear,
But for your own sake) to forbear;
And for the Churches, which may chance
From hence to spring a variance,
And raise among themselves new scruples,
Whom common danger hardly couples.
Remember how in arms and politics
We still have worsted all your holy tricks;
Trepann'd your party with intrigue,
And took your Grandees down a peg;
New-modell'd th' army, and cashier'd
All that to Legion Smec adher'd;
Made a mere utensil o' your Church,
And after left it in the lurch,
A scaffold to build up our own,
And when w' had done with 't pull'd it down;

Capoch'd your Rabbins of the Synod,
And snapp'd their Canons with a Why-not
(Grave Synod-men, that were rever'd
For solid face and depth of beard);
Their Classic model prov'd a maggot,
Their Direct'ry an Indian pagod;
And drown'd their Discipline like a kitten,
On which th' had been so long a-sitting;
Decry'd it as a holy cheat
Grown out of date and obsolete,
And all the Saints of the first grass
As castling foals of Balaam's ass.
  At this the Knight grew high in chafe,
And, staring furiously on Ralph,
He trembled and look'd pale with ire,
Like ashes first, then red as fire.
Have I (quoth he) been ta'en in fight,
And for so many moons lain by 't,
And when all other means did fail
Have been exchang'd for tubs of ale
(Not but they thought me worth a ransom
Much more consid'rable and handsome,
But for their own sakes, and for fear
They were not safe when I was there),
Now to be baffled by a scoundrel,
An upstart Sect'ry and a Mongrel,
Such as breed out of peccant humours
Of our own Church, like wens or tumours,

V. 529. Var. 'O'er-reach'd.' 'Capoch'd' signifies hooded, or blindfolded.

And, like a maggot in a sore,
Would that which gave it life devour?
It never shall be done or said.
With that he seiz'd upon his blade;
And Ralpho too, as quick and bold,
Upon his basket-hilt laid hold
With equal readiness, prepar'd
To draw and stand upon his guard:
When both were parted on the sudden
With hideous clamour and a loud one,
As if all sorts of noise had been
Contracted into one loud din;
Or that some member to be chosen
Had got the odds above a thousand,
And by the greatness of his noise
Prov'd fittest for his country's choice.
This strange surprisal put the Knight
And wrathful Squire into a fright;
And though they stood prepar'd, with fatal
Impetuous rancour, to join battle,
Both thought it was the wisest course
To wave the fight and mount to horse,
And to secure by swift retreating
Themselves from danger of worse beating:
Yet neither of them would disparage,
By utt'ring of his mind, his courage,
Which made them stoutly keep their ground,
With horror and disdain wind-bound.
And now the cause of all their fear
By slow degrees approach'd so near

They might distinguish diff'rent noise
Of horns, and pans, and dogs, and boys,
And kettle-drums, whose sullen dub
Sounds like the hooping of a tub.
But when the sight appear'd in view,
They found it was an antique shew;
A triumph that for pomp and state
Did proudest Roman's emulate.
For as the Aldermen of Rome,
Their foes at training overcome
(And not enlarging territory,
As some mistaken write in story),
Being mounted in their best array
Upon a car — and who but they? —
And follow'd with a world of tall lads
That merry ditties troll'd and ballads,
Did ride with many a Good-morrow,
Crying, Hey for our town! through the Borough;
So when this triumph drew so nigh
They might particulars descry,
They never saw two things so pat
In all respects as this and that.
First, he that led the cavalcate
Wore a sow-gelder's flagellate,
On which he blew so strong a levet
As well-feed lawyer on his brev'ate
When over one another's heads

V. 587. Var. 'They might discern respective noise.'
V. 596. Var. 'For foes.'
V. 609, 610. Var. 'cavalcade,' 'flagellet.'

They charge (three ranks at once) like Sweads.
Next pans and kettles of all keys,
From trebles down to double base;
And after them, upon a nag
That might pass for a forehand stag,
A cornet rode, and on his staff
A smock display'd did proudly wave:
Then bagpipes of the loudest drones
With snuffling broken-winded tones,
Whose blasts of air, in pockets shut,
Sound filthier than from the gut,
And make a viler noise than swine
In windy weather when they whine.
Next one upon a pair of panniers,
Full fraught with that which for good manners
Shall here be nameless, mix'd with grains,
Which he dispens'd among the swains,
And busily upon the crowd
At random round about bestow'd.
Then, mounted on a horned horse,
One bore a gauntlet and gilt spurs,
Ty'd to the pummel of a long sword
He held revers'd, the point turn'd downward.
Next after, on a raw-bon'd steed,
The conqu'ror's Standard-bearer rid,
And bore aloft before the champion
A petticoat display'd, and rampant;
Near whom the Amazon triumphant

V. 614. Var. 'Swedes.'

Bestrid her beast, and on the rump on't
Sat, face to tail and bum to bum,
The warrior whilom overcome,
Arm'd with a spindle and a distaff,
Which as he rode she made him twist off;
And when he loiter'd, o'er her shoulder
Chastis'd the reformado soldier.
Before the Dame and round about
March'd whifflers and Staffiers on foot,
With lacquies, grooms, valets, and pages,
In fit and proper equipages;
Of whom some torches bore, some links,
Before the proud virago minx,
That was both Madam and a Don,
Like Nero's Sporus or Pope Joan;
And at fit periods the whole rout
Set up their throats with clam'rous shout.
The Knight transported, and the Squire,
Put up their weapons and their ire;
And Hudibras, who us'd to ponder
On such sights with judicious wonder,
Could hold no longer to impart
His an'madversions, for his heart.
Quoth he, In all my life till now
I ne'er saw so profane a show:
It is a Paganish invention
Which Heathen writers often mention;
And he who made it had read Goodwin,
Or Ross, or Cælius Rhodogine,
With all the Grecian Speeds and Stows

That best describe those ancient shows,
And has observ'd all fit decorums
We find describ'd by old historians.
For as the Roman conqueror
That put an end to foreign war,
Ent'ring the town in triumph for it,
Bore a slave with him in his chariot;
So this insulting female brave
Carries behind her here a slave:
And as the Ancients long ago,
When they in field defy'd the foe,
Hung out their mantles *della guerre*,
So her proud Standard-bearer here
Waves on his spear, in dreadful manner,
A Tyrian petticoat for banner.
Next links and torches, heretofore
Still borne before the emperor:
And, as in antique triumph eggs
Were borne for mystical intrigues,
There 's one in truncheon, like a ladle,
That carries eggs too, fresh or addle;
And still at random as he goes
Among the rabble-rout bestows.
  Quoth Ralpho, You mistake the matter;
For all th' antiquity you smatter
Is but a riding us'd of course
When The grey mare 's the better horse;
When o'er the breeches greedy women
Fight to extend their vast dominion,
And in the cause impatient Grizel

Has drubb'd her husband with bull's pizzle,
And brought him under Covert-baron,
To turn her vassal with a murrain;
When wives their sexes shift, like hares,
And ride their husbands, like night-mares,
And they in mortal battle vanquish'd
Are of their charter disenfranchis'd,
And by the right of war, like gills,
Condemn'd to distaff, horns, and wheels:
For when men by their wives are cow'd,
Their horns of course are understood.
Quoth Hudibras, Thou still giv'st sentence
Impertinently, and against sense:
'Tis not the least disparagement
To be defeated by th' event,
Nor to be beaten by main force;
That does not make a man the worse,
Although his shoulders with battoon
Be claw'd and cudgel'd to some tune.
A tailor's prentice has no hard
Measure that 's bang'd with a true yard;
But to turn tail or run away,
And without blows give up the day,
Or to surrender ere th' assault,
That 's no man's fortune, but his fault;
And renders men of honour less
Than all th' adversity of success:
And only unto such this shew
Of horns and petticoats is due.
There is a lesser profanation,

Like that the Romans call'd Ovation:
For as ovation was allow'd
For conquest purchas'd without blood
So men decree those lesser shows
For vict'ry gotten without blows,
By dint of sharp hard words, which some
Give battle with and overcome:
These mounted in a chair-curule,
Which Moderns call a Cuckling-stool,
March proudly to the river side,
And o'er the waves in triumph ride;
Like dukes of Venice, who are said
The Adriatic sea to wed,
And have a gentler wife than those
For whom the state decrees those shows.
But both are Heathenish, and come
From th' Whores of Babylon and Rome,
And by the Saints should be withstood,
As antichristian and lewd;
And we as such should now contribute
Our utmost strugglings to prohibit.
 This said, they both advanc'd, and rode
A dog-trot through the bawling crowd
T' attack the leader, and still prest
Till they approach'd him breast to breast.
Then Hudibras with face and hand
Made signs for silence; which obtain'd:
What means (quoth he) this devil's procession
With men of orthodox profession?
'Tis ethnique and idolatrous,

From Heathenism deriv'd to us.
Does not the Whore of Bab'lon ride
Upon her horned Beast astride
Like this proud Dame, who either is
A type of her, or she of this?
Are things of superstitious function
Fit to be us'd in Gospel sunshine?
It is an antichristian opera,
Much us'd in midnight times of Popery;
Of running after self-inventions
Of wicked and profane intentions;
To scandalize that sex for scolding,
To whom the Saints are so beholden.
Women, who were our first apostles,
Without whose aid we 'ad all been lost else;
Women, that left no stone unturn'd
In which the Cause might be concern'd;
Brought in their children's spoons and whistles
To purchase swords, carbines, and pistols;
Their husbands' cullies and sweethearts,
To take the Saints' and Churches' parts;
Drew several Gifted Brethren in,

V. 775. The women were zealous contributors to the Good Cause, as they called it. Mr. James Howel observes, "That unusual voluntary collections were made both in town and country; the seamstress brought in her silver thimble, the chambermaid her bodkin, the cook her silver spoon, into the common treasury of war. — And some sort of females were freer in their contributions, so far as to part with their rings and earrings, as if some golden calf were to be molten and set up to be idolized."

That for the Bishops would have been,
And fix'd 'em constant to the party
With motives powerful and hearty;
Their husbands robb'd, and made hard shifts
T' administer unto their Gifts
All they could rap, and rend, and pilfer,
To scraps and ends of gold and silver;
Rubb'd down the Teachers, tir'd and spent
With holding forth for Parl'ament;
Pamper'd and edify'd their zeal
With marrow puddings many a meal;
Enabled them, with store of meat,
On controverted points to eat;
And cramm'd 'em till their guts did ake
With caudle, custard, and plum-cake.
What have they done or what left undone
That might advance the Cause at London?
March'd rank and file with drum and ensign,
T' intrench the City for defence in;
Rais'd rampiers with their own soft hands,
To put the Enemy to stands:
From ladies down to oyster wenches
Labour'd like pioneers in trenches,
Fall'n to their pickaxes and tools,
And help'd the men to dig like moles.
Have not the handmaids of the City
Chose of their Members a Committee,
For raising of a common purse,

V. 807. Var. 'Fell.'

Out of their wages, to raise horse?
And do they not as triers sit,
To judge what officers are fit?
Have they — At that an egg let fly
Hit him directly o'er the eye,
And, running down his cheek, besmear'd
With orange-tawny slime his beard;
But beard and slime being of one hue,
The wound the less appear'd in view.
Then he that on the panniers rode
Let fly on th' other side a load,
And, quickly charg'd again, gave fully
In Ralpho's face another volley.
The Knight was startled with the smell,
And for his sword began to feel;
And Ralpho, smother'd with the stink,
Grasp'd his, when one that bore a link
O' th' sudden clapp'd his flaming cudgel,
Like linstock, to the horse's touch-hole;
And straight another with his flambeau
Gave Ralpho o'er the eyes a damn'd blow.
The beasts began to kick and fling,
And forc'd the rout to make a ring;

V. 813, 814. "The House considered, in the next place, that divers weak persons have crept into places beyond their abilities; and, to the end that men of greater parts may be put into their rooms, they appointed the Lady Middlesex, Mrs. Dunch, the Lady Foster, and the Lady Anne Waller, by reason of their great experience in soldiery in the kingdom, to be a Committee of Triers for the business." See "The Parliament of Ladies," p. 6.

Through which they quickly broke their way,
And brought them off from further fray.
And though disorder'd in retreat,
Each of them stoutly kept his seat:
For quitting bòth their swords and reins,
They grasp'd with all their strength the manes,
And, to avoid the foe's pursuit,
With spurring put their cattle to 't;
And till all four were out of wind,
And danger too, ne'er look'd behind.
After they 'ad paus'd awhile, supplying
Their spirits spent with fight and flying,
And Hudibras recruited force
Of lungs for action or discourse:
  Quoth he, That man is sure to lose
That fouls his hands with dirty foes:
For where no honour 's to be gain'd,
'Tis thrown away in being maintain'd.
'Twas ill for us we had to do
With so dishon'rable a foe:
For though the law of arms doth bar
The use of venom'd shot in war,
Yet by the nauseous smell and noisom
Their case-shot savour strong of poison,
And doubtless have been chew'd with teeth
Of some that had a stinking breath;
Else when we put it to the push,
They had not giv'n us such a brush.

V. 839. Var. 'Rains.'

But as those pultroons that fling dirt
Do but defile, but cannot hurt;
So all the honour they have won,
Or we have lost, is much at one.
'Twas well we made so resolute
A brave retreat without pursuit,
For if we had not, we had sped
Much worse, to be in triumph led;
Than which the ancients held no state
Of man's life more unfortunate.
But if this bold adventure e'er
Do chance to reach the widow's ear,
It may, being destin'd to assert
Her sex's honour, reach her heart:
And as such homely treats (they say)
Portend good fortune, so this may.
Vespasian being daub'd with dirt
Was destin'd to the empire for 't;
And from a scavenger did come
To be a mighty prince in Rome:
And why may not this foul address
Presage in love the same success?
Then let us straight, to cleanse our wounds,
Advance in quest of nearest ponds;
And after (as we first design'd)
Swear I've perform'd what she enjoin'd.

V. 868. Var. 'T' avoid pursuit.'

PART II. CANTO III.

THE ARGUMENT.

The Knight, with various doubts possest,
To win the Lady goes in quest
Of Sidrophel the Rosycrucian,
To know the Dest'nies' resolution:
With whom b'ing met, they both chop logic
About the science astrologic;
Till, falling from dispute to fight,
The Conj'rer's worsted by the Knight.

DOUBTLESS the pleasure is as great
Of being cheated, as to cheat;
As lookers-on feel most delight
That least perceive a juggler's sleight,
And still, the less they understand,
The more they' admire his sleight of hand,
Some with a noise and greasy light
Are snapt, as men catch larks by night,
Ensnar'd and hamper'd by the soul,
As nooses by the legs catch fowl.
Some with a med'cine and receipt
Are drawn to nibble at the bait;
And though it be a two-foot trout,
'Tis with a single hair pull'd out.
Others believe no voice t' an organ
So sweet as lawyer's in his bar-gown,

Until with subtle cobweb-cheats
They're catch'd in knotted law like nets;
In which, when once they are imbrangled,
The more they stir the more they're tangled;
And while their purses can dispute,
There's no end of th' immortal suit.
  Others still gape t' anticipate
The cabinet-designs of Fate,
Apply to wizards to foresee
What shall and what shall never be;
And, as those vultures do forebode,
Believe events prove bad or good:
A flam more senseless than the roguery
Of old auruspicy and aug'ry,
That out of garbages of cattle
Presag'd th' events of truce or battle;
From flight of birds, or chickens' pecking,
Success of great'st attempts would reckon:
Though cheats, yet more intelligible
Than those that with the stars do fribble.
This Hudibras by proof found true,
As in due time and place we'll shew:
For he, with beard and face made clean,
Being mounted on his steed agen,
(And Ralpho got a-cock-horse too
Upon his beast, with much ado),
Advanc'd on for the Widow's house,
T' acquit himself and pay his vows:

V. 25. Var. 'Run after wizards.'

When various thoughts began to bustle,
And with his inward man to justle.
He thought what danger might accrue,
If she should find he swore untrue;
Or if his Squire or he should fail,
And not be punctual in their tale,
It might at once the ruin prove
Both of his honour, faith, and love.
But if he should forbear to go,
She might conclude he 'ad broke his vow;
And that he durst not now for shame
Appear in court to try his claim:
This was the penn'worth of his thought,
To pass time, and uneasy trot.
  Quoth he, In all my past adventures
I ne'er was set so on the tenters,
Or taken tardy with dilemma
That ev'ry way I turn does hem me,
And with inextricable doubt
Besets my puzzled wits about:
For though the Dame has been my bail,
To free me from enchanted jail,
Yet as a dog, committed close
For some offence, by chance breaks loose,
And quits his clog; but all in vain,
He still draws after him his chain:
So, though my ankle she has quitted,
My heart continues still committed;
And, like a bail'd and mainpriz'd lover,
Although at large, I am bound over;

And when I shall appear in court
To plead my cause and answer for 't,
Unless the judge do partial prove,
What will become of me and love?
For, if in our account we vary,
Or but in circumstance miscarry;
Or if she put me to strict proof,
And make me pull my doublet off
To shew, by evident record
Writ on my skin, I've kept my word,
How can I e'er expect to have her,
Having demurr'd unto her favour?
But, faith and love and honour lost,
Shall be reduc'd t' a Knight o' th' Post?
Beside, that stripping may prevent
What I'm to prove by argument,
And justify I have a tail,
And that way too my proof may fail.
Oh, that I could enucleate,
And solve the problems of my fate!
Or find by necromantic art
How far the Dest'nies take my part!
For if I were not more than certain
To win and wear her and her fortune,
I'd go no farther in this courtship,
To hazard soul, estate, and Worship:
For though an oath obliges not
Where any thing is to be got
(As thou hast prov'd), yet 'tis profane
And sinful when men swear in vain.

Quoth Ralph, Not far from hence doth dwell
A cunning man, hight Sidrophel,
That deals in Destiny's dark counsels,
And sage opinions of the Moon sells;
To whom all people, far and near,
On deep importances repair:
When brass and pewter hap to stray,
And linen slinks out o' the way;
When geese and pullen are seduc'd,
And sows of sucking pigs are chous'd;
When cattle feel indisposition,
And need th' opinion of physician;
When murrain reigns in hogs or sheep,
And chickens languish of the pip;
When yest and outward means do fail,
And have no pow'r to work on ale;
When butter does refuse to come,
And love proves cross and humoursome;
To him with questions, and with urine,
They for discov'ry flock, or curing.
Quoth Hudibras, This Sidrophel
I've heard of, and should like it well,
If thou canst prove the Saints have freedom
To go to sorc'rers when they need 'em.
Says Ralpho, There 's no doubt of that;
Those principles I quoted late

V. 106. William Lilly, the famous astrologer of those times, who in his yearly almanacks foretold victories for the Parliament with as much certainty as the preachers did in their sermons.

Prove that the Godly may allege
For any thing their privilege,
And to the dev'l himself may go
If they have motives thereunto:
For, as there is a war between
The dev'l and them, it is no sin
If they by subtle stratagem
Make use of him, as he does them.
Has not this present Parl'ament
A ledger to the devil sent,
Fully empower'd to treat about
Finding revolted witches out?
And has not he, within a year,
Hang'd threescore of 'em in one shire?
Some only for not being drown'd,
And some for sitting above ground,
Whole days and nights, upon their breeches,
Not feeling pain, were hang'd for witches;
And some for putting knavish tricks
Upon green geese and turkey-chicks,
Or pigs that suddenly deceast
Of griefs unnat'ral, as he guest;
Who after prov'd himself a witch,
And made a rod for his own breech.
Did not the dev'l appear to Martin
Luther in Germany, for certain?
And would have gull'd him with a trick,
But Mart. was too, too politic.
Did he not help the Dutch to purge,
At Antwerp, their cathedral church?

Sing catches to the Saints at Mascon,
And tell them all they came to ask him?
Appear in divers shapes to Kelly,
And speak i' th' Nun of Loudon's belly?
Meet with the Parl'ament's Committee,
At Woodstock, on a pers'nal treaty?
At Sarum take a cavalier,
I' th' Cause's service, prisoner?
As Withers in immortal rhyme
Has register'd to aftertime.
Do not our great Reformers use
This Sidrophel to forebode news;
To write of victories next year,
And castles taken, yet i' th' air?
Of battles fought at sea, and ships
Sunk two years hence the last eclipse?
A total o'erthrow giv'n the King
In Cornwall, horse and foot, next Spring?
And has not he point-blank foretold
Whats'e'er the Close Committee would?
Made Mars and Saturn for the Cause?
The Moon for fundamental laws?
The Ram, the Bull, and Goat, declare
Against the Book of Common Pray'r?
The Scorpion take the Protestation,
And Bear engage for Reformation?
Made all the Royal stars recant,
Compound, and take the Covenant?

V. 169. This Withers was a Puritanical officer in the Parliament army, and a great pretender to poetry, as appears from his poems enumerated by A. Wood.

Quoth Hudibras, The case is clear.
The Saints may 'mploy a conjurer,
As thou hast prov'd it by their practice
No argument like matter of fact is;
And we are best of all led to
Men's principles by what they do.
Then let us straight advance in quest
Of this profound gymnosophist,
And, as the Fates and he advise,
Pursue or wave this enterprise.
This said, he turn'd about his steed,
And eftsoons on th' adventure rid;
Where leave we him and Ralph awhile,
And to the conj'rer turn our style,
To let our reader understand
What 's useful of him beforehand.
He had been long t'wards mathematics,
Optics, philosophy, and statics,
Magic, horoscopy, astrology,
And was old dog at physiology;
But as a dog that turns the spit
Bestirs himself, and plies his feet
To climb the wheel, but all in vain,
His own weight brings him down again,
And still he 's in the self-same place
Where at his setting out he was;
So in the circle of the arts
Did he advance his nat'ral parts,
Till falling back still, for retreat,
He fell to juggle, cant, and cheat.
For as those fowls that live in water

Are never wet, he did but smatter;
Whate'er he labour'd to appear,
His understanding still was clear;
Yet none a deeper knowledge boasted,
Since old Hodge Bacon, and Bob Grosted.
Th' intelligible world he knew,
And all men dream on 't to be true,
That in this world there 's not a wart
That has not there a counterpart;
Nor can there on the face of ground
An individual beard be found
That has not in that foreign nation
A fellow of the self-same fashion;
So cut, so colour'd, and so curl'd,
As those are in th' inferior world.
He 'ad read Dee's prefaces before
The Dev'l, and Euclid, o'er and o'er;

V. 224. Roger Bacon, commonly called 'Friar Bacon,' lived in the reign of our Edward I., and, for some little skill he had in the mathematics, was by the rabble accounted a conjurer, and had the sottish story of the Brazen Head fathered upon him by the ignorant Monks of those days.

Ib. Bishop Grosted was Bishop of Lincoln, 20th Henry III. A. D. 1235. "He was suspected by the clergy to be a conjurer; for which crime he was deprived by Pope Innocent IV. and summoned to appear at Rome." But this is a mistake; for the Pope's antipathy to him was occasioned by his frankly expostulating with him (both personally and by letter) on his encroachments upon the English church and monarchy. He was persecuted by Pope Innocent, but it is not certain that he was deprived, though Bale thinks he was.

V. 235. Dee was a Welshman, and educated at Oxford,

And all th' intrigues 'twixt him and Kelly,
Lascus and th' Emperor, would tell ye:
But with the moon was more familiar
Than e'er was almanack well-willer;
Her secrets understood so clear,
That some believ'd he had been there;
Knew when she was in fittest mood
For cutting corns or letting blood;
When for anointing scabs or itches,
Or to the bum applying leeches;
When sows and bitches may be spay'd,
And in what sign best cyder 's made;
Whether the wane be, or increase,
Best to set garlic or sow pease;
Who first found out the man i' th' moon,
That to the Ancients was unknown;
How many Dukes, and Earls, and Peers,
Are in the planetary spheres;
Their airy empire, and command;
Their sev'ral strengths by sea and land;
What factions they 've, and what they drive at
In public vogue, or what in private;
With what designs and interests
Each party manages contests.
He made an instrument to know
If the moon shine at full or no;

where he commenced Doctor, and afterwards travelled into foreign parts in quest of chemistry, &c.

V. 238. Albertus Lascus, Lasky, or Alasco, Prince Palatine of Poland, concerned with Dee and Kelly.

That would, as soon as e'er she shone, straight
Whether 'twere day or night demonstrate;
Tell what her d'ameter to an inch is,
And prove that she 's not made of greeen cheese.
It would demonstrate that the man in
The moon 's a sea Mediterranean;
And that it is no dog nor bitch
That stands behind him at his breech,
But a huge Caspian sea or lake,
With arms, which men for legs mistake;
How large a gulf his tail composes,
And what a goodly bay his nose is;
How many German leagues by th' scale
Cape Snout 's from Promontory Tail.
He made a planetary gin,
Which rats would run their own heads in,
And come on purpose to be taken,
Without th' expense of cheese or bacon.
With lutestrings he would counterfeit
Maggots that crawl on dish of meat;
Quote moles and spots on any place
O' th' body, by the index face;
Detect lost maidenheads by sneezing,
Or breaking wind of dames, or pissing;
Cure warts and corns with application
Of med'cines to th' imagination:
Fright agues into dogs, and scare
With rhymes the toothach and catarrh;
Chase evil spirits away by dint
Of sickle, horse-shoe, hollow flint;

Spit fire out of a walnut-shell,
Which made the Roman slaves rebel;
And fire a mine in China here
With sympathetic gunpowder.
He knew whats'ever 's to be known,
But much more than he knew would own.
What med'cine 'twas that Paracelsus
Could make a man with, as he tells us;
What figur'd slates are best to make
On wat'ry surface duck or drake;
What bowling-stones, in running race
Upon a board, have swiftest pace;
Whether a pulse beat in the black
List of a dappled louse's back;
If systole or diastole move
Quickest when he 's in wrath, or love;
When two of them do run a race,
Whether they gallop, trot, or pace;
How many scores a flea will jump
Of his own length from head to rump,
Which Socrates and Chærephon
In vain assay'd so long agone;
Whether his snout a perfect nose is,
And not an elephant's proboscis;
How many diff'rent specieses
Of maggots breed in rotten cheeses;
And which are next of kin to those
Engender'd in a chandler's nose;
Or those not seen, but understood,
That live in vinegar and wood.

A paltry wretch he had, half-starv'd,
That him in place of zany serv'd,
Hight Whachum, bred to dash and draw,
Not wine, but more unwholesome law;
To make 'twixt words and lines huge gaps,
Wide as meridians in maps;
To squander paper and spare ink,
Or cheat men of their words, some think.
From this, by merited degrees,
He 'd to more high advancement rise,
To be an under conjurer,
Or journeyman astrologer:
His bus'ness was to pump and wheedle,
And men with their own keys unriddle;
To make them to themselves give answers,
For which they pay the necromancers;
To fetch and carry' intelligence
Of whom, and what, and where, and whence,
And all discoveries disperse
Among th' whole pack of conjurers;
What cut-purses have left with them
For the right owners to redeem,
And what they dare not vent, find out,
To gain themselves and th' art repute;

V. 325. 'Whachum,' journeyman to Sidrophel, who was one 'Tom Jones,' a foolish Welshman. In a key to a poem of Mr. Butler's, Whachum is said to be one 'Richard Green,' who published a pamphlet of about five sheets of base ribaldry, and called 'Hudibras in a snare.' It was printed about the year 1667.

Draw figures, and schemes, and horoscopes,
Of Newgate, Bridewell, brokers' shops,
Of thieves ascendant in the cart,
And find out all by rules of art:
Which way a serving-man, that's run
With clothes or money away, is gone;
Who pick'd a fob at Holding-forth,
And where a watch for half the worth
May be redeem'd; or stolen plate
Restor'd at conscionable rate.
Beside all this he serv'd his master
In quality of poetaster,
And rhymes appropriate could make
To ev'ry month i' th' almanack;
When terms begin and end could tell,
With their returns, in doggerel;
When the Exchequer opes and shuts,
And sow-gelder with safety cuts;
When men may eat and drink their fill,
And when be temp'rate if they will;
When use, and when abstain from, vice,
Figs, grapes, phlebotomy, and spice.
And as in prison mean rogues beat
Hemp for the service of the great,
So Whachum beat his dirty brains
T' advance his master's fame and gains;
And, like the devil's oracles,
Put into dogg'rel rhymes his spells,
Which, over ev'ry month's blank page
I' th' almanack, strange bilks presage.

He would an elegy compose
On maggots squeez'd out of his nose;
In lyric numbers write an ode on
His mistress eating a black pudden;
And when imprison'd air escap'd her,
It puft him with poetic rapture:
His sonnets charm'd th' attentive crowd,
By wide-mouth'd mortal troll'd aloud,
That, circled with his long-ear'd guests,
Like Orpheus look'd among the beasts:
A carman's horse could not pass by,
But stood ty'd up to poetry;
No porter's burthen pass'd along,
But serv'd for burthen to his song:
Each window like a pill'ry appears,
With heads thrust through, nail'd by the ears;
All trades run in as to the sight
Of monsters, or their dear delight
The gallow-tree, when cutting purse
Breeds bus'ness for heroic verse,
Which none does hear but would have hung
T' have been the theme of such a song.
  Those two together long had liv'd
In mansion prudently contriv'd,
Where neither tree nor house could bar
The free detection of a star;
And nigh an ancient obelisk
Was rais'd by him, found out by Fisk,

V. 404. Mr. Butler alludes to one 'Fisk,' of whom Lilly observes, that he was a licentiate in physic, and born near

On which was written, not in words,
But hieroglyphic mute of birds,
Many rare pithy saws concerning
The worth of astrologic learning:
From top of this there hung a rope,
To which he fasten'd telescope,
The spectacles with which the stars
He reads in smallest characters.
It happen'd as a boy one night
Did fly his tarsel of a kite,
The strangest long-wing'd hawk that flies,
That, like a bird of Paradise,
Or herald's martlet, has no legs,
Nor hatches young ones, nor lays eggs;
His train was six yards long, milk-white,
At th' end of which there hung a light,
Enclos'd in lantern made of paper,
That far off like a star did appear:
This Sidrophel by chance espy'd,
And, with amazement staring wide,
Bless us! quoth he, what dreadful wonder
Is that appears in heaven yonder?
A comet, and without a beard!
Or star that ne'er before appear'd?
I'm certain 'tis not in the scrowl

Framlingham in Suffolk; was bred at a country-school, and designed for the university, but went not thither, studying physic and astrology at home, which afterwards he practised at Colchester; after which he came to London, and practised there.

Of all those beasts, and fish, and fowl,
With which, like Indian plantations,
The learned stock the constellations;
Nor those that drawn for signs have bin
To th' houses where the planets inn.
It must be supernatural,
Unless it be that cannon-ball
That, shot i' th' air point-blank upright,
Was borne to that prodigious height
That learn'd philosophers maintain,
It ne'er came backwards down again,
But in the airy region yet
Hangs, like the body of Mahomet:
For if it be above the shade
That by the earth's round bulk is made,
'Tis probable it may from far
Appear no bullet, but a star.
This said, he to his engine flew,
Plac'd near at hand, in open view,
And rais'd it till it levell'd right
Against the glow-worm tail of kite,
Then peeping through, Bless us! (quoth he)
It is a planet now, I see;
And, if I err not, by his proper
Figure, that 's like tobacco-stopper,
It should be Saturn: yes, 'tis clear
'Tis Saturn, but what makes him there?
He 's got between the Dragon's tail
And farther leg behind o' th' Whale;
Pray Heav'n divert the fatal omen,

For 'tis a prodigy not common,
And can no less than the world's end,
Or Nature's funeral, portend.
With that he fell again to pry
Through perspective more wistfully,
When, by mischance, the fatal string,
That kept the tow'ring fowl on wing,
Breaking, down fell the star. Well shot,
Quoth Whachum, who right wisely thought
He 'ad levell'd at a star, and hit it;
But Sidrophel, more subtil-witted,
Cry'd out, What horrible and fearful
Portent is this, to see a star fall!
It threatens Nature, and the doom
Will not be long before it come!
When stars do fall, 'tis plain enough
The day of judgment 's not far off;
As lately 'twas reveal'd to Sedgwick,
And some of us find out by magic:

V. 477. William Sedgwick, a whimsical enthusiast, sometimes a Presbyterian, sometimes an Independent, and at other times an Anabaptist; sometimes a prophet, and pretended to foretell things, out of the pulpit, to the destruction of ignorant people; at other times pretended to revelations; and, upon pretence of a vision that Doomsday was at hand, he retired to the house of Sir Francis Russel, in Cambridgeshire; and finding several gentlemen at bowls, called upon them to prepare for their dissolution; telling them that he had lately received a revelation that Doomsday would be some day the week following. Upon which they ever after called him 'Doomsday Sedgwick.'

Then since the time we have to live
In this world 's shorten'd, let us strive
To make our best advantage of it,
And pay our losses with our profit.
  This feat fell out not long before
The Knight, upon the forenam'd score,
In quest of Sidrophel advancing,
Was now in prospect of the mansion;
Whom he discov'ring, turn'd his glass,
And found far off 'twas Hudibras.
  Whachum (quoth he), look yonder, some
To try or use our art are come:
The one 's the learned Knight; seek out,
And pump 'em what they come about.
Whachum advanc'd with all submiss'ness
T' accost 'em, but much more their bus'ness:
He held a stirrup, while the Knight
From leathern Bare-bones did alight;
And taking from his hand the bridle,
Approach'd, the dark Squire to unriddle.
He gave him first the time o' the day,
And welcom'd him as he might say:
He ask'd him whence they came, and whither
Their bus'ness lay?—Quoth Ralpho, Hither.—
Did you not lose—Quoth Ralpho, Nay—
Quoth Whachum, Sir, I meant your way.
Your knight—Quoth Ralpho, is a lover,
And pains intol'rable doth suffer;
For lovers' hearts are not their own hearts,
Nor lights, nor lungs, and so forth downwards.—

What time — Quoth Ralpho, Sir, too long;
Three years it off and on has hung. —
Quoth he, I meant what time o' th' day 'tis. —
Quoth Ralpho, Between seven and eight 'tis. —
Why then (quoth Whachum) my small art
Tells me the dame has a hard heart,
Or great estate. — Quoth Ralph, A jointer,
Which makes him have so hot a mind t' her. —
Meanwhile the Knight was making water,
Before he fell upon the matter;
Which having done, the Wizard steps in,
To give him suitable reception;
But kept his bus'ness at a bay,
Till Whachum put him in the way;
Who having now, by Ralpho's light,
Expounded th' errand of the Knight,
And what he came to know, drew near,
To whisper in the conj'rer's ear,
Which he prevented thus: what was 't,
Quoth he, that I was saying last,
Before these gentlemen arriv'd?
Quoth Whachum, Venus you retriev'd,
In opposition with Mars,
And no benign and friendly stars
T' allay the effect. Quoth Wizard, So!
In Virgo? Ha! quoth Whachum, No.
Has Saturn nothing to do in it?
One tenth of 's circle to a minute.
'Tis well, quoth he. — Sir, you'll excuse
This rudeness I am forc'd to use;

It is a scheme and face of heaven,
As th' aspects are dispos'd this even,
I was contemplating upon
When you arriv'd; but now I've done.
  Quoth Hudibras, if I appear
Unseasonable in coming here
At such a time, to interrupt
Your speculations, which I hop'd
Assistance from, and come to use,
'Tis fit that I ask your excuse.
  By no means, Sir, quoth Sidrophel,
The stars your coming did foretell;
I did expect you here, and knew,
Before you spake, your bus'ness too.
  Quoth Hudibras, Make that appear,
And I shall credit whatsoe'er
You tell me after, on your word,
Howe'er unlikely or absurd.
  You are in love, Sir, with a widow,
Quoth he, that does not greatly heed you,
And for three years has rid your wit
And passion without drawing bit;
And now your bus'ness is to know
If you shall carry her or no.
  Quoth Hudibras, You 're in the right,
But how the devil you come by 't
I can't imagine; for the stars
I 'm sure can tell no more than a horse;
Nor can their aspects (though you pore
Your eyes out on them) tell you more

Than th' oracle of sieve and sheers
That turns as certain as the spheres:
But if the devil 's of your counsel
Much may be done, my noble Donzel;
And 'tis on his account I come,
To know from you my fatal doom.
  Quoth Sidrophel, If you suppose,
Sir Knight, that I am one of those,
I might suspect, and take th' alarm,
Your bus'ness is but to inform;
But if it be, 'tis ne'er the near,
You have a wrong sow by the ear;
For I assure you, for my part,
I only deal by rules of art,
Such as are lawful, and judge by
Conclusions of astrology;
But for the devil know nothing by him,
But only this, that I defy him.
  Quoth he, Whatever others deem ye,
I understand your metonymy;
Your words of second-hand intention,
When things by wrongful names you mention;
The mystic sense of all your terms,
That are indeed but magic charms
To raise the devil, and mean one thing,
And that is downright conjuring;
And in itself more warrantable
Than cheat, or canting to a rabble,
Or putting tricks upon the moon,
Which by confed'racy are done.

Your ancient conjurers were wont
To make her from her sphere dismount,
And to their incantations stoop;
They scorn'd to pore through telescope,
Or idly play at bo-peep with her,
To find out cloudy or fair weather,
Which ev'ry almanack can tell
Perhaps as learnedly and well
As you yourself. Then, friend, I doubt
You go the farthest way about.
Your modern Indian magician
Makes but a hole in th' earth to piss in,
And straight resolves all questions by 't,
And seldom fails to be i' th' right.
The Rosycrucian way 's more sure
To bring the devil to the lure;
Each of 'em has a sev'ral gin
To catch intelligences in.
Some by the nose with fumes trepan 'em,
As Dunstan did the devil's grannam;
Others with characters and words
Catch 'em, as men in nets do birds;
And some with symbols, signs, and tricks,
Engrav'd in planetary nicks,
With their own influences will fetch 'em

V. 618. St. Dunstan was made Archbishop of Canterbury anno 961. His skill in the liberal arts and sciences (qualifications much above the genius of the age he lived in) gained him first the name of a Conjurer, and then of a Saint: he is revered as such by the Romanists, who keep a holiday in honour of him yearly, on the 19th of May.

Down from their orbs, arrest, and catch 'em:
Make 'em depose and answer to
All questions ere they let them go.
Bumbastus kept a devil's bird
Shut in the pummel of his sword,
That taught him all the cunning pranks
Of past and future mountebanks.
Kelly did all his feats upon
The devil's looking-glass, a stone,
Where, playing with him at bo-peep,
He solv'd all problems, ne'er so deep.
Agrippa kept a Stygian pug
I' th' garb and habit of a dog,
That was his tutor, and the cur
Read to th' occult philosopher,
And taught him subt'ly to maintain
All other sciences are vain.
  To this quoth Sidrophello, Sir,
Agrippa was no conjurer,

V. 631. This Kelly was chief seer, or, as Lilly calls him, Speculator, to Dr. Dee; was born at Worcester, and bred an apothecary, and was a good proficient in chemistry, and pretended to have the grand elixir, or philosopher's stone, which Lilly tells us he made, or at least received ready made from a Friar in Germany, on the confines of the Emperor's dominions. He pretended to see apparitions in a crystal or beryl looking-glass (or a round stone like a crystal). Alasco, Palatine of Poland; Pucel, a learned Florentine; and Prince Rosemberg of Germany, the Emperor's Viceroy in Bohemia; were long of the society with him and Dr. Dee, and often present at their apparitions, as was once the King of Poland himself. But Lilly observes that he was so wicked that the angels would not appear to him willingly, nor be obedient to him.

Nor Paracelsus, no, nor Behmen;
Nor was the dog a cacodæmon,
But a true dog, that would shew tricks
For th' Emperor, and leap o'er sticks;
Would fetch and carry, was more civil
Than other dogs, but yet no devil;
And whatsoe'er he 's said to do,
He went the self-same way we go.
As for the Rosycross philosophers,
Whom you will have to be but sorcerers,
What they pretend to is no more
Than Trismegistus did before,
Pythagoras, old Zoroaster,
And Apollonius their master,
To whom they do confess they owe
All that they do, and all they know.
Quoth Hudibras, Alas! what is 't t' us
Whether 'twas said by Trismegistus,
If it be nonsense, false, or mystic,
Or not intelligible, or sophistic?
'Tis not antiquity, nor author,
That makes truth Truth, although Time's daughter;
'Twas he that put her in the pit
Before he pull'd her out of it;
And as he eats his sons, just so
He feeds upon his daughters too.
Nor does it follow, 'cause a herald
Can make a gentleman, scarce a year old,

V. 669, 670. Such gentry were Thomas Pury, the elder, first a weaver in Gloucester, then an ignorant solicitor; John

To be descended of a race
Of ancient kings in a small space,
That we should all opinions hold
Authentic that we can make old.
Quoth Sidrophel, it is no part
Of prudence to cry down an art,
And what it may perform deny
Because you understand not why
(As Averrhois play'd but a mean trick
To damn our whole art for eccentric);
For who knows all that knowledge contains?
Men dwell not on the tops of mountains,
But on their sides or rising's seat;
So 'tis with knowledge's vast height.
Do not the hist'ries of all ages
Relate miraculous presages
Of strange turns in the world's affairs
Foreseen b' astrologers, soothsayers,
Chaldeans, learn'd Genethliacks,
And some that have writ almanacks?
The Median Emp'ror dream'd his daughter

Blackston, a poor shopkeeper of Newcastle; John Birch, formerly a carrier, afterwards Colonel; Richard Salway, Colonel, formerly a grocer's man; Thomas Rainsborough, a skipper of Lynn, Colonel and Vice-Admiral of England; Colonel Thomas Scot, a brewer's clerk; Colonel Philip Skippon, originally a waggoner to Sir Francis Vere; Colonel John Jones, a serving-man; Colonel Barkstead, a pitiful thimble and bodkin goldsmith; Colonel Pride, a foundling and drayman; Colonel Hewson, a one-eyed cobbler; and Colonel Harrison, a butcher. These and hundreds more affected to be thought gentlemen, and lorded it over persons of the first rank and quality.

Had piss'd all Asia under water,
And that a vine, sprung from her haunches,
O'erspread his empire with its branches;
And did not soothsayers expound it
As after by th' event he found it?
When Cæsar in the senate fell,
Did not the sun eclips'd foretell,
And in resentment of his slaughter
Look'd pale for almost a year after?
Augustus having, by' oversight,
Put on his left shoe 'fore his right,
Had like to have been slain that day
By soldiers mutin'ing for pay.
Are there not myriads of this sort
Which stories of all times report?
Is it not ominous in all countries
When crows and ravens croak upon trees?
The Roman senate, when within
The city walls an owl was seen,
Did cause their clergy, with lustrations
(Our Synod calls Humiliations),
The round-fac'd prodigy t' avert
From doing town or country hurt.
And if an owl have so much pow'r,
Why should not planets have much more,
That in a region far above
Inferior fowls of the air move,
And should see further, and foreknow
More than their augury below?
Though that once serv'd the polity

Of mighty states to govern by ;
And this is what we take in hand
By pow'rful art to understand;
Which how we have perform'd all ages
Can speak th' events of our presages.
Have we not lately in the moon
Found a new world, to th' old unknown?
Discover'd sea and land Columbus
And Magellan could never compass?
Made mountains with our tubes appear,
And cattle grazing on 'em there?
Quoth Hudibras, You lie so ope
That I, without a telescope
Can find your tricks out, and descry
Where you tell truth and where you lye:
For Anaxagoras, long agon,
Saw hills, as well as you, i' th' moon,
And held the sun was but a piece
Of red-hot ir'n as big as Greece;
Believ'd the heav'ns were made of stone,
Because the sun had voided one;
And, rather than he would recant
Th' opinion, suffer'd banishment.
But what, alas! is it to us
Whether i' th' moon men thus or thus
Do eat their porridge, cut their corns,
Or whether they have tails or horns ?
What trade from thence can you advance
But what we nearer have from France?
What can our travellers bring home

That is not to be learnt at Rome?
What politics or strange opinions
That are not in our own dominions?
What science can be brought from thence
In which we do not here commence?
What revelations or religions
That are not in our native regions?
Are sweating-lanterns or screen-fans
Made better there than th' are in France?
Or do they teach to sing and play
O' th' guitar there a newer way?
Can they make plays there that shall fit
The public humour with less wit;
Write wittier dances, quainter shows,
Or fight with more ingenious blows?
Or does the man i' th' moon look big,
And wear a huger periwig?
Shew in his gate or face more tricks
Than our own native lunatics?
But if w' outdo him here at home,
What good of your design can come?
As wind i' th' hypocondres pent
Is but a blast if downward sent,
But if it upward chance to fly
Becomes new light and prophecy;
So when your speculations tend
Above their just and useful end,
Although they promise strange and great
Discoveries of things far fet,
They are but idle dreams and fancies,

And savour strongly of the ganzas.
Tell me but what 's the natural cause
Why on a sign no painter draws
The full-moon ever, but the half?
Resolve that with your Jacob's staff;
Or why wolves raise a hubbub at her,
And dogs howl when she shines in water?
And I shall freely give my vote
You may know something more remote.
  At this deep Sidrophel look'd wise,
And, staring round with owl-like eyes,
He put his face into a posture
Of sapience, and began to bluster;
For having three times shook his head,
To stir his wit up, thus he said:
Art has no mortal enemies
Next ignorance, but owls and geese;
Those consecrated geese in orders
That to the capitol were warders,
And, being then upon patrol,
With noise alone beat off the Gaul,
Or those Athenian sceptic owls
That will not credit their own souls,
Or any science understand
Beyond the reach of eye or hand,
But, meas'ring all things by their own
Knowledge, hold nothing 's to be known;
Those wholesale critics, that in coffee-
Houses cry down all philosophy,
And will not know upon what ground

In Nature we our doctrine found,
Although with pregnant evidence
We can demonstrate it to sense,
As I just now have done to you,
Foretelling what you came to know.
Were the stars only made to light
Robbers and burglarers by night?
To wait on drunkards, thieves, gold-finders,
And lovers solacing behind doors,
Or giving one another pledges
Of matrimony under hedges?
Or witches simpling, and on gibbets
Cutting from malefactors snippets,
Or from the pill'ry tips of ears
Of rebel saints and perjurers?
Only to stand by and look on,
But not know what is said or done?
Is there a constellation there
That was not born and bred up here,
And therefore cannot be to learn
In any inferior concern?
Were they not, during all their lives,
Most of them pirates, whores, and thieves?
And is it like they have not still
In their old practices some skill?
Is there a planet that by birth
Does not derive its house from earth,
And therefore probably must know
What is and hath been done below?
Who made the Balance, or whence came

The Bull, the Lion, and the Ram?
Did not we here the Argo rig,
Make Berenice's periwig?
Whose liv'ry does the Coachman wear?
Or who made Cassiopeia's chair?
And therefore, as they came from hence,
With us may hold intelligence.
Plato deny'd the world can be
Govern'd without geòmetry
(For money b'ing the common scale
Of things by measure, weight, and tale,
In all th' affairs of church and state
'Tis both the balance and the weight);
Then much less can it be without
Divine astrology made out,
That puts the other down in worth
As far as heaven 's above the earth.
These reasons (quoth the knight) I grant
Are something more significant
Than any that the learned use
Upon this subject to produce;
And yet th' are far from satisfactory
T' establish and keep up your factory.
Th' Egyptians say, the sun has twice
Shifted his setting and his rise;
Twice has he risen in the west,
As many times set in the east:
But whether that be true or no
The devil any of you know.
Some hold the heavens, like a top,

Are kept by circulation up,
And, were 't not for their wheeling round,
They 'd instantly fall to the ground;
As sage Empedocles of old,
And, from him, modern authors hold.
Plato believ'd the sun and moon
Below all other planets run.
Some Mercury, some Venus, seat
Above the sun himself in height.
The learned Scaliger complain'd,
'Gainst what Copèrnicus maintain'd,
That, in twelve hundred years and odd,
The sun had left its ancient road,
And nearer to the earth is come
'Bove fifty thousand miles from home;
Swore 'twas a most notorious flam,
And he that had so little shame
To vent such fopperies abroad
Deserv'd to have his rump well claw'd;
Which Monsieur Bodin hearing, swore
That he deserv'd the rod much more
That durst upon a truth give doom
He knew less than the Pope of Rome.
Cardan believ'd great states depend
Upon the tip o' th' Bear's tail's end,
That, as she whisk'd it t'wards the sun,
Strew'd mighty empires up and down;

V. 873. Var. 'And, 'twere not.'
V. 894. Var. 'He knew no more,' &c.

Which others say must needs be false,
Because your true bears have no tails.
Some say the Zodiac constellations
Have long since chang'd their antique stations
Above a sign, and prove the same
In Taurus now, once in the Ram;
Affirm the Trigons chopp'd and chang'd,
The wat'ry with the fiery rang'd:
Then how can their effects still hold
To be the same they were of old?
This, though the art were true, would make
Our modern soothsayers mistake,
And is one cause they tell more lies
In figures and nativities
Than th' old Chaldean conjurers
In so many hundred thousand years;
Beside their nonsense in translating,
For want of Accidence and Latin,
Like Idus and Calendæ, Englisht
The Quarter-days by skilful linguist:
And yet with canting, sleight, and cheat,
'Twill serve their turn to do the feat;
Make fools believe in their foreseeing
Of things before they are in being;
To swallow gudgeons ere they 're catch'd,
And count their chickens ere they 're hatch'd;

V. 901. Var. 'Some say the stars i' th' Zodiac
Are more than a whole sign gone back
Since Ptolemy; and prove the same
In Taurus now, then in the Ram.'

Make them the constellations prompt,
And give them back their own accompt;
But still the best to him that gives
The best price for 't, or best believes.
Some towns, some cities, some, for brevity,
Have cast the versal world's nativity,
And made the infant-stars confess,
Like fools or children, what they please.
Some calculate the hidden fates
Of monkeys, puppy-dogs, and cats;
Some running-nags and fighting-cocks;
Some love, trade, law-suits, and the pox;
Some take a measure of the lives
Of fathers, mothers, husbands, wives,
Make opposition, trine, and quartile,
Tell who is barren and who fertile.
As if the planet's first aspect
The tender infant did infect
In soul and body, and instill
All future good and future ill;
Which, in their dark fatal'ties lurking,
At destin'd periods fall a-working,
And break out, like the hidden seeds
Of long diseases, into deeds,
In friendships, enmities, and strife,
And all th' emergencies of life:
No sooner does he peep into
The world but he has done his do,
Catch'd all diseases, took all physic
That cures or kills a man that is sick,

Marry'd his punctual dose of wives,
Is cuckolded, and breaks or thrives.
There 's but the twinkling of a star
Between a man of peace and war,
A thief and justice, fool and knave,
A huffing officer and a slave,
A crafty lawyer and pick-pocket,
A great philosopher and a blockhead,
A formal preacher and a player,
A learn'd physician and man-slayer;
As if men from the stars did suck
Old age, diseases, and ill-luck,
Wit, folly, honour, virtue, vice,
Trade, travel, women, claps, and dice,
And draw, with the first air they breathe,
Battle and murder, sudden death.
Are not these fine commodities
To be imported from the skies,
And vended here among the rabble
For staple goods and warrantable?
Like money by the Druids borrow'd,
In th' other world to be restored.
 Quoth Sidrophel, To let you know
You wrong the art and artists too,
Since arguments are lost on those
That do our principles oppose,
I will (although I 've done 't before)
Demonstrate to your sense once more,

V. 956. Var. 'Cookolded.'

And draw a figure that shall tell you
What you perhaps forget befell you,
By way of horary inspection,
Which some account our worst erection.
With that he circles draws and squares,
With ciphers, astral characters,
Then looks 'em o'er to understand 'em,
Although set down hab-nab at random.
Quoth he, This scheme of th' heavens set
Discovers how in fight you met
At Kingston with a May-pole idol,
And that y' were bang'd both back and side well;
And, though you overcame the Bear,
The dogs beat you at Brentford fair,
Where sturdy butchers broke your noddle,
And handled you like a fop-doodle.
Quoth Hudibras, I now perceive
You are no conj'rer : by your leave:
That paltry story is untrue,
And forg'd to cheat such gulls as you.
Not true! quoth he ; Howe'er you vapour,
I can what I affirm make appear;
Whachum shall justify 't t' your face,
And prove he was upon the place:
He play'd the saltinbancho's part,
Transform'd t' a Frenchman by my art;
He stole your cloak, and pick'd your pocket,
Chous'd and caldes'd you like a blockhead,

V. 1010. Var. 'Caldes'd.' Put the fortune-teller on him.

And what you lost I can produce,
If you deny it, here i' th' house.
Quoth Hudibras, I do believe
That argument 's demonstrative;
Ralpho, bear witness, and go fetch us
A constable to seize the wretches:
For though th' are both false knaves and cheats,
Impostors, jugglers, counterfeits,
I 'll make them serve for perpendic'lars
As true as e'er were us'd by bricklayers.
They 're guilty by their own confessions,
Of felony, and at the Sessions,
Upon the bench, I will so handle 'em,
That the vibration of this pendulum
Shall make all tailors' yards of one
Unanimous opinion;
A thing he long has vapour'd of,
But now shall make it out by proof.
Quoth Sidrophel, I do not doubt
To find friends that will bear me out;
Nor have I hazarded my art
And neck so long on the State's part
To be expos'd i' th' end to suffer
By such a braggadocio huffer.
Huffer! quoth Hudibras, this sword
Shall down thy false throat cram that word.
Ralpho, make haste, and call an officer
To apprehend this Stygian sophister;
Meanwhile I 'll hold 'em at a bay,
Lest he and Whachum run away.

But Sidrophel, who from th' aspect
Of Hudibras did now erect
A figure worse portending far
Than that of most malignant star,
Believ'd it now the fittest moment
To shun the danger that might come on 't,
While Hudibras was all alone,
And he and Whachum two to one.
This being resolv'd, he spy'd by chance
Behind the door an iron lance,
That many a sturdy limb had gor'd,
And legs, and loins, and shoulders bor'd;
He snatch'd it up, and made a pass
To make his way through Hudibras.
Whachum had got a fire-fork,
With which he vow'd to do his work;
But Hudibras was well prepar'd,
And stoutly stood upon his guard:
He put by Sidrophello's thrust,
And in right manfully he rusht;
The weapon from his gripe he wrung,
And laid him on the earth along.
Whachum his sea-coal prong threw by,
And basely turn'd his back to fly;
But Hudibras gave him a twitch,
As quick as lightning, in the breech,
Just in the place where honour 's lodg'd,
As wise philosophers have judg'd.
Because a kick in that place more
Hurts honour than deep wounds before.

Quoth Hudibras, The stars determine
You are my prisoners, base vermine:
Could they not tell you so, as well
As what I came to know foretell?
By this what cheats you are we find,
That in your own concerns are blind.
Your lives are now at my dispose,
To be redeem'd by fine or blows;
But who his honour would defile
To take or sell two lives so vile?
I 'll give you quarter; but your pillage,
The conqu'ring warrior's crop and tillage
Which with his sword he reaps and plows,
That 's mine, the law of arms allows.
This said in haste, in haste he fell
To rummaging of Sidrophel.
First he expounded both his pockets,
And found a watch, with rings and lockets,
Which had been left with him t' erect
A figure for, and so detect;
A copper-plate, with almanacks
Engrav'd upon 't, with other knacks
Of Booker's, Lilly's, Sarah Jimmers',
And blank schemes to discover nimmers;

V. 1093. John Booker was born in Manchester, and was a famous astrologer in the time of the civil wars. He was a great acquaintance of Lilly's; and so was this Sarah Jimmers, whom Lilly calls 'Sarah Shelhorn,' a great speculatrix. He owns he was very familiar with her ('quod nota'), so that it is no wonder that the Knight found several of their knick-knacks in Sidrophel's cabinet.

A moon-dial, with Napier's bones,
And several constellation-stones,
Engrav'd in planetary hours,
That over mortals had strange powers
To make them thrive in law or trade,
And stab or poison to evade,
In wit or wisdom to improve,
And be victorious in love.
Whachum had neither cross nor pile,
His plunder was not worth the while.
All which the conqu'ror did discompt,
To pay for curing of his rump.
But Sidrophel, as full of tricks
As Rota-men of politics,
Straight cast about to overreach
Th' unwary conqu'ror with a fetch,
And make him glad at least to quit
His victory, and fly the pit,
Before the secular prince of darkness
Arriv'd to seize upon his carcass:
And as a fox, with hot pursuit
Chas'd through a warren, casts about
To save his credit, and among
Dead vermine on a gallows hung,
And while the dogs run underneath,
Escap'd (by counterfeiting death),
Not out of cunning, but a train
Of atoms justling in his brain,
As learn'd philosophers give out;
So Sidrophello cast about,

And fell t' his wonted trade again
To feign himself in earnest slain.
First stretch'd out one leg, then another,
And, seeming in his breast to smother
A broken sigh; quoth he, Where am I?
Alive or dead? or which way came I
Through so immense a space so soon?
But now I thought myself i' th' moon,
And that a monster, with huge whiskers
More formidable than a Switzer's,
My body through and through had drill'd,
And Whachum by my side had kill'd;
Had cross-examin'd both our hose,
And plunder'd all we had to lose:
Look! there he is! I see him now,
And feel the place I am run through!
And there lies Whachum by my side
Stone dead, and in his own blood dy'd!
Oh! oh! — With that he fetch'd a groan,
And fell again into a swoon,
Shut both his eyes, and stopp'd his breath,
And to the life outacted death,
That Hudibras, to all appearing,
Believ'd him to be dead as herring.
He held it now no longer safe
To tarry the return of Ralph,
But rather leave him in the lurch:
Thought he, He has abus'd our Church,
Refus'd to give himself one firk
To carry on the Public Work;

Despis'd our Synod-men like dirt,
And made their discipline his sport;
Divulg'd the secrets of their Classes,
And their Conventions prov'd high-places;
Disparag'd their tithe-pigs as Pagan,
And set at nought their cheese and bacon;
Rail'd at their Covenant, and jeer'd
Their rev'rend Parsons to my beard;
For all which scandals to be quit
At once this juncture falls out fit.
I 'll make him henceforth to beware,
And tempt my fury if he dare:
He must at least hold up his hand,
By twelve freeholders to be scann'd,
Who, by their skill in palmistry,
Will quickly read his destiny,
And make him glad to read his lesson,
Or take a turn for 't at the Session,
Unless his Light and gifts prove truer
Than ever yet they did, I 'm sure:
For if he 'scape with whipping now,
'Tis more than he can hope to do;
And that will disengage my Conscience
Of th' obligation, in his own sense.
I 'll make him now by force abide,
What he by gentle means deny'd,
To give my honour satisfaction,
And right the Brethren in the action.
This being resolv'd, with equal speed
And conduct he approach'd his steed,

And, with activity unwont,
Assay'd the lofty beast to mount;
Which once achiev'd, he spurr'd his palfry
To get from th' enemy and Ralph free;
Left dangers, fears, and foes behind,
And beat at least three lengths the wind.

AN HEROICAL EPISTLE*

OF HUDIBRAS TO SIDROPHEL.

Ecce iterum Crispinus. . . .

WELL, Sidrophel, though 'tis in vain
To tamper with your crazy brain,
Without trepanning of your scull
As often as the moon 's at full,
'Tis not amiss, ere y' are giv'n o'er,
To try one desp'rate med'cine more;
For where your case can be no worse
The desp'rat'st is the wisest course.
Is 't possible that you, whose ears
Are of the tribe of Issachar's,
And might (with equal reason) either

* This Epistle was published ten years after the Third Canto of the Second Part, to which it is now annexed, namely, in the year 1674; and is said, in a Key to a Burlesque Poem of Mr. Butler's, published 1706, p. 13, to have been occasioned by Sir Paul Neal, a conceited virtuoso, and member of the Royal Society, who constantly affirmed that Mr. Butler was not the author of Hudibras, which gave rise to this Epistle; and by some he has been taken for the real Sidrophel of the poem. This was the gentleman, who, I am told, made a great discovery of an elephant in the moon, which, upon examination, proved to be no other than a mouse which had mistaken its way, and got into his telescope. See 'The Elephant in the Moon,' vol. ii.

For merit or extent of leather,
With William Pryn's, before they were
Retrench'd and crucify'd, compare,
Should yet be deaf against a noise
So roaring as the public voice?
That speaks your virtues free and loud,
And openly in every crowd,
As loud as one that sings his part
T' a wheelbarrow or turnip-cart,
Or your new nick-nam'd old invention
To cry green hastings with an engine
(As if the vehemence had stunn'd
And torn your drum-heads with the sound);
And 'cause your folly 's now no news,
But overgrown and out of use,
Persuade yourself there 's no such matter,
But that 'tis vanish'd out of Nature;
When Folly, as it grows in years,
The more extravagant appears;
For who but you could be possest
With so much ignorance and beast,
That neither all men's scorn and hate,
Nor being laugh'd and pointed at,
Nor bray'd so often in a mortar,
Can teach you wholesome sense and nurture,
But (like a reprobate) what course
Soever us'd, grow worse and worse?
Can no transfusion of the blood,
That makes fools cattle, do you good?
Nor putting pigs t' a bitch to nurse,

To turn them into mongrel curs,
Put you into a way at least
To make yourself a better beast?
Can all your critical intrigues
Of trying sound from rotten eggs;
Your sev'ral new-found remedies
Of curing wounds and scabs in trees;
Your arts of fluxing them for claps,
And purging their infected saps;
Recov'ring shankers, chrystallines,
And nodes and blotches in their rinds;
Have no effect to operate
Upon that duller block, your pate?
But still it must be lewdly bent
To tempt your own due punishment;
And, like your whimsy'd chariots, draw
The boys to course you without law;
As if the art you have so long
Profess'd, of making old dogs young,
In you had virtue to renew
Not only youth but childhood too.
Can you, that understand all books,
By judging only with your looks,
Resolve all problems with your face,
As others do with B's and A's;
Unriddle all that mankind knows
With solid bending of your brows;
All arts and sciences advance
With screwing of your countenance,
And with a penetrating eye

Into th' abstrusest learning pry;
Know more of any trade b' a hint
Than those that have been bred up in 't,
And yet have no art, true or false,
To help your own bad naturals?
But still the more you strive t' appear
Are found to be the wretcheder:
For fools are known by looking wise,
As men find woodcocks by their eyes.
Hence 'tis that 'cause y' have gain'd o' th' college
A quarter share (at most) of knowledge,
And brought in none, but spent repute,
Y' assume a pow'r as absolute
To judge, and censure, and control,
As if you were the sole Sir Poll,
And saucily pretend to know
More than your dividend comes to.
You 'll find the thing will not be done
With ignorance and face alone;
No, though y' have purchas'd to your name
In history so great a fame;

V. 86. Sir Politic Would-be, in "Volpone."

V. 91, 92. These two lines, I think, plainly discover that Lilly, and not Sir Paul Neal, was here lashed under the name of 'Sidrophel;' for Lilly's fame abroad was indisputable. Mr. Strickland, who was many years agent for the Parliament in Holland, thus publishes it: "I came purposely into the committee this day to see the man who is so famous in those parts where I have so long continued: I assure you his name is famous all over Europe. I came to do him justice." Lilly is also careful to tell us, that the King of Sweden sent him a gold chain and medal, worth about fifty pounds, for making hon-

That now your talent 's so well known
For having all belief outgrown,
That ev'ry strange prodigious tale
Is measur'd by your German scale —
By which the virtuosi try
The magnitude of ev'ry lie,
Cast up to what it does amount,
And place the bigg'st to your account:
That all those stories that are laid
Too truly to you, and those made,
Are now still charg'd upon your score,
And lesser authors nam'd no more.
Alas! that faculty betrays
Those soonest it designs to raise;
And all your vain renown will spoil,
As guns o'ercharg'd the more recoil;
Though he that has but impudence
To all things has a fair pretence;
And put among his wants but shame,
To all the world may lay his claim:
Though you have try'd that nothing 's borne
With greater ease than public scorn,
That all affronts do still give place
To your impenetrable face;
That makes your way through all affairs,

ourable mention of his Majesty in one of his almanacks, which, he says, was translated into the language spoken at Hamburgh, and printed and cried about the streets, as it was in London.. Thus he trumpets to the world the fame he acquired by his infamous practices, if we may credit his own history.

V. 105. Var. 'Destroys.'

As pigs through hedges creep with theirs:
Yet as 'tis counterfeit, and brass,
You must not think 'twill always pass;
For all impostors, when they 're known,
Are past their labour and undone;
And all the best that can befall
An artificial natural,
Is that which madmen find as soon
As once they 're broke loose from the moon,
And, proof against her influence,
Relapse to e'er so little sense,
To turn stark fools, and subjects fit
For sport of boys and rabble-wit.

PART III. CANTO I.

THE ARGUMENT.

The Knight and Squire resolve at once,
The one the other to renounce;
They both approach the Lady's bower,
The Squire t' inform, the Knight to woo her.
She treats them with a masquerade,
By Furies and Hobgoblins made;
From which the Squire conveys the Knight,
And steals him from himself by night.

'Tis true no lover has that pow'r
T' enforce a desperate amour,
As he that has two strings t' his bow,
And burns for love and money too;
For then he 's brave and resolute,
Disdains to render in his suit;
Has all his flames and raptures double,
And hangs or drowns with half the trouble;
While those who sillily pursue
The simple downright way and true,
Make as unlucky applications,
And steer against the stream, their passions.
Some forge their mistresses of stars,
And when the ladies prove averse,
And more untoward to be won
Than by Caligula the moon,

Cry out upon the stars for doing
Ill offices, to cross their wooing,
When only by themselves they 're hind'red,
For trusting those they made her kindred,
And still the harsher and hide-bounder
The damsels prove, become the fonder;
For what mad lover ever dy'd
To gain a soft and gentle bride?
Or for a lady tender-hearted,
In purling streams or hemp departed?
Leap'd headlong int' Elysium,
Through th' windows of a dazzling room?
But for some cross ill-natur'd dame,
The am'rous fly burnt in his flame.
This to the Knight could be no news,
With all mankind so much in use,
Who therefore took the wiser course,
To make the most of his amours,
Resolv'd to try all sorts of ways,
As follows in due time and place.
  No sooner was the bloody fight
Between the Wizard and the Knight,
With all th' appurtenances, over,
But he relaps'd again t' a lover,
As he was always wont to do
When h' had discomfited a foe,
And us'd the only antique philters
Deriv'd from old heroic tilters.

V. 43. Var. 'And us'd as.'

But now triumphant and victorious,
He held th' achievement was too glorious
For such a conqueror to meddle
With petty constable or beadle,
Or fly for refuge to the hostess
Of th' inns of Court and Chancery, Justice;
Who might perhaps reduce his cause
To th' ordeal trial of the laws,
Where none escape but such as branded
With red-hot irons have past bare-handed;
And, if they cannot read one verse
I' th' Psalms, must sing it, and that 's worse.
He, therefore, judging it below him
To tempt a shame the dev'l might owe him,
Resolv'd to leave the Squire for bail
And mainprize for him to the jail,
To answer with his vessel all
That might disastrously befall,
And thought it now the fittest juncture
To give the Lady a rencounter,
T' acquaint her with his expedition,
And conquest o'er the fierce magician;
Describe the manner of the fray,
And shew the spoils he brought away;
His bloody-scourging aggravate,
The number of the blows, and weight;
All which might probably succeed,
And gain belief he 'ad done the deed:
Which he resolv'd t' enforce, and spare
No pawning of his soul to swear;

But rather than produce his back,
To set his conscience on the rack;
And, in pursuance of his urging
Of articles perform'd, and scourging,
And all things else, upon his part
Demand deliv'ry of her heart,
Her goods, and chattels, and good graces,
And person, up to his embraces.
Thought he, The ancient errant knights
Won all their ladies' hearts in fights,
And cut whole giants into fritters,
To put them into am'rous twitters;
Whose stubborn bowels scorn'd to yield,
Until their gallants were half kill'd;
But when their bones were drubb'd so sore,
They durst not woo one combat more,
The ladies' hearts began to melt,
Subdu'd by blows their lovers felt.
So Spanish heroes with their lances,
At once wound bulls and ladies' fancies;
And he acquires the noblest spouse
That widows greatest herds of cows;
Then what may I expect to do,
Wh' have quell'd so vast a buffalo?
  Meanwhile the Squire was on his way,
The Knight's late orders to obey;
Who sent him for a strong detachment
Of beadles, constables, and watchmen,
T' attack the cunning-man, for plunder
Committed falsely on his lumber;

When he who had so lately sack'd
The enemy, had done the fact;
Had rifled all his pokes and fobs
Of gimcracks, whims, and jiggumbobs,
Which he by hook or crook had gather'd,
And for his own inventions father'd;
And when they should, at gaol delivery,
Unriddle one another's thievery,
Both might have evidence enough
To render neither halter-proof:
He thought it desperate to tarry,
And venture to be accessary;
But rather wisely slip his fetters,
And leave them for the Knight, his betters.
He call'd to mind th' unjust foul play,
He would have offer'd him that day,
To make him curry his own hide,
Which no beast ever did beside
Without all possible evasion,
But of the riding dispensation:
And therefore much about the hour
The Knight (for reasons told before)
Resolv'd to leave him to the fury
Of Justice, and an unpack'd jury,
The Squire concurr'd t' abandon him,
And serve him in the self-same trim;
T' acquaint the Lady what h' had done,
And what he meant to carry on;
What project 'twas he went about,
When Sidrophel and he fell out:

His firm and steadfast resolution,
To swear her to an execution;
To pawn his inward ears to marry her,
And bribe the devil himself to carry her;
In which both dealt, as if they meant
Their party-saints to represent,
Who never fail'd upon their sharing
In any prosperous arms-bearing,
To lay themselves out, to supplant
Each other cousin-german saint.
But ere the Knight could do his part,
The Squire had got so much the start,
H' had to the Lady done his errand,
And told her all his tricks aforehand.
Just as he finish'd his report,
The Knight alighted in the court,
And having ty'd his beast t' a pale,
And taking time for both to stale,
He put his band and beard in order,
The sprucer to accost and board her:
And now began t' approach the door,
When she, wh' had spy'd him out before,
Convey'd th' informer out of sight,
And went to entertain the Knight;
With whom encount'ring, after longees
Of humble and submissive congees,
And all due ceremonies paid,
He strok'd his beard, and thus he said:
Madam, I do, as is my duty,
Honour the shadow of your shoe-tye;

And now am come to bring your ear
A present you 'll be glad to hear;
At least I hope so: the thing 's done,
Or may I never see the sun;
For which I humbly now demand
Performance at your gentle hand;
And that you 'd please to do your part
As I have done mine, to my smart.
 With that he shrugg'd his sturdy back,
As if he felt his shoulders ake:
But she, who well enough knew what
(Before he spoke) he would be at,
Pretended not to apprehend
The mystery of what he mean'd.
And therefore wish'd him to expound
His dark expressions less profound.
 Madam, quoth he, I come to prove
How much I 've suffer'd for your love,
Which (like your votary) to win,
I have not spar'd my tatter'd skin:
And, for those meritorious lashes,
To claim your favour and good graces.
 Quoth she, I do remember once
I freed you from th' inchanted sconce,
And that you promis'd for that favour
To bind your back to th' good behaviour;
And, for my sake and service, vow'd
To lay upon 't a heavy load,
And what 't would bear t' a scruple prove,
As other knights do oft make love;

Which, whether you have done or no,
Concerns yourself, not me, to know;
But if you have, I shall confess
Y' are honester than I could guess.
Quoth he, If you suspect my troth,
I cannot prove it but by oath;
And if you make a question on 't,
I 'll pawn my soul that I have done 't:
And he that makes his soul his surety,
I think, does give the best security.
Quoth she, Some say the soul 's secure
Against distress and forfeiture;
Is free from action, and exempt
From execution and contempt;
And to be summon'd to appear
In th' other world 's illegal here,
And therefore few make any account
Int' what incumbrances they run 't
For most men carry things so even
Between this world, and hell, and heaven,
Without the least offence to either,
They freely deal in all together,
And equally abhor to quit
This world for both, or both for it;
And when they pawn and damn their souls,
They are but pris'ners on paroles.
For that, quoth he, 'tis rational,
They may b' accomptable in all:
For when there is that intercourse
Between divine and human pow'rs,

That all that we determine here
Commands obedience every-where;
When penalties may be commuted
For fines, or ears, and executed,
It follows nothing binds so fast
As souls in pawn and mortgage past;
For oaths are th' only tests and seals
Of right and wrong, and true and false;
And there 's no other way to try
The doubts of law and justice by.
  Quoth she, What is it you would swear?
There 's no believing till I hear:
For till they 're understood, all tales
(Like nonsense) are not true nor false.
  Quoth he, When I resolv'd t' obey
What you commanded th' other day,
And to perform my exercise
(As schools are wont) for your fair eyes,
T' avoid all scruples in the case,
I went to do 't upon the place
But as the castle is inchanted
By Sidrophel the witch, and haunted
With evil spirits, as you know,
Who took my Squire and me for two,
Before I 'ad hardly time to lay
My weapons by, and disarray,
I heard a formidable noise,
Loud as the Stentrophonic voice,
That roar'd far off, Dispatch, and strip,
I 'm ready with th' infernal whip,

That shall divest thy ribs of skin,
To expiate thy ling'ring sin;
Th' hast broke perfidiously thy oath,
And not perform'd thy plighted troth,
But spar'd thy renegado back,
Where th' hadst so great a prize at stake,
Which now the Fates have order'd me,
For penance and revenge to flee,
Unless thou presently make haste;
Time is, time was: and there it ceast.
With which, though startled, I confess,
Yet th' horror of the thing was less
Than th' other dismal apprehension
Of interruption or prevention;
And therefore snatching up the rod,
I laid upon my back a load,
Resolv'd to spare no flesh and blood,
To make my word and honour good:
Till tir'd, and taking truce at length,
For new recruits of breath and strength,
I felt the blows still ply'd as fast
As if th' had been by lovers plac'd
In raptures of Platonic lashing,
And chaste contemplative bardashing;
When facing hastily about,
To stand upon my guard and scout,
I found th' infernal cunning-man,
And th' under-witch, his Caliban,
With scourges (like the Furies) arm'd,
That on my outward quarters storm'd.

In haste I snatch'd my weapon up,
And gave their hellish rage a stop;
Call'd thrice upon your name, and fell
Courageously on Sidrophel;
Who now transform'd himself t' a bear,
Began to roar aloud and tear;
When I as furiously press'd on,
My weapon down his throat to run,
Laid hold on him, but he broke loose,
And turn'd himself into a goose,
Div'd under water in a pond,
To hide himself from being found.
In vain I sought him; but as soon
As I perceiv'd him fled and gone,
Prepar'd, with equal haste and rage,
His under-sorcerer t' engage;
But bravely scorning to defile
My sword with feeble blood, and vile,
I judg'd it better from a quick-
Set hedge to cut a knotted stick;
With which I furiously laid on,
Till in a harsh and doleful tone
It roar'd, O hold, for pity, Sir!
I am too great a sufferer,
Abus'd, as you have been, b' a witch,
But conjur'd into a worse caprich:
Who sends me out on many a jaunt,
Old houses in the night to haunt,
For opportunities t' improve
Designs of thievery or love;

With drugs convey'd in drink or meat,
All feats of witches counterfeit,
Kill pigs and geese with powder'd glass,
And make it for inchantment pass;
With cow-itch measle like a leper,
And choke with fumes of Guinea-pepper;
Make lechers, and their punks, with dewtry,
Commit phantastical advowtry;
Bewitch Hermetic-men to run
Stark staring mad with manicon;
Believe mechanic virtuosi
Can raise them mountains in Potosi;
And, sillier than the antic fools,
Take treasure for a heap of coals;
Seek out for plants with signatures,
To quack off universal cures;
With figures ground on panes of glass,
Make people on their heads to pass;
And mighty heaps of coin increase,
Reflected from a single piece;
To draw in fools, whose nat'ral itches
Incline perpetually to witches,
And keep me in continual fears,
And danger of my neck and ears;
When less delinquents have been scourg'd,
And hemp on wooden anvils forg'd,
Which others for cravats have worn
About their necks, and took a turn.
I pity'd the sad punishment
The wretched caitiff underwent,

And held my drubbing of his bones
Too great an honour for pultroons;
For knights are bound to feel no blows
From paltry and unequal foes,
Who, when they slash and cut to pieces,
Do all with civilest addresses:
Their horses never give a blow,
But when they make a leg and bow.
I therefore spar'd his flesh, and prest him
About the witch with many a question.
  Quoth he, For many years he drove
A kind of broking-trade in love:
Employ'd in all th' intrigues and trust,
Of feeble speculative lust;
Procurer to th' extravagancy
And crazy ribaldry of fancy,
By those the devil had forsook,
As things below him, to provoke;
But b'ing a virtuoso, able
To smatter, quack, and cant, and dabble,
He held his talent most adroit,
For any mystical exploit,
As others of his tribe had done,
And rais'd their prices three to one:
For one predicting pimp has th' odds
Of chaldrons of plain downright bawds,
But as an elf (the dev'l's valet)
Is not so slight a thing to get,
For those that do his bus'ness best,
In hell are us'd the ruggedest,

Before so meriting a person
Could get a grant, but in reversion,
He serv'd two prenticeships, and longer,
I' th' myst'ry of a lady-monger.
For (as some write) a witch's ghost,
As soon as from the body loos'd,
Becomes a puiney imp itself,
And is another witch's elf.
He, after searching far and near,
At length found one in Lancashire,
With whom he bargain'd before-hand,
And, after hanging, entertain'd:
Since which h' has play'd a thousand feats,
And practis'd all mechanic cheats;
Transform'd himself to th' ugly shapes
Of wolves, and bears, baboons, and apes,
Which he has vary'd more than witches,
Or Pharaoh's wizards, could their switches;
And all with whom h' has had to do,
Turn'd to as monstrous figures too;
Witness myself, whom h' has abus'd,
And to this beastly shape reduc'd,
By feeding me on beans and pease
He crams in nasty crevices,
And turns to comfits by his arts,
To make me relish for deserts,
And one by one, with shame and fear,
Lick up the candy'd provender.
Beside — But as h' was running on,
To tell what other feats h' had done,

The Lady stopt his full career,
And told him now 'twas time to hear.
If half those things (said she) be true —
They 're all (quoth he), I swear by you: —
Why then (said she) that Sidrophel
Has damn'd himself to th' pit of hell,
Who, mounted on a broom, the nag
And hackney of a Lapland hag,
In quest of you came hither post,
Within an hour (I 'm sure) at most,
Who told me all you swear and say,
Quite contrary another way;
Vow'd that you came to him, to know
If you should carry me or no;
And would have hir'd him and his imps,
To be your match-makers and pimps,
T' engage the devil on your side,
And steal (like Proserpine) your bride;
But he disdaining to embrace
So filthy a design and base,
You fell to vapouring and huffing,
And drew upon him like a ruffin;
Surpris'd him meanly, unprepar'd,
Before h' had time to mount his guard,
And left him dead upon the ground,
With many a bruise and desp'rate wound:
Swore you had broke and robb'd his house,
And stole his talismanic louse,
And all his new-found old inventions,
With flat felonious intentions;

Which he could bring out where he had,
And what he bought them for, and paid:
His flea, his morpion, and punese,
H' had gotten for his proper ease,
And all in perfect minutes made,
By th' ablest artist of the trade;
Which (he could prove it) since he lost
He has been eaten up almost;
And altogether might amount
To many hundreds on account:
For which h' had got sufficient warrant
To seize the malefactors errant,
Without capacity of bail,
But of a cart's or horse's tail;
And did not doubt to bring the wretches
To serve for pendulums to watches;
Which, modern virtuosis say,
Incline to hanging every way.
Beside, he swore, and swore 'twas true,
That ere he went in quest of you,
He set a figure to discover
If you were fled to Rye or Dover;
And found it clear that, to betray
Yourselves and me, you fled this way;
And that he was upon pursuit,
To take you somewhere hereabout.
He vow'd he had intelligence
Of all that pass'd before and since,
And found that, ere you came to him,
Y' had been engaging life and limb

About a case of tender conscience,
Where both abounded in your own sense,
Till Ralpho, by his light and grace,
Had clear'd all scruples in the case;
And prov'd that you might swear and own
Whatever 's by the Wicked done;
For which, most basely to requite
The service of his gifts and light,
You strove t' oblige him, by main force,
To scourge his ribs instead of yours;
But that he stood upon his guard,
And all your vapouring out-dar'd;
For which, between you both, the feat
Has never been perform'd as yet.
While thus the Lady talk'd, the Knight
Turn'd th' outside of his eyes to white
(As men of inward light are wont
To turn their optics in upon 't);
He wonder'd how she came to know
What he had done, and meant to do:
Held up his affidavit-hand,
As if h' had been to be arraign'd;
Cast towards the door a ghastly look,
In dread of Sidrophel, and spoke:
Madam, if but one word be true
Of all the wizard has told you,
Or but one single circumstance
In all th' apocryphal romance,
May dreadful earthquakes swallow down
This vessel, that is all your own;

Or may the heavens fall and cover
These reliques of your constant lover.
  You have provided well (quoth she),
(I thank you) for yourself and me,
And shewn your Presbyterian wits
Jump punctual with the Jesuits';
A most compendious way and civil,
At once to cheat the world, the devil,
And heaven and hell, yourselves, and those
On whom you vainly think t' impose.
Why then (quoth he), may hell surprise —
That trick (said she) will not pass twice:
I 've learn'd how far I 'm to believe
Your pinning oaths upon your sleeve;
But there 's a better way of clearing
What you would prove, than downright swearing;
For if you have perform'd the feat,
The blows are visible as yet,
Enough to serve for satisfaction
Of nicest scruples in the action;
And if you can produce those knobs,
Although they 're but the witch's drubs,
I 'll pass them all upon account,
As if your nat'ral self had done 't;
Provided that they pass th' opinion
Of able juries of old women;
Who, us'd to judge all matter of facts
For bellies, may do so for backs.
  Madam (quoth he), your love 's a million,
To do is less than to be willing,

As I am, were it in my power
T' obey what you command, and more;
But for performing what you bid,
I thank you as much as if I did.
You know I ought to have a care
To keep my wounds from taking air;
For wounds in those that are all heart,
Are dangerous in any part.
  I find (quoth she) my goods and chattels
Are like to prove but mere drawn battles;
For still the longer we contend,
We are but farther off the end;
But granting now we should agree,
What is it you expect from me?
Your plighted faith (quoth he) and word
You past in heaven on record,
Where all contracts, to have and t' hold,
Are everlastingly enroll'd;
And if 'tis counted treason here
To raze records, 'tis much more there.
  Quoth she, There are no bargains driv'n
Nor marriages clapp'd up in heav'n,
And that 's the reason, as some guess,
There is no heav'n in marriages;
Two things that naturally press
Too narrowly to be at ease;
Their bus'ness there is only love,
Which marriage is not like t' improve;
Love, that 's too generous t' abide
To be against its nature ty'd;

For where 'tis of itself inclin'd,
It breaks loose when it is confin'd,
And like the soul, its harbourer,
Debarr'd the freedom of the air,
Disdains against its will to stay,
But struggles out and flies away;
And therefore never can comply
T' endure the matrimonial tie,
That binds the female and the male,
Where th' one is but the other's bail;
Like Roman gaolers, when they slept
Chain'd to the prisoners they kept.
Of which the true and faithful'st lover,
Gives best security to suffer.
Marriage is but a beast some say,
That carries double in foul way,
And therefore 'tis not to b' admir'd
It should so suddenly be tir'd:
A bargain, at a venture made,
Between two partners in a trade;
(For what 's inferr'd by t' have and t' hold,
But something past away, and sold?)
That, as it makes but one of two,
Reduces all things else as low;
And at the best is but a mart,
Between the one and th' other part,
That on the marriage-day is paid,
Or hour of death, the bet is laid;
And all the rest of better or worse,
Both are but losers out of purse:

For when upon their ungot heirs
Th' entail themselves, and all that 's theirs,
What blinder bargain e'er was driv'n,
Or wager laid at six and sev'n?
To pass themselves away, and turn
Their children's tenants ere they 're born?
Beg one another idiot
To guardians, ere they are begot;
Or ever shall, perhaps, by th' one
Who 's bound to vouch 'em for his own,
Though got b' implicit generation,
And gen'ral club of all the nation;
For which she 's fortify'd no less
Than all the island, with four seas;
Exacts the tribute of her dower,
In ready insolence and power,
And makes him pass away, to have
And hold, to her, himself, her slave,
More wretched than an ancient villain,
Condemn'd to drudgery and tilling:
While all he does upon the by,
She is not bound to justify,
Nor at her proper cost and charge
Maintain the feats he does at large.
Such hideous sots were those obedient
Old vassals, to their ladies regent,
To give the cheats the eldest hand
In foul play, by the laws o' th' land;
For which so many a legal cuckold
Has been run down in courts, and truckled:

A law that most unjustly yokes
All Johns of Stiles to Joans of Noakes,
Without distinction of degree,
Condition, age, or quality;
Admits no pow'r of revocation,
Nor valuable consideration,
Nor writ of Error, nor reverse
Of judgment past, for better or worse;
Will not allow the privileges
That beggars challenge under hedges,
Who, when they 're griev'd, can make dead horses
Their sp'ritual judges of divorces,
While nothing else but *rem* in *re*
Can set the proudest wretches free;
A slavery beyond enduring,
But that 'tis of their own procuring.
As spiders never seek the fly,
But leave him of himself t' apply;
So men are by themselves employ'd,
To quit the freedom they enjoy'd,
And run their necks into a noose,
They 'd break 'em after to break loose.
As some whom death would not depart,
Have done the feat themselves by art:
Like Indian widows, gone to bed,
In flaming curtains, to the dead;
And men as often dangled for 't,
And yet will never leave the sport.
Nor do the ladies want excuse
For all the stratagems they use,

To gain th' advantage of the set,
And lurch the amorous rook and cheat.
For as the Pythagorean soul
Runs through all beasts, and fish, and fowl,
And has a smack of ev'ry one,
So love does, and has ever done;
And therefore though 'tis ne'er so fond,
Takes strangely to the vagabond.
'Tis but an ague that 's reverst,
Whose hot fit takes the patient first,
That after burns with cold as much
As iron in Greenland does the touch;
Melts in the furnace of desire
Like glass, that 's but the ice of fire;
And when his heat of fancy 's over,
Becomes as hard and frail a lover:
For when he 's with love-powder laden,
And prim'd and cock'd by Miss or Madam,
The smallest sparkle of an eye
Gives fire to his artillery,
And off the loud oaths go, but, while
They 're in the very act, recoil:
Hence 'tis so few dare take their chance
Without a sep'rate maintenance;
And widows, who have try'd one lover,
Trust none again till they 've made over;
Or if they do, before they marry
The foxes weigh the geese they carry;
And ere they venture o'er a stream,
Know how to size themselves and them.

Whence wittiest ladies always choose
To undertake the heaviest goose:
For now the world is grown so wary,
That few of either sex dare marry,
But rather trust on tick t' amours,
The cross and pile for bett'r or worse;
A mode that is held honourable
As well as French and fashionable:
For when it falls out for the best,
Where both are incommoded least,
In soul and body two unite
To make up one hermaphrodite;
Still amorous, and fond, and billing,
Like Philip and Mary on a shilling,
They 've more punctilios and capriches
Between the petticoat and breeches;
More petulent extravagances
Than poets make 'em in romances;
Though when their heroes 'spouse the dames,
We hear no more of charms and flames;
For then their late attracts decline
And turn as eager as prick'd wine;
And all their caterwauling tricks,
In earnest to as jealous piques:
Which th' ancients wisely signify'd
By th' yellow manteaus of the bride;
For jealousy is but a kind
Of clap and grincam of the mind,
The natural effects of love,
As other flames and aches prove:

But all the mischief is the doubt
On whose account they first broke out.
For though Chineses go to bed
And lie-in, in their ladies' stead;
And, for the pains they took before,
Are nurs'd and pamper'd to do more;
Our green-men do it worse, when th' hap
To fall in labour of a clap;
Both lay the child to one another,
But who 's the father? who the mother?
'Tis hard to say in multitudes,
Or who imported the French goods.
But health and sickness b'ing all one,
Which both engag'd before to own,
And are not with their bodies bound
To worship, only when they 're sound;
Both give and take their equal shares
Of all they suffer by false wares;
A fate no lover can divert
With all his caution, wit, and art:
For 'tis in vain to think to guess
At women by appearances;
That paint and patch their imperfections,
Of intellectual complexions,
And daub their tempers o'er with washes
As artificial as their faces:
Wear, under vizard-masks, their talents
And mother-wits, before their gallants;
Until they 're hamper'd in the noose,
Too fast to dream of breaking loose:

When all the flaws they strove to hide
Are made unready with the bride,
That with her wedding-clothes undresses
Her complaisance and gentilesses;
Tries all her arts to take upon her
The government from th' easy owner;
Until the wretch is glad to wave
His lawful right, and turn her slave;
Find all his having and his holding
Reduc'd t' eternal noise and scolding;
The conjugal petard, that tears
Down all portcullices of ears,
And makes the volley of one tongue
For all their leathern shields too strong.
When only arm'd with noise and nails,
The female silk-worms ride the males;
Transform 'em into rams and goats
Like Syrens, with their charming notes;
Sweet as the screech-owl's serenade,
Or those enchanting murmurs made
By th' husband mandrake, and the wife,
Both bury'd (like themselves) alive.
  Quoth he, These reasons are but strains
Of wanton, over-heated brains,
Which ralliers in their wit or drink
Do rather wheedle with than think.
Man was not man in Paradise,
Until he was created twice;
And had his better half, his bride,
Carv'd from th' original, his side,

T' amend his natural defects,
And perfect his recruiting sex;
Enlarge his breed at once, and lessen
The pains and labour of increasing,
By changing them for other cares,
As by his dried-up paps appears.
His body, that stupendous frame,
Of all the world the anagram,
Is of two equal parts compact,
In shape and symmetry exact;
Of which the left and female side
Is to the manly right a bride;
Both join'd together with such art,
That nothing else but death can part.
Those heav'nly attracts of yours, your eyes,
And face, that all the world surprise,
That dazzle all that look upon ye,
And scorch all other ladies tawny;
Those ravishing and charming graces,
Are all made up of two half-faces,
That, in a mathematic line,
Like those in other heavens, join:
Of which, if either grew alone,
'Twould fright as much to look upon:
And so would that sweet bud, your lip,
Without the other's fellowship.
Our noblest senses act by pairs,
Two eyes to see; to hear, two ears;
Th' intelligencers of the mind,
To wait upon the soul design'd:

But those that serve the body' alone
Are single and confin'd to one.
The world is but two parts, that meet
And close at th' equinoctial fit;
And so are all the works of Nature,
Stamp'd with her signature on matter;
Which all her creatures, to a leaf,
Or smallest blade of grass, receive.
All which sufficiently declare
How entirely marriage is her care,
The only method that she uses
In all the wonders she produces;
And those that take their rules from her
Can never be deceiv'd, nor err:
For what secures the civil life,
But pawns of children, and a wife?
That lie, like hostages, at stake,
To pay for all men undertake;
To whom it is as necessary,
As to be borne and breathe, to marry;
So universal, all mankind
In nothing else is of one mind;
For in what stupid age or nation
Was marriage ever out of fashion?
Unless among the Amazons,
Or cloister'd Friars and Vestal nuns,
Or Stoics, who, to bar the freaks
And loose excesses of the sex,
Prepost'rously would have all women
Turn'd up to all the world in common.

Though men would find such mortal feuds
In sharing of their public goods,
'Twould put them to more charge of lives
Than they 're supply'd with now by wives,
Until they graze, and wear their clothes,
As beasts do, of their native growths;
For simple wearing of their horns
Will not suffice to serve their turns.
For what can we pretend t' inherit,
Unless the marriage-deed will bear it?
Could claim no right to lands or rents,
But for our parents' settlements;
Had been but younger sons o' th' earth
Debarr'd it all, but for our birth.
What honours, or estates of peers,
Could be preserv'd but by their heirs?
And what security maintains
Their right and title, but the banns?
What crowns could be hereditary,
If greatest monarchs did not marry,
And with their consorts consummate
Their weightiest interests of state?
For all th' amours of princes are
But guarantees of peace or war.
Or what but marriage has a charm,
The rage of empires to disarm?
Make blood and desolation cease,
And fire and sword unite in peace;
When all their fierce contests for forage
Conclude in articles of marriage.

Nor does the genial bed provide
Less for the int'rests of the bride,
Who else had not the least pretence
T' as much as due benevolence;
Could no more title take upon her
To virtue, quality, and honour,
Than ladies errant unconfin'd,
And feme-coverts to all mankind.
All women would be of one piece,
The virtuous matron, and the miss;
The nymphs of chaste Diana's train,
The same with those in Lewkner's lane;
But for the diff'rence marriage makes
'Twixt wives and ladies of the Lakes:
Besides the joys of place and birth,
The sex's paradise on earth,
A privilege so sacred held
That none will to their mothers yield,
But, rather than not go before,
Abandon heaven at the door:
And if th' indulgent law allows
A greater freedom to the spouse,
The reason is, because the wife
Runs greater hazards of her life;
Is trusted with the form and matter
Of all mankind by careful Nature;
Where man brings nothing but the stuff
She frames the wondrous fabric of;
Who therefore, in a strait, may freely
Demand the clergy of her belly;

And make it save her the same way
It seldom misses to betray,
Unless both parties wisely enter
Into the Liturgy indenture.
And though some fits of small contest
Sometimes fall out among the best,
That is no more than every lover
Does from his hackney-lady suffer;
That makes no breach of faith and love,
But rather sometimes serves t' improve:
For as, in running, every pace
Is but between two legs a race,
In which both do their uttermost
To get before and win the post,
Yet, when they 're at their races' ends,
They 're still as kind and constant friends,
And, to relieve their weariness,
By turns give one another ease;
So all those false alarms of strife
Between the husband and the wife,
And little quarrels, often prove
To be but new recruits of love,
When those who 're always kind or coy
In time must either tire or cloy.
Nor are the loudest clamours more
Than as they 're relish'd sweet or sour;
Like music, that proves bad or good
According as 'tis understood.
In all amours a lover burns
With frowns, as well as smiles, by turns;

And hearts have been as oft with sullen
As charming looks surpris'd and stolen:
Then why should more bewitching clamour
Some lovers not as much enamour?
For discords make the sweetest airs,
And curses are a kind of pray'rs;
Two slight alloys for all those grand
Felicities by marriage gain'd:
For nothing else has power to settle
The interests of love perpetual.
An act and deed that makes one heart
Become another's counter-part,
And passes fines on faith and love,
Inroll'd and register'd above,
To seal the slippery knots of vows,
Which nothing else but death can loose.
And what security 's too strong
To guard that gentle heart from wrong
That to its friend is glad to pass
Itself away and all it has,
And, like an anchorite, gives over
This world for th' heaven of a lover?
 I grant (quoth she) there are some few
Who take that course, and find it true,
But millions whom the same does sentence
To heav'n b' another way, repentance.
Love's arrows are but shot at rovers,
Though all they hit they turn to lovers,
And all the weighty consequents
Depend upon more blind events

Than gamesters, when they play a set
With greatest cunning at Piquet,
Put out with caution, but take in
They know not what, unsight unseen.
For what do lovers, when they 're fast
In one another's arms embrac'd,
But strive to plunder, and convey
Each other, like a prize, away?
To change the property of selves,
As sucking children are by elves?
And if they use their persons so,
What will they to their fortunes do?
Their fortunes! the perpetual aims
Of all their ecstasies and flames.
For when the money 's on the book,
And 'All my worldly goods' but spoke
(The formal livery and seisin
That puts a lover in possession),
To that alone the bridegroom 's wedded,
The bride a flam that 's superseded:
To that their faith is still made good,
And all the oaths to us they vow'd;
For when we once resign our pow'rs,
We 've nothing left we can call ours;
Our money 's now become the Miss
Of all your lives and services,
And we, forsaken and postpon'd,
But bawds to what before we own'd;
Which, as it made y' at first gallant us,
So now hires others to supplant us,

Until 'tis all turn'd out of doors
(As we had been) for new amours.
For what did ever heiress yet,
By being born to lordships, get?
When, the more lady she 's of manors,
She 's but expos'd to more trepanners,
Pays for their projects and designs,
And for her own destruction fines;
And does but tempt them with her riches,
To use her as the dev'l does witches,
Who takes it for a special grace
To be their cully for a space,
That, when the time 's expir'd, the drazels
For ever may become his vassals;
So she, bewitch'd by rooks and spirits,
Betrays herself and all sh' inherits;
Is bought and sold, like stolen goods,
By pimps, and match-makers, and bawds;
Until they force her to convey
And steal the thief himself away.
These are the everlasting fruits
Of all your passionate love-suits,
Th' effects of all your am'rous fancies
To portions and inheritances;
Your love-sick rapture, for fruition
Of dowry, jointure, and tuition;
To which you make address and courtship,
And with your bodies strive to worship,
That th' infant's fortunes may partake
Of love too for the mother's sake.

For these you play at purposes,
And love your loves with A's and B's;
For these at Beste and L'Ombre woo,
And play for love and money too:
Strive who shall be the ablest man
At right gallanting of a fan;
And who the most genteelly bred
At sucking of a vizard-bead;
How best t' accost us in all quarters,
T' our question-and-command new garters;
And solidly discourse upon
All sorts of dresses *pro* and *con*:
For there 's no mystery nor trade
But in the art of love is made;
And when you have more debts to pay
Than Michaelmas and Lady-day,
And no way possible to do 't
But love and oaths, and restless suit,
To us y' apply to pay the scores
Of all your cully'd past amours;
Act o'er your flames and darts again,
And charge us with your wounds and pain,
Which others' influences long since
Have charm'd your noses with and shins,
For which the surgeon is unpaid,
And like to be without our aid.
Lord! what an am'rous thing is want!
How debts and mortgages inchant!
What graces must that lady have
That can from executions save!

What charms that can reverse extent,
And null degree and exigent!
What magical attracts and graces
That can redeem from *Scire facias*,
From bonds and statutes can discharge,
And from contempts of courts enlarge!
These are the highest excellences
Of all your true or false pretences;
And you would damn yourselves, and swear
As much t' an hostess dowager,
Grown fat and pursy by retail
Of pots of beer and bottled ale,
And find her fitter for your turn,
For fat is wondrous apt to burn;
Who at your flames would soon take fire,
Relent and melt to your desire,
And, like a candle in the socket,
Dissolve her graces int' your pocket.
  By this time 'twas grown dark and late,
When they' heard a knocking at the gate,
Laid on in haste, with such a powder,

V. 1053, 1054. The persons who knocked at the gate were, probably, two of the lady's own servants: for as she and Ralpho (who all the time lay in ambuscade) had been descanting on the Knight's villanies, so they had undoubtedly laid this scheme to be revenged of him: the servants were disguised, and acted in a bold and hectoring manner, pursuant to the instructions given them by the Widow. The Knight was to be made believe they were Sidrophel and Whachum, which made his fright and consternation so great that we find him falling into a swoon.

The blows grew louder still and louder;
Which Hudibras, as if they 'd been
Bestow'd as freely on his skin,
Expounding by his inward light,
Or rather more prophetic fright,
To be the Wizard come to search,
And take him napping in the lurch,
Turn'd pale as ashes or a clout,
But why or wherefore is a doubt;
For men will tremble, and turn paler,
With too much or too little valour.
His heart laid on, as if it try'd
To force a passage through his side,
Impatient (as he vow'd) to wait 'em,
But in a fury to fly at 'em;
And therefore beat and laid about,
To find a cranny to creep out.
But she, who saw in what a taking
The Knight was by his furious quaking,
Undaunted cry'd, Courage, Sir Knight,
Know I 'm resolv'd to break no rite
Of hospital'ty to a stranger,
But, to secure you out of danger,
Will here myself stand sentinel
To guard this pass 'gainst Sidrophel.
Women, you know, do seldom fail
To make the stoutest men turn tail,
And bravely scorn to turn their backs
Upon the desp'ratest attacks.
At this the Knight grew resolute

As Ironside or Hardiknute;
His fortitude began to rally,
And out he cry'd aloud to sally:
But she besought him to convey
His courage rather out o' th' way,
And lodge in ambush on the floor,
Or fortify'd behind a door,
That, if the enemy should enter,
He might relieve her in th' adventure.
  Meanwhile they knock'd against the door
As fierce as at the gate before;
Which made the renegado Knight
Relapse again t' his former fright.
He thought it desperate to stay
Till th' enemy had forc'd his way,
But rather post himself, to serve
The Lady for a fresh reserve.
His duty was not to dispute,
But what sh' had order'd execute;
Which he resolv'd in haste t' obey,
And therefore stoutly march'd away,
And all h' encounter'd fell upon,
Though in the dark, and all alone;
Till fear, that braver feats performs
Than ever courage dar'd in arms,
Had drawn him up before a pass,
To stand upon his guard, and face:

V. 1086. Two famous and valiant princes of this country, the one a Saxon, the other a Dane.

This he courageously invaded,
And, having enter'd, barricaded;
Insconc'd himself as formidable
As could be underneath a table,
Where he lay down in ambush close,
T' expect th' arrival of his foes.
Few minutes he had lain perdue,
To guard his desp'rate avenue,
Before he heard a dreadful shout,
As loud as putting to the rout,
With which impatiently alarm'd,
He fancy'd th' enemy had storm'd,
And, after ent'ring, Sidrophel
Was fall'n upon the guards pell-mell:
He therefore sent out all his senses
To bring him in intelligences,
Which vulgars, out of ignorance,
Mistake for falling in a trance;
But those that trade in geomancy
Affirm to be the strength of fancy,
In which the Lapland Magi deal,
And things incredible reveal.
Meanwhile the foe beat up his quarters,
And storm'd the outworks of his fortress;
And as another of the same
Degree and party in arms and fame,
That in the same cause had engag'd,
And war with equal conduct wag'd,
By vent'ring only but to thrust
His head a span beyond his post,

B' a general of the Cavaliers
Was dragg'd through a window by the ears;
So he was serv'd in his redoubt,
And by the other end pull'd out.
  Soon as they had him at their mercy,
They put him to the cudgel fiercely,
As if they 'd scorn'd to trade or barter,
By giving or by taking quarter;
They stoutly on his quarters laid,
Until his scouts came in t' his aid:
For when a man is past his sense,
There 's no way to reduce him thence
But twinging him by th' ears or nose,
Or laying on of heavy blows;
And, if that will not do the deed,
To burning with hot irons proceed.
No sooner was he come t' himself,
But on his neck a sturdy elf
Clapp'd, in a trice, his cloven hoof,
And thus attack'd him with reproof:
  Mortal, thou art betray'd to us
B' our friend, thy evil genius,
Who, for thy horrid perjuries,
Thy breach of faith, and turning lies,
The Brethren's privilege (against
The Wicked), on themselves, the Saints,
Has here thy wretched carcase sent
For just revenge and punishment,
Which thou hast now no way to lessen
But by an open free confession;

For if we catch thee failing once,
'Twill fall the heavier on thy bones.
What made thee venture to betray
And filch the Lady's heart away,
To spirit her to matrimony? —
That which contracts all matches, money.
It was th' inchantment of her riches
That made m' apply t' your crony witches;
That in return would pay th' expense,
The wear and tear of conscience,
Which I could have patch'd up and turn'd
For th' hundredth part of what I earn'd. —
Didst thou not love her then? speak true. —
No more (quoth he) than I love you. —
How would'st thou 'ave us'd her and her money? —
First turn'd her up to alimony,
And laid her dowry out in law
To null her jointure with a flaw,
Which I beforehand had agreed
T' have put on purpose in the deed,
And bar her widow's making over
T' a friend in trust, or private lover. —
What made thee pick and choose her out
T' employ their sorceries about? —
That which makes gamesters play with those
Who have least wit, and most to lose. —
But didst thou scourge thy vessel thus,
As thou hast damn'd thyself to us? —
I see you take me for an ass:
'Tis true, I thought the trick would pass

Upon a woman well enough,
As 't has been often found by proof,
Whose humours are not to be won
But when they are impos'd upon;
For Love approves of all they do
That stand for candidates, and woo.—
  Why didst thou forge those shameful lies
Of bears and witches in disguise?—
  That is no more than authors give
The rabble credit to believe;
A trick of following their leaders
To entertain their gentle readers:
And we have now no other way
Of passing all we do or say;
Which, when 'tis natural and true,
Will be believ'd b' a very few,
Beside the danger of offence,
The fatal enemy of sense.—
  Why didst thou choose that cursed sin,
Hypocrisy, to set up in?—
  Because it is the thriving'st calling,
The only saints'-bell that rings all in;
In which all Churches are concern'd,
And is the easiest to be learn'd:
For no degrees, unless they employ 't,
Can ever gain much or enjoy 't:
A gift that is not only able
To domineer among the rabble,
But by the laws impower'd to rout
And awe the greatest that stand out;

Which few hold forth against, for fear
Their hands should slip and come too near;
For no sin else, among the Saints,
Is taught so tenderly against. —
  What made thee break thy plighted vows? —
That which makes others break a house,
And hang, and scorn you all, before
Endure the plague of being poor.
  Quoth he, I see you have more tricks
Than all our doting politics,
That are grown old and out of fashion,
Compar'd with your new Reformation;
That we must come to school to you
To learn your more refin'd and new.
  Quoth he, If you will give me leave
To tell you what I now perceive,
You 'll find yourself an errant chouse
If y' were but at a Meeting-house.
  'Tis true (quoth he), we ne'er come there,
Because w' have let 'em out by th' year.
  Truly (quoth he), you can't imagine
What wondrous things they will engage in;
That as your fellow fiends in hell
Were angels all before they fell,
So are you like to be agen
Compar'd with th' angels of us men.
  Quoth he, I am resolv'd to be
Thy scholar in this mystery;
And therefore first desire to know
Some principles on which you go.

What makes a knave a child of God,
And one of us? — A livelihood. —
What renders beating out of brains
And murther godliness? — Great gains.
What 's tender conscience? — 'Tis a botch
That will not bear the gentlest touch;
But, breaking out, dispatches more
Than th' epidemical'st plague-sore.
What makes y' incroach upon our trade,
And damn all others? — To be paid. —
What 's orthodox and true believing
Against a conscience? — A good living.
What makes rebelling against kings
A good old Cause? — Administ'rings.
What makes all doctrines plain and clear? —
About two hundred pounds a-year.
And that which was prov'd true before
Prove false again? — Two hundred more.
What makes the breaking of all oaths
A holy duty? — Food and clothes.
What laws and freedom persecution? —
B'ing out of power and contribution.
What makes a church a den of thieves? —
A dean and Chapter and white sleeves.
And what would serve, if those were gone,
To make it orthodox? — Our own.
What makes morality a crime
The most notorious of the time;
Morality, which both the Saints
And Wicked too cry out against? —

'Cause grace and virtue are within
Prohibited degrees of kin;
And therefore no true Saint allows
They shall be suffer'd to espouse;
For Saints can need no conscience
That with morality dispense;
As virtue 's impious when 'tis rooted
In nature only, and not imputed:
But why the Wicked should do so
We neither know, nor care to do.
What 's liberty of conscience,
I' th' natural and genuine sense?—
'Tis to restore with more security
Rebellion to its ancient purity;
And Christian liberty reduce
To th' elder practice of the Jews:
For a large conscience is all one
And signifies the same with none.
It is enough (quoth he) for once,
And has repriev'd thy forfeit bones:
Nick Machiavel had ne'er a trick
(Though he gave his name to our Old Nick)
But was below the least of these
That pass i' th' world for holiness.
This said, the Furies and the light
In th' instant vanish'd out of sight,
And left him in the dark alone,
With stinks of brimstone and his own.
The Queen of Night, whose large command
Rules all the sea and half the land,

And over moist and crazy brains,
In high spring-tides, at midnight reigns,
Was now declining to the west,
To go to bed and take her rest;
When Hudibras, whose stubborn blows
Deny'd his bones that soft repose,
Lay still, expecting worse and more,
Stretch'd out at length upon the floor;
And, though he shut his eyes as fast
As if h' had been to sleep his last,
Saw all the shapes that fear or wizards
Do make the devil wear for vizards,
And, pricking up his ears to hark
If he could hear too in the dark,
Was first invaded with a groan,
And after, in a feeble tone,
These trembling words: Unhappy wretch!
What hast thou gotten by this fetch,
Or all thy tricks, in this new trade,
Thy holy Brotherhood o' th' blade?
By saunt'ring still on some adventure,
And growing to thy horse a Centaur?
To stuff thy skin with swelling knobs
Of cruel and hard-wooded drubs?
For still th' hast had the worst on 't yet,
As well in conquest as defeat.
Night is the sabbath of mankind,
To rest the body and the mind,
Which now thou art deny'd to keep,
And cure thy labour'd corpse with sleep,

The Knight, who heard the words, explain'd
As meant to him this reprimand,
Because the character did hit
Point-blank upon his case so fit;
Believ'd it was some drolling spright
That stay'd upon the guard that night,
And one of those h' had seen, and felt
The drubs he had so freely dealt;
When, after a short pause and groan,
The doleful Spirit thus went on:
This 'tis t' engage with Dogs and Bears
Pell-mell together by the ears,
And, after painful bangs and knocks,
To lie in limbo in the stocks,
And from the pinnacle of glory
Fall headlong into purgatory —
(Thought he, This devil 's full of malice,
That on my late disaster rallies;) —
Condemn'd to whipping, but declin'd it,
By being more heroic-minded;
And at a riding handled worse,
With treats more slovenly and coarse;
Engag'd with fiends in stubborn wars,
And hot disputes with conjurers;
And, when th' hadst bravely won the day,
Wast fain to steal thyself away —
(I see, thought he, this shameless elf
Would fain steal me too from myself,
That impudently dares to own
What I have suffer'd for and done) —

And now, but vent'ring to betray,
Hast met with vengeance the same way.
Thought he, How does the devil know
What 'twas that I design'd to do?
His office of intelligence,
His oracles are ceas'd long since;
And he knows nothing of the Saints,
But what some treach'rous spy acquaints.
This is some pettifogging fiend,
Some under door-keeper's friend's friend,
That undertakes to understand,
And juggles at the second-hand,
And now would pass for Spirit Po,
And all men's dark concerns foreknow.
I think I need not fear him for 't;
These rallying devils do no hurt.
With that he rous'd his drooping heart,
And hastily cry'd out, What art?
A wretch (quoth he) whom want of grace
Has brought to this unhappy place. —
I do believe thee, quoth the Knight;
Thus far I 'm sure thou 'rt in the right,
And know what 'tis that troubles thee
Better than thou hast guess'd of me.
Thou art some paltry blackguard spright,
Condemn'd to drudg'ry in the night;
Thou hast no work to do in th' house,
Nor halfpenny to drop in shoes;
Without the raising of which sum
You dare not be so troublesome,

To pinch the slatterns black and blue,
For leaving you their work to do.
This is your bus'ness, good Pug-Robin,
And your diversion dull dry bobbing,
T' entice fanatics in the dirt,
And wash 'em clean in ditches for 't;
Of which conceit you are so proud,
At ev'ry jest you laugh aloud,
As now you would have done by me,
But that I barr'd your raillery.
Sir (quoth the Voice), y' are no such sophi
As you would have the world judge of ye.
If you design to weigh our talents
I' th' standard of your own false balance,
Or think it possible to know
Us ghosts, as well as we do you,
We who have been the everlasting
Companions of your drubs and basting,
And never left you in contest,
With male or female, man or beast,
But prov'd as true t' ye, and entire,
In all adventures as your Squire.
Quoth he, That may be said as true
By th' idlest pug of all your crew:
For none could have betray'd us worse
Than those allies of ours and yours.
But I have sent him for a token
To your low country Hogen-Mogen,
To whose infernal shores I hope
He 'll swing like skippers in a rope:

And if y' have been more just to me
(As I am apt to think) than he,
I am afraid it is as true
What th' ill-affected say of you;
Ye 've 'spous'd the Covenant and Cause,
By holding up your cloven paws.
Sir (quoth the Voice), 'tis true, I grant,
We made and took the Covenant;
But that no more concerns the Cause,
Than other perj'ries do the laws,
Which, when they 're prov'd in open court,
Wear wooden peccadilloes for 't:
And that 's the reason Cov'nanters
Hold up their hands like rogues at bars.
I see (quoth Hudibras) from whence
These scandals of the Saints commence,
That are but natural effects
Of Satan's malice and his sects,
Those spider-saints that hang by threads
Spun out o' th' entrails of their heads.
Sir (quoth the Voice), that may as true
And properly be said of you,
Whose talents may compare with either,
Or both the other put together:
For all the Independents do
Is only what you forc'd 'em to;
You, who are not content alone
With tricks to put the devil down,
But must have armies rais'd to back
The gospel-work you undertake;

As if artillery and edge-tools
Were th' only engines to save souls:
While he, poor devil, has no pow'r
By force to run down and devour;
Has ne'er a Classis, cannot sentence
To stools, or poundage of repentance;
Is ty'd up only to design
T' entice and tempt and undermine:
In which you all his arts outdo,
And prove yourselves his betters too.
Hence 'tis possessions do less evil
Than mere temptations of the devil,
Which all the horrid'st actions done
Are charg'd in courts of law upon;
Because, unless they help the elf,
He can do little of himself;
And therefore where he 's best possest
Acts most against his interest;
Surprises none but those who 've priests
To turn him out, and exorcists,
Supply'd with spiritual provision,
And magazines of ammunition;
With crosses, relics, crucifixes,
Beads, pictures, rosaries, and pixes;
The tools of working out salvation
By mere mechanic operation:
With holy water, like a sluice,
To overflow all avenues:
But those who 're utterly unarm'd,
T' oppose his entrance if he storm'd;

He never offers to surprise,
Although his falsest enemies;
But is content to be their drudge,
And on their errands glad to trudge:
For where are all your forfeitures
Intrusted in safe hands, but ours?
Who are but jailors of the holes
And dungeons where you clap up souls;
Like under-keepers, turn the keys
T' your mittimus anathemas,
And never boggle to restore
The members you deliver o'er,
Upon demand, with fairer justice
Than all your covenanting Trustees;
Unless, to punish them the worse,
You put them in the secular pow'rs,
And pass their souls, as some demise
The same estate in mortgage twice;
When to a legal utlegation
You turn your excommunication,
And for a groat unpaid that 's due,
Distrain on soul and body too.
  Thought he, 'Tis no mean part of civil
State-prudence to cajole the devil,
And not to handle him too rough,
When h' has us in his cloven hoof.
  'Tis true (quoth he), that intercourse
Has pass'd between your friends and ours,
That, as you trust us, in our way,
To raise your members and to lay,

We send you others of our own,
Denounc'd to hang themselves or drown,
Or, frighted with our oratory,
To leap down headlong many a story;
Have us'd all means to propagate
Your mighty interests of state,
Laid out our sp'ritual gifts to further
Your great designs of rage and murther.
For if the Saints are nam'd from blood,
We only 've made that title good;
And, if it were but in our power,
We should not scruple to do more,
And not be half a soul behind
Of all Dissenters of mankind.
Right (quoth the Voice), and, as I scorn
To be ungrateful, in return
Of all those kind good offices,
I'll free you out of this distress,
And set you down in safety, where
It is no time to tell you here.
The cock crows, and the morn draws on,
When 'tis decreed I must be gone;
And if I leave you here till day,
You'll find it hard to get away.
With that the Spirit grop'd about
To find th' inchanted hero out,
And try'd with haste to lift him up,
But found his forlorn hope, his crup,
Unserviceable with kicks and blows
Receiv'd from harden'd hearted foes.

He thought to drag him by the heels,
Like Gresham-carts with legs for wheels;
But fear, that soonest cures those sores,
In danger of relapse to worse,
Came in t' assist him with his aid,
And up his sinking vessel weigh'd.
No sooner was he fit to trudge,
But both made ready to dislodge;
The Spirit hors'd him like a sack,
Upon the vehicle his back,
And bore him headlong into th' hall,
With some few rubs against the wall;
Where, finding out the postern lock'd,
And th' avenues as strongly block'd,
H' attack'd the window, storm'd the glass,
And in a moment gain'd the pass;
Through which he dragg'd the worsted soldier's
Fore-quarters out by th' head and shoulders,
And cautiously began to scout
To find their fellow-cattle out;
Nor was it half a minute's quest
Ere he retriev'd the champion's beast,
Ty'd to a pale, instead of rack,
But ne'er a saddle on his back,
Nor pistols at the saddle bow,
Convey'd away, the Lord knows how.
He thought it was no time to stay,
And let the night too steal away;

V. 1575. Var. 'th' outer postern.'

But in a trice advanc'd the Knight
Upon the bare ridge, bolt upright,
And, groping out for Ralpho's jade,
He found the saddle too was stray'd,
And in the place a lump of soap,
On which he speedily leap'd up;
And, turning to the gate the rein,
He kick'd and cudgel'd on amain;
While Hudibras with equal haste
On both sides laid about as fast,
And spurr'd, as jockeys use to break,
Or padders to secure, a neck:
Where let us leave 'em for a time,
And to their Churches turn our rhyme;
To hold forth their declining state,
Which now come near an even rate.

END OF VOL. I.

www.ingramcontent.com/pod-product-compliance
Lightning Source LLC
LaVergne TN
LVHW010141110826
845151LV00002B/396

* 9 7 8 1 4 2 5 5 3 9 2 4 5 *